Early Childhood in the Anglosphere

Early Childhood in the Anglosphere

Systemic failings and transformative possibilities

Peter Moss and Linda Mitchell

First published in 2024 by
UCL Press
University College London
Gower Street
London WC1E 6BT

Available to download free: www.uclpress.co.uk

ISBN: 978-1-80008-255-7 (Hbk.)
ISBN: 978-1-80008-254-0 (Pbk.)
ISBN: 978-1-80008-253-3 (PDF)
ISBN: 978-1-80008-256-4 (epub)
DOI: https://doi.org/10.14324/111.9781800082533

Contents

List of tables

About the authors

Linda Mitchell is Professor of Early Childhood Education at the Wilf Malcolm Institute of Educational Research, University of Waikato. She joined the university in 2008, after 15 years in leadership positions with the New Zealand early childhood teachers' union and seven years as a senior researcher with the New Zealand Council for Educational Research. She has spent many years researching early childhood education policy and practice, critiquing the marketisation and privatisation of early childhood education and advocating for policy change. She was Leverhulme Visiting Professor at Manchester Metropolitan University (2022/23), working with colleagues on the project 'Democracy and Education across the Lifespan'. Her most recent books are *Democratic Practices and Policies in Early Childhood Education: An Aotearoa New Zealand case study* (Springer, 2019) and *The Decommodification of Early Childhood Education and Care: Resisting neoliberalism* (the latter co-authored with Michel Vandenbroeck and Joanne Lehrer, Routledge, 2022).

Peter Moss is Emeritus Professor of Early Childhood Provision at the Thomas Coram Research Unit, UCL Institute of Education, having joined TCRU in 1973. He co-founded the International Network on Leave Policies and, for 10 years, co-edited the book series *Contesting Early Childhood*. Much of his work has been cross-national and his interests include early childhood education, democracy in education and the relationship between employment, care and gender. His most recent books are *Parental Leave and Beyond* (edited with Alison Koslowski and Ann-Zofie Duvander, Policy Press, 2019), *Neoliberalism and Early Childhood Education* (with Guy Roberts-Holmes, Routledge, 2021) and *Transforming Early Childhood in England* (edited with Claire Cameron, UCL Press, 2020).

Acknowledgements

The authors have benefitted greatly from the knowledge and feedback of a number of colleagues from the countries covered in this book, including Gordon Cleveland, Sue Colley, Aline-Gunilla Dahlberg, Wendy Dunlop, Nóirín Hayes, Christa Japel, Neil Leitch, Caitlin McLean, Helen May, Frances Press, Sylvie Reyna, Beth Blue Swadener, Marcy Whitebook, Toby Wolfe, Christine Woodrow and Nicola Yelland. Any errors of fact and all opinions expressed in this book are solely the responsibility of the authors.

1

The Anglosphere in a time of crises

This book is about 'early childhood systems' in the 'Anglosphere'. It is about what these systems have in common, their shared and substantial failings, and the causes and consequences of these failings. But it is also about how these failings might be made good through major changes. In other words, it is a book about transformation, about why transformation is needed and why it is possible and necessary at this particular time, and about what transformation might look like and how it might happen. Part of that transformation is about policies and structures, how things are organised and done. But part is about how the Anglosphere thinks about early childhood systems, for, as the French philosopher Michel Foucault (1988: 155) has so aptly written, 'as soon as one can no longer think things as one formerly thought them, transformation becomes both very urgent, very difficult, and quite possible'. So we will argue to no longer think of early childhood services as 'childcare', as businesses and as marketised commodities, and think of them instead as education with an ethics of care, as public goods and as a universal entitlement for children.

Full definitions of 'early childhood systems' and the 'Anglosphere' will follow shortly, but suffice it to say for now that 'early childhood systems' spans both early childhood education and care services, and parenting leave (including maternity, paternity and parental leave), while the 'Anglosphere' covers a number of high-income countries where English is the most commonly spoken language: Australia, Canada, England, Ireland, Aotearoa New Zealand,[1] Scotland and the United States. This book, therefore, is a comparative study, whose purpose is to analyse, to explain, and to provoke: that is, to provoke critical thought about what exists and what could be by 'challeng[ing] taken-for-granted assumptions, [and] expand[ing] the menu of the possible' (J. Tobin, 2022: 298). The book does that by highlighting not only some striking similarities but also some important differences of experience within the Anglosphere, and by offering the contrasting examples of two other high-income countries, both outside the Anglosphere. Our hope is to encourage readers to ask: Why do we think and do things like this? What do we really want for our children, families and societies? Why and how might we think and do things differently?

We also hope to provoke critical thought by situating our discussion of the Anglosphere's early childhood systems in a political context. These systems did not just fall from a clear blue sky. They are the products of particular and prevalent ways of thinking, at least among those who influence and determine policy. They are therefore neither natural nor inevitable, and are by implication changeable, albeit with great difficulty. The failings and adverse consequences of the Anglosphere's early childhood systems are many, varied and historical; they have accumulated over many years, as the systems themselves have grown in piecemeal fashion, rarely benefitting from comprehensive review or planning. But our further contention is that the situation has been exacerbated in recent years by a profound political change, the rise of 'a thought collective and political movement combined' (Mirowski, 2014: 2): neoliberalism.

We will discuss 'neoliberalism', as well as its associated concept of 'human capital', in more detail in Chapter 4, but here we briefly introduce it as a set of ideas and a movement that has become increasingly influential globally since the 1970s, to the extent that Stephen Ball, a leading scholar on neoliberalism and education, concludes that

> Neoliberalism now configures great swathes of our daily lives and structures our experience of the world – how we understand the way the world works, how we understand ourselves and others, and how we relate to ourselves and others. … We are produced by it. (Ball, 2020: xv)

Neoliberalism has achieved these profound effects through what the American political theorist Wendy Brown (2016: 3) has called a 'crucial signature of neoliberalism' – economisation. Brown describes this as

> the conversion of non-economic domains, activities and subjects into economic ones …. [This is] the ascendency of a form of normative reason that extends market metrics and practices to every dimension of human life; political, cultural, personal, vocational, educational. … [T]his form of reason displaces other modes of valuation for judgment and action, displaces basic liberal democratic criteria for justice, with business metrics, transforms the state itself into a firm,

produces everyday norms of identity and conduct that configure the subject as human capital, and configures every kind of human activity in terms of rational self-investment and entrepreneurship. (Brown, 2016: 3, 5, 8)

Economisation under neoliberalism has manifested itself in distinct and varied ways, including: the introduction of markets into all social domains and opening up previously public services to private business and profit; attacking regulation and trade unions, both viewed as imposing harmful constraints on markets, enterprise and profit; the primacy given to competition, individual choice and constant calculation of benefit as values; and the production of an ideal subject, *homo economicus*, self-interested and competitive, independent and self-reliant, an informed consumer and flexible worker constantly calculating what is in their best interests – in other words, the economised human being incarnate.

The results have been brutal and shocking, including

staggering levels of wealth and income inequality, the disappearance or significant shredding of even the most grudging social safety net provisions, the loss of the 'commons' in virtually all sectors, and the truncation (ideally to zero) of public expectations for anything that might be provided by something called 'society'. (Chomsky and Waterstone, 2021: x–xi)

To this we might add the undermining and weakening of trade unions and other forms of social solidarity, of regulation and other social protections, and of democracy and the public domain.

Although neoliberalism is global in its influence, the Anglosphere has been its epicentre. It has also found its educational expression in what has been termed GERM, or the Global Education Reform Movement, which has 'emerged since the 1980s and has increasingly become adopted as an educational reform orthodoxy within many education systems throughout the world, including in the U.S., England [and] Australia' (Sahlberg, 2012). GERM, with its contagious symptoms of market logic, standardisation, focus on a few core subjects, business management models, and test-based accountability, has infected all sectors of education, from higher to early childhood. The Australian academic Margaret Sims, stung by experience from her own country, has bitingly observed how neoliberalism has had 'a devastating impact on the early childhood sector with its focus on standardisation, push-down curriculum and its positioning of children as investments for future economic productivity'

(Sims, 2017: 1). As this comment suggests, neoliberalism's impact has not been confined to education policy and practice. It has produced a way of thinking about children and their parents, and teachers and their schools, a way of thinking that has in turn produced a certain approach to educational policy and practice, an impoverished and impoverishing approach that is narrow and technical, instrumental and above all economised. We shall explore this way of thinking further in Chapter 4.

This book takes an unapologetically critical approach towards neoliberalism and the educational turn guided by this movement and ideology. For it seems to us that the early childhood systems in the countries of the Anglosphere were already on the wrong track, but that under neoliberalism they have taken a further wrong turning that has led them down a blind alley. With a partial exception, these countries have not stopped to appreciate that the alley they are headed down is a blind one, nor to contemplate what other directions they could choose to take or how to extract themselves from the blind alley. Processes of collective, critical and democratic thought, deliberation and decision-making have been largely absent. The result has been early childhood systems that are increasingly flawed and dysfunctional.

Of course, the seven countries on which we focus are by no means identical. They differ in important respects, some of which we flag up later in this chapter, and their early childhood systems are not identical. In particular, one of them, Aotearoa New Zealand, has made substantial efforts to transform itself, and has been partially successful, though without managing to escape neoliberalism's damaging influence. But, as we shall document both in comparing the Anglosphere countries and in comparing them with other countries, they share significant features that taken together make them distinctive – and not in a good way. Three are of particular note, and are major contributors to the common identity of the Anglosphere's early childhood systems. The first might be termed childcare-dominated split systems; the second is the important part played by the marketisation and privatisation of services; the third is the inadequacy of parenting leave.

Early childhood systems in all countries start out split: split between services that have a predominantly employment or welfare function (providing 'childcare for working mothers' and support for poor or otherwise disadvantaged families), and others that have a predominantly educational function. The former services have often come within the purview of the 'welfare' system, are viewed as and often termed 'day care', 'childcare' or 'nursery' services, and have usually taken children from an early age, well before 3 years; there are centres, gathering groups of children together in non-domestic settings, but these are also complemented by individuals providing services in their own homes, with names like 'childminder' or 'family day carer'. The latter services have been more likely to come under the 'education' system, have been viewed as primarily 'educational' in purpose and are termed, for example, 'kindergartens' or 'nursery schools', or 'kindergarten classes' or 'nursery classes' located within primary schools. They have usually been for older pre-school children, from 3 or 4 years, and available on a sessional (part-time) basis or for school hours.

Over time, and especially in recent decades, 'childcare' services have been overlaid with an 'educational' veneer. There is a growing awareness, too, that schools or kindergartens can provide important support for employed parents; this has become especially apparent when they have been unable to open, for example because of Covid restrictions. Many countries have taken steps to narrow the split between childcare and education; in Chapters 3, 6 and 7 we will give some examples of these movements towards greater integration, and the limited progress that has been made in most cases. But overall, with a few exceptions (one of which, Sweden, we consider in detail in Chapter 5), early childhood systems not only in the Anglosphere but elsewhere in the world remain substantially split between the two groups of services – childcare, and school-based or kindergartens – in ways we will explore in more detail in subsequent chapters.

But what marks out the Anglosphere countries from many others is how the split in their systems manifests itself. For example, in Continental European countries (except for the Netherlands and the Nordic countries) and many other countries around the world, most early childhood services and places are in schools or kindergartens, as we shall illustrate in Chapter 5 with the case of France. But the Anglosphere is different. Here childcare/day care/nursery/family day care services account for most of the available places: 'childcare', in short, is dominant; services in schools or kindergartens, in other words services that are primarily educational in purpose and identity, form the minority. Mirroring the division of services, the workforce in the Anglosphere (with Aotearoa New Zealand the one exception) is dominated by 'childcare' workers, a universally undervalued group characterised by low qualifications, low pay and low status.

This structural imbalance is matched by a dominating 'childcare' discourse, in which individuals, organisations, media and policy makers talk endlessly about 'childcare' – about the insufficiency of 'childcare' places, the excessive expense parents incur using 'childcare', the need for 'quality childcare', and so on. We will be highly critical of this Anglosphere preoccupation with 'childcare', which drives a wedge through early childhood systems with all sorts of adverse consequences. We will argue that the Anglosphere needs to give up its interminable talk about 'childcare' and its recurrent attempts to make adjustments to 'childcare', and ditch 'childcare' altogether; instead, it should focus its attention on 'early childhood education' and on transforming early childhood systems accordingly. We shall argue that, paradoxically, this would mean paying more, not less, attention to care, because it would acknowledge the importance of care for *all* children and *all* parents, including (but not only) those who are in paid employment. The time has come to get beyond 'childcare'.

But to return to where we are today. The current dominance of 'childcare' feeds into the second distinctive feature of the Anglosphere: marketisation and privatisation. For reasons we shall explore, 'childcare' services have come to be widely viewed in the countries of the Anglosphere as, first and foremost, traders in a private commodity, namely 'childcare for working parents', to be purchased by parents (in practice, usually assumed to be mothers) as a necessary condition for employment. For this reason, these services have been mainly supplied by private providers, which are often, and increasingly, for-profit businesses, and have operated in a 'childcare market' in which they compete to sell their wares to parent-consumers. There is little public 'childcare' provision in the Anglosphere, for example services run by local authorities (communes, municipalities, councils), and the presence of non-profit private providers varies: it is highest in Canada, lowest in England. School or kindergarten provision is more likely to be publicly provided, but such services find themselves in some Anglosphere countries competing with each other and with 'childcare services', in a wider 'early childhood education' market.

The third feature of the typical Anglosphere early childhood system is inadequate parenting leave. Adequate leave, in our view, would have several components: leave for parents that runs for at least 12 months; leave that is well paid, by which we mean income replacement of at least two-thirds; leave that is designed to encourage the sharing of leave between fathers and mothers; and leave that is universally available, not restricted by eligibility conditions. Overall, too, an adequate early childhood system would see an integration of policies on early childhood services and parenting leave, so that an entitlement to the former is available once the latter comes to an end. On these criteria, all Anglosphere countries fall short[2] – as, it must be conceded, do most other countries.

Division and fragmentation, an obsession with childcare, the spread of markets and privatised provision, inadequate parenting leave and, to round things off, relatively low public funding: these are the most distinctive features of early childhood systems in the Anglosphere. These might be said to constitute an 'Anglosphere model'. We will delve further into these features in the next three chapters, while also noting (in Chapter 3) that they are not exclusive to the Anglosphere, but can also be found in some other countries.

As we have indicated above, other models are available. Chapter 5 includes an example, France, of another type of split system, one in which school-based services are predominant. It also includes an example, Sweden, of a third model, the product of successful transformative change, which over time has moved that country from a split early childhood system to an almost fully integrated system of early childhood education and parenting leave; despite pressures to privatise, it can still be described as a public system. Sweden, therefore, matters both as an example of possibility, of *what* a different type of system looks like, and as an example of process, of *how* wholesale change can be brought about: examples, it should be emphasised, not blueprints.

There have been some attempts at change within the Anglosphere, and we examine in greater detail two of these which we consider of particular significance: England (Chapter 6) and Aotearoa New Zealand (Chapter 7). Both chapters describe and analyse the history of these attempts, considering the conditions and forces driving and impeding change, in particular the conflict between altruistic aims and financial gain. Although neither country has achieved transformation, it will be apparent that Aotearoa New Zealand has got considerably further than England, not least with its innovative early years curriculum and its major reform of the workforce, which has led to a world-leading position, with graduate early years teachers constituting over 70 per cent of the early childhood workforce. Moreover, although the language of 'childcare' is still to be heard, the terminology in widespread use today is 'early childhood education'. England's reform movement stalled at an earlier stage; for example, it did not touch the workforce and left the discourse of 'childcare' dominant and uncontested. However, unlike in Aotearoa New Zealand, a radical new type of integrated public provision was introduced and rapidly expanded: community-based and multi-purpose 'Children's Centres', open to all families, were introduced, only to be decimated in a subsequent era of government disfavour and austerity.

This can all seem very disheartening, and there is much to be depressed and angry about in the Anglosphere. But that is not the end of the story, and the book ends in Chapter 8 on a hopeful note. We consider future transformative possibilities for early childhood systems in the Anglosphere; our approach assumes that these must be one part of a wider transformation of the welfare state and society, a necessary and important part of rising to the challenge of the immense social, political, economic, health and environmental crises that are enveloping and imperilling us, as societies, but also as a species. The extreme danger of the times is reflected in the Doomsday Clock of the Bulletin of the Atomic Scientists, which today (2023) is set at just 90 seconds to midnight, the closest to midnight the clock has been since it was established in 1947. Announcing the latest move of the clock in January 2023, Rachel Bronson, president and CEO of the Bulletin, commented, 'We are living in a time of unprecedented danger, and the Doomsday Clock time reflects that reality. Ninety seconds to midnight is the closest the clock has ever been set to midnight, and it's a decision our experts do not take lightly' (quoted in Borger, 2023).

Converging crises are not the only conditions of our times; we are also, as we shall argue in Chapter 8, living through the end days of the neoliberal hegemony, its credibility in ruins, its devastating consequences apparent for all to see and contributing to the converging crises that are jeopardising humankind and the planet. This context of multiple crises and regime failure makes transformative change of early childhood systems, and much else besides, very urgent: we cannot go on as we are, the time for tweaking and more of the same is over. But it also makes transformative change, which is always very difficult, very possible, providing openings for rethinking, reconceptualising and reforming early childhood systems, and much else besides. Rethinking calls for asking political questions and making political choices, not only about the diagnosis of our times, but also about paradigms, images, purposes, meanings, values and ethics. Reconceptualising involves working with those choices, emerging from the process of rethinking to create new understandings and discourses, while reforming means operationalising choices and implementing a new early childhood system: getting beyond split systems, the domination of 'childcare' services, devalued workforces, marketisation and reliance on private services operating as businesses, and a disjointed relationship between early childhood services and parenting leave.

We will argue in the final chapter that three of the countries featured earlier in the book – England, Aotearoa New Zealand and Sweden – between them can suggest some transformative possibilities, while recent policy developments in Canada provide rich food for thought about a particularly challenging part of transformation, namely, de-privatising the system. Working with such possibilities would create transformative change that leads to:

- an integrated and public early childhood system, with its services reconceptualised as 'early childhood education', an education infused with care and recognised as the first stage of the education system;
- a graduate workforce of early childhood teachers, having parity with other teachers;
- a universal, multi-purpose and community-based form of early childhood education provision; and
- synergy between well-paid parenting leave and children's entitlement to education.

All this is inscribed, we will also argue, with a new culture that values democracy, cooperation, diversity and experimentation, regards early childhood services as a universal public good, and embeds this transformed early childhood system in a transformed education system and a strong, renewed welfare state, able and willing to care for all its citizens and enable them to live flourishing lives.

These, at least, are the choices, the possibilities to which rethinking, reconceptualising and reforming lead us ... but alternatives are available, our riposte to the neoliberal mantra that there is no alternative. Implementing our choices, we recognise, will create many challenges, not least how to de-privatise, but also de-marketise, early childhood services. We will take up these challenges.

Some definitions

We started by saying that this book is about the early childhood systems in an Anglosphere of high-income Anglophone countries. The terms used here, and therefore the parameters of this book, need defining so as to be clear about what is and is not included. In 'early childhood systems' we include formal services providing education and care for children up to compulsory school age, in both centre-based and domestic settings; such services go under a variety of names, including (and this is just in the English language) nursery, crèche, childcare or (long) day care centre, education or early learning and care centre, kindergarten, nursery class and nursery school, childminder, family day care and home-based care. For the moment, this group of services will be labelled 'early childhood education and care services' or 'ECEC services'. But later we will question this term and propose, for a transformed system, the term 'early childhood education', not to ditch care or deny its importance, but to reconceptualise its meaning and its relationship to education. And if here and subsequently we labour this point, it is because we want to leave no room for misunderstanding about what we are saying: no to 'childcare' for some, but yes to 'care' for all.

But when we refer to 'early childhood systems', or 'EC systems', we cover more than ECEC services, including another policy area and form of provision: statutory parenting leaves. We use the term 'parenting leave(s)' to cover legal entitlements for employed parents to take time away from their jobs because of pregnancy and parenthood: such leaves include maternity leave, paternity leave, parental leave and leave to care for sick children.[3] In an ideal world, both these provisions – ECEC services and parenting leave – would be complementary and synchronised, so that, as one entitlement (to well-paid leave) ends, another (to ECEC services) begins; there should be no gap. But except in a few countries (one of which, Sweden, we discuss later), such synergy does not happen, neither in the Anglosphere nor beyond.

While our definition of 'early childhood system' is therefore broader than just early childhood education and care services, being ECEC services plus parenting leaves, we acknowledge it is not a comprehensive account of all policies and provisions that are or could be made for young children and their families. There are many others that could form part of a truly comprehensive account of an early childhood system, including a wide range of financial benefits and health and family support services. These are important and, in general, not the subjects of this book, which adopts a relatively narrow definition of 'early childhood system'; our later discussion and advocacy of the 'Children's Centre' as a model for a transformed early childhood system will offer a type of multi-purpose provision capable of including a wide range of other services pursuing a variety of projects.

We also acknowledge that setting 'compulsory school age' as the upper limit of our enquiry produces different ages in the nine countries we cover, being 5 years in some and 6 years in others. Moreover, defining 'early childhood systems' in relation to the beginning of compulsory schooling goes counter to definitions that take 'early childhood' up to 8 years of age (as adopted by, for example, organisations such as UNICEF and UNESCO). We understand the rationale for this wider age span, but have adopted a narrower definition on the grounds that we want to focus on a particular sector and period of the education system, namely early childhood education, as opposed to including part of primary or elementary education. However, we recognise that the relationship between early childhood and primary/elementary education, is an important issue that needs to figure in any transformative agenda, so we will return to this relationship at a later stage in the book.

Our concern with 'early childhood *systems*' means, as defined, a focus on structures, organisation and policy, rather than on early childhood *pedagogical* theories and practices. It would be misleading to argue a simple relationship between these two domains, the systemic and the pedagogical. Instances of good pedagogical work can be found in poorly conceived systems, while the best-designed system is no guarantee of perfect pedagogy. Our contention, however, would be that a well-conceived and effectively implemented system is one of the conditions that make good pedagogy – however defined – more possible and more likely. We shall, in later chapters, give some examples that support this contention.

Another frequently used term in this book is 'the Anglosphere'. As we said earlier, we have chosen to focus our attention on this part of the world because of the many similarities in its early childhood policies and systems and their many common failings, and because of the positive innovations to be found within the Anglosphere that could provide the basis for transformative change. But what and where is the Anglosphere? We have taken it to include a group of English-speaking nations that share common cultural and historical ties to England or the United Kingdom broadly, and which today maintain close political, diplomatic and, in most cases, military cooperation. More specifically, for our purposes we have taken the 'Anglosphere' to consist of seven high-income nations where English is the predominant language: Aotearoa New Zealand, Australia, Canada, England, the Republic of Ireland, Scotland and the United States. This definition excludes a few smaller or lower-income nations, namely Northern Ireland and Wales within the United Kingdom, Malta and some Caribbean islands. It excludes, too, the many countries where English is an official but not the majority language, including South Africa, Nigeria and some other African countries, as well as India, Pakistan and a number of other countries in Asia and Oceania. It is also important to acknowledge that while English is the most widely spoken language in the seven countries that are the focus of this book, other languages are spoken and some indeed have the status of official languages, for example

French in Canada, Irish (*Gaeilge*) in the Republic of Ireland, and Māori in Aotearoa New Zealand.

Some other terms used in the book should be defined at this early stage. A 'publicly provided service' is owned and managed by a democratically accountable public body such as a local authority or school board, though a 'public service' may include a publicly provided service or any other service that has entered into an agreement with a public body to provide a service on behalf of that body. We use the term 'community-based service' for a service that is not publicly provided, but that is prohibited from making, or is not intended to make, financial gains for distribution to owners or shareholders; it may, for example, be a registered charity, a cooperative, or a community organisation. A 'private service', by contrast, can make financial gains and distribute these to owners or shareholders, and may be owned by a private company, a publicly listed company, a private trust, a partnership, or an individual.

The book also makes frequent reference to 'entitlement' (e.g., a leave entitlement or an entitlement to an ECEC service). By 'entitlement' we mean a statutory or legal right to a benefit (such as leave) or a service. So, for example, England and Scotland provide an entitlement to ECEC for all 3- and 4-year-old children, but in New Zealand, while the government funds services that provide 20 hours' free early childhood education to 3- and 4-year-olds, accessing such services depends on local availability and is not an entitlement.

A final term needing definition early on is 'transformation/al', since the book makes the case for the transformation of early childhood systems in the Anglosphere. It carries for us the idea of making deep or fundamental changes so that the system – its components and how they relate – is completely rethought and reformed. Transformation is the antithesis of merely tweaking or modifying the existing system, an adjustment of the status quo that Roberto Unger describes as 'reformist tinkering with the established system ... [consisting] simply in the accumulation of practical solutions to practical problems' (Unger, 2004: lviii); similarly, Foucault refers to 'superficial transformation', which is 'transformation that remains within the same mode of thought, a transformation that is only a way of adjusting the same thought more closely to the reality of things' (Foucault, 1988: 155). As we shall see, there is quite a lot of 'reformist tinkering' and 'superficial transformation' going on in the Anglosphere, but precious little fundamental change. The case of Sweden will give some idea of what that can look like.

Diversity in the Anglosphere

There are a variety of historical, cultural, social and political connections and similarities across the Anglosphere as defined in this book, beyond sharing English as the main official language, enjoying high levels of income and wealth, and (in the case of Australia, Canada, Ireland, Aotearoa New Zealand and the US) having been governed at some stage by the United Kingdom as part of the British Empire. In later chapters we will look at some other similarities, especially in their early childhood systems and a shared susceptibility to neoliberalism.

But there are also significant differences. There are large variations in population size, ranging in 2022 from the US (333.3 million) through England (56.5 million), Canada (38.9 million) and Australia (26 million) to Scotland, Aotearoa New Zealand and the Republic of Ireland (5.5, 5.1 and 5.1 million respectively) (Office of National Statistics, 2022a; World Bank, 2023). Geographical size is also very different.

Three of the seven countries – Australia, Canada and the United States – are federal nations, with a federal (national) government and a union of partially self-governing provinces, states or territories; in these three countries, primary responsibility for ECEC services resides with provincial, state or territorial governments, rather than at the federal level, though the latter (as we will see) may well exert some influence, for example through federal funding programmes. Both Aotearoa New Zealand and the Republic of Ireland are unitary nation states, where the national government has primary responsibility for early childhood systems. The United Kingdom has four constituent nations (England, Northern Ireland, Scotland, Wales[4]), each of which has primary responsibility for most aspects of its early childhood systems; however, the overall United Kingdom government (which also, confusingly, acts as the English government for devolved policy areas) retains responsibility across the whole of the United Kingdom for subsidies paid to parents who use 'childcare' services, as well as for parenting leave. It should be noted that in no Anglosphere countries, except Scotland, do local authorities play a substantial role in early childhood systems: there is, in short, little democratic accountability to local communities for the early childhood services that serve them, a feature compounded by the high level of private services in the countries of the Anglosphere.

A final point of difference concerns the diversity of population. All countries of the Anglosphere have ethnically diverse populations, with migration in recent years contributing much to this. But there is another element to this diversity, which varies in significance between countries.

Australia, Canada, Aotearoa New Zealand and the United States are all settler countries, colonised mainly by European migrants, with seriously adverse consequences for their indigenous populations. In Australia, Canada and the United States, these indigenous populations now account for fewer than 5 per cent of the total population; but in Aotearoa New Zealand the indigenous Māori population is significantly higher, at 17.4 per cent (New Zealand Government, 2022). Another differentiating feature of Aotearoa New Zealand is Te Tiriti o Waitangi, an agreement made in 1840 between representatives of the British Crown and around 500 Māori chiefs. More will be said about this in Chapter 7.

By contrast, the United Kingdom has not been colonised, at least not for many hundreds of years, while the Republic of Ireland, though experiencing successive waves of British settler colonisation up to the end of the seventeenth century, has maintained an indigenous majority.

With these important contextual similarities and differences in mind, we turn now to consider the early childhood systems in our seven Anglosphere countries, their similarities (and some differences), and the consequences and causes of the 'Anglosphere model'.

Notes

1   Aotearoa is the Māori name for New Zealand and is increasingly used alongside the English name.
2   A partial exception, as we shall see in Chapter 2, is Canada, but only in the province of Québec, which is in any case a Francophone, rather than an Anglophone, part of the country.
3   The International Network on Leave Policies and Research adopts the following definitions for different types of parenting leave (https://www.leavenetwork.org/annual-review-reports/defining-policies/, accessed 3 October 2023). Maternity leave is 'generally available to mothers only (except in a few cases where part of the leave can be transferred to other carers under certain circumstances). It is usually understood to be a health and welfare measure, intended to protect the health of the mother and newborn child, and to be taken just before, during and immediately after childbirth.' Paternity leave is 'generally available to fathers only, usually to be taken soon after the birth of a child and intended to enable the father to spend time with his partner, new child and older children'. Parental leave is 'available equally to mothers and fathers, either as: (i) a non-transferable individual right (i.e. both parents have an entitlement to an equal amount of leave); or (ii) an individual right that can be transferred to the other parent; or (iii) a family right that parents can divide between themselves as they choose. … It is generally understood to be a care measure, intended to give both parents an equal opportunity to spend time caring for a young child; it usually can only be taken after the end of Maternity leave.'
4   In the rest of this book, the focus for the United Kingdom is on two of its nations, England, which accounts for nearly 85 per cent of the UK's population, and Scotland, which accounts for just over 8 per cent. Reference will not be made to Northern Ireland or Wales (which account for just under 3 and 5 per cent respectively of the UK's population), where there are substantial differences from England.

2
Early childhood systems in the Anglosphere: seven national summaries

In the next three chapters we analyse and compare the early childhood systems of the seven countries of the Anglosphere that are the main focus of this book. These countries, as indicated in Chapter 1, are not identical; they differ in important ways. The same applies to their early childhood systems, where there are a number of differences, most obviously in the case of Aotearoa New Zealand (the subject of Chapter 7). Yet our contention is that these systems have more similarities than differences, enough to justify our referring to an 'Anglosphere model', a model that is distinct from systems in most other countries; this will become apparent in Chapter 5, where we use France and Sweden to exemplify two other models.

In Chapter 3, we build up a picture of the 'Anglosphere model' through analysis of the early childhood systems of the seven Anglosphere countries. We also assess how far changes that are underway or proposed in individual countries reinforce the model or show signs of contesting it. We then consider some of the consequences of this model, in particular the adverse effects that it has on children, families, workers and societies. In Chapter 4, we attempt to understand the causes of this distinctive approach to early childhood systems. Why are Anglosphere countries like this? Why do they follow similar paths? The answers to these questions also bear on the issue of transformation. Any discussion of transformation – we shall embark on one later in this book – must not only address the nature of transformation, and what the desired alternative is, but also why and how that transformation may come about: this means an analysis of why things are as they are and, equally important, why that may change.

We base our analysis and comparison of early childhood systems in the seven Anglosphere nations on detailed 'national profiles' that we have built up through consulting documentation from each country and then checking our initial understandings with 'critical friends'. These full 'national profiles' can be found in Annex A, available at https://discovery.ucl.ac.uk/id/eprint/10180525/. We have also drawn, for a few items, on the OECD's Family Database, which provides comparable data for a number of metrics about ECEC services (https://www.oecd.org/els/family/database.htm),[1] and on the annual review of leave policies produced by the International Network on Leave Policies & Research (https://www.leavenetwork.org).

But in this chapter we provide a series of 'national summaries' that outline the salient features of each country, giving readers some basics about and a flavour of Aotearoa New Zealand, Australia, Canada, England, Ireland, Scotland and the United States. Similar summaries for France and Sweden appear in Chapter 5, and their 'national profiles' are also in Annex A. Readers may want to read through all of these summaries before moving on to the next chapter, which contains our analysis of the Anglosphere model and its consequences; alternatively, readers may choose to go straight to that analysis in Chapter 3, referring back to these 'national summaries' (in this chapter) or to the fuller 'national profiles' (Annex A) to check the bases for our conclusions.

National summaries

Aotearoa New Zealand

Aotearoa New Zealand has a population of 5.1 million, including a large Māori indigenous minority. It is a unitary state, and, though there are regional and local authorities, they play a minor role in ECEC services compared to the national government. At national level, responsibility for the early childhood system is split between the Ministry of Education (for ECEC services) and the Ministry for Business, Innovation and Employment (for parenting leave).

Aotearoa New Zealand offers 12 months of parenting leave, though none of this is well paid.[2] (In all of these summary profiles, the period of parenting leave is the maximum length of continuous leave that parents in a two-parent family can take following the birth of a child; 'well paid' is defined as payment to a parent on leave equivalent to at least two-thirds of their earnings.) Compulsory school age is 6 years, but most children enter the first class of primary education when they are 5 years. There is no entitlement to an ECEC place, but all 3- to 5-year-olds can have 20 hours of free ECEC if their parents can secure a place in a service that offers this. Such a place may be in an early childhood education service – which include kindergartens, education and care centres, playcentres and licensed home-based services – or in *kōhanga reo* (total immersion Māori-language services; family and whānau are responsible for the management and operation of their *kōhanga reo* and are encouraged to take part in the daily programme).

According to OECD data for 2020, 46 per cent of children under 3 years attended an ECEC service (with no information on average hours of attendance), and 89 per cent of children aged 3 to 5 years. ECEC services are provided in both 'teacher-led' and 'parent/whānau-led' services ('whānau' means extended family). 'Teacher-led' services include 'education and care centres', 'home-based services' (family day care) and hospital-based services, all of which may take children from a few months to 5 years old, and 'kindergartens', which are mainly available sessionally or for a school day for children from 2 to 5 years old. 'Parent/whānau-led' services include playcentres, playgroups and *kōhanga reo*. Children attending ECEC do not go to school; there is, instead, separate kindergarten provision, but this accounts for a minority of ECEC places. Until recently, 'early childhood education' was the official term for early childhood services, but this was changed to 'early learning' in the 2019 Early Learning Action Plan and subsequent official documentation, a change that has been contested by some advocates. Nearly all services are privately owned:[3] kindergartens, parent/whānau-led services and a small proportion of education and care centres and home-based services are 'community-based', not run for profit: playcentres and playgroups are usually run by parents, and *kōhanga reo* managed by whānau; most education and care centres and home-based services are businesses run for profit.

All services are regulated by the Ministry of Education, with an Education Review Office inspecting all ECEC services as well as schools. There is a national curriculum for all ECEC services. *Te Whāriki (Early Childhood Curriculum)* (Ministry of Education (New Zealand), 1996 ', 2017b') is a bicultural curriculum for children from birth; it provides a framework of four principles, five strands and 23 goals that services are expected to use to weave their own unique curriculum (*whāriki* means a woven mat). Learning outcomes include knowledge, skills and attitudes, which combine as learning dispositions and working theories. *Kōhanga reo* have their own curriculum, *Te Whāriki a te kōhanga reo*, which has the same principles and strands. There are no statutory assessment requirements; most services use narrative approaches to assessment, predominantly in the form of learning stories, particularly focused on dispositions and to a lesser extent, working theories.

According to OECD data, public funding of ECEC is relatively high, above the OECD average. All licensed ECEC services are directly funded through the ECE Funding Subsidy, for which a complex formula applies: payments vary according to enrolment, service type, percentage of qualified teachers, whether the service is all-day or sessional, or for children over 2 or under 2, and whether '20 hours ECE' is offered. All teacher-led services, except kindergartens (where the subsidy rate is higher, all teachers are qualified and teachers are paid on a national collective agreement), get higher rates if they pay their teachers at or above certain minimum salary levels (connected to the kindergarten teachers' salary scale). There is additional 'Equity Funding' for provision serving certain groups (for example, of low socio-economic status, isolated, requiring teaching in a language other than English) and 'Targeted Funding for Disadvantage' for services where 20 per cent of the children attending have spent the largest portion of their life as the dependants of a welfare beneficiary. For the remainder, parents pay fees, though targeted, means-tested 'childcare subsidies' are also available, administered by the Ministry of Work and Income and paid to the service, not the parent. According to OECD data, the net cost of 'childcare services' for two-parent and single-parent families is relatively high.

Nearly three-quarters of the workforce in 'teacher-led' services are graduate early childhood teachers, except in home-based services. Here, service coordinators are nearly all teachers but 'educators' (family day carers) have lower levels of qualification; additional funding is paid to the service if the educators have approved qualifications (level 3). In parent/whānau-led services, the workforce in kōhanga reo require the qualification recognised by the Kōhanga Reo National Trust Board, playcentres have different qualification requirements, and playgroups have no qualification requirements. Teachers in kindergartens have pay parity with primary school teachers. The pay of graduate teachers in education and care centres is lower, just over three-quarters of that of kindergarten teachers, while home-based educators receive, on average, just over the national minimum wage if they have four children (the maximum permitted).

The outgoing Labour government was committed to teachers in education and care centres having pay parity with kindergarten teachers (and therefore with primary school teachers), and had begun the process by introducing 'parity funding rates' for centres that agree to adopt this goal. It also proposed increasing the required proportion of qualified teachers in all teacher-led services from the current 50 per cent to 80 per cent. These proposals for the teaching workforce are in question, as a new coalition government, elected in October 2023, seeks to reverse fair pay agreements and to review regulations in early childhood education.

Australia

Australia has a population of 25.7 million, with an indigenous minority of under 5 per cent and an ethnically diverse majority. It is a federal state, comprising six states and two self-governing territories, and around 560 local councils. The federal government provides funding for non-government schools, for the early childhood education entitlement and to subsidise parents' use of childcare services. Individual states and territory governments have responsibility for ECEC services, regulating services and funding pre-schools, and, along with local councils, may provide some services. At federal level, responsibility for the early childhood system is split between the Department of Education, Skills and Employment (for ECEC) and the Department of Social Services (for parenting leave), while state education departments are mostly responsible at state level for ECEC services. The nine ministers for education (the federal one plus the six state-level and two territory-level ones) work collaboratively in an Education Council to develop national policies and respond to matters that require national collaboration and coordination; the Council provides a forum through which strategic policy on ECEC, school education and higher education can be coordinated at the national level and through which information can be shared, and resources used collaboratively, to address issues of national significance.

Australia offers 24 months of parenting leave, none of which is well paid. Compulsory school age is 6 years (except in Tasmania, where it is 5 years), though most children start primary education earlier, entering a class variously termed 'kindergarten', 'reception', 'pre-primary', 'prep' or 'transition'. All children are entitled to 600 hours of free early childhood education in the year before they start full-time primary school, that is, when they are 4 to 5 years old; this 'pre-school' is provided in schools and stand-alone provision, but mostly in childcare centres.

According to OECD data for 2020, 45 per cent of children under 3 years attended ECEC (with no information on average hours of attendance), and 82 per cent of children aged 3 to 5 years, below the average for OECD member states. Most ECEC is not school-based but is mainly in 'long day care centres' and 'family day care', which provide for children from a few months to 5 years old; 'childcare' or 'day care' is widely used to describe these services. In addition to children entering school before the compulsory school age, there is some limited 'pre-school' provision in schools; schools are mostly provided by state government agencies (about two-thirds) or by independent bodies with public funding, the largest provider being the Catholic Church. Over 80 per cent of non-school services are privately owned, with the majority run as businesses for profit.

State and territory authorities are responsible for regulating ECEC services. The national Australian Children's Education and Care Quality Authority supports the monitoring and quality improvement activities of state and territory regulators. There is a National Quality Framework, a national quality standard covering long day care, family day care, pre-school/kindergarten, and outside-school-hours care services. There is a national curriculum framework, the Early Years Learning Framework, which covers all children from birth to primary school entry age and is compulsory for all settings under the National Quality Framework. In addition, individual states and territories may choose to have a state-specific approved learning framework such as the Victorian Early Years Learning and Development Framework for children from birth to 8 years. Individual states have various reporting, testing and diagnostic regimes that are implemented in the year before school commencement or in the first year of schooling, while the Australian Early Development Census, which takes place every three years, assesses the developmental outcomes of children in their first year of school.

According to OECD data, public funding of ECEC in Australia is low, below the OECD average. School-based services are directly publicly funded; so too are non-school services that offer the early childhood education entitlement. The federal government also supports access to non-school services through the 'Child Care Package', which includes: the means-tested Child Care Subsidy providing families with financial assistance to help with the cost of ECEC and to encourage workforce participation, paid directly to providers to reduce the fees they charge parents; the Additional Child Care Subsidy, a top-up payment in addition to the Child Care Subsidy that provides targeted fee assistance to vulnerable or disadvantaged families and children facing barriers in accessing affordable ECEC; the Community Child Care Fund, which provides grants to ECEC services to reduce barriers to accessing childcare, particularly in disadvantaged, regional and remote communities; and the Inclusion Support Program, which improves access to ECEC for children with additional needs through tailored inclusion advice and support and by reducing more challenging inclusion barriers. According to OECD data, overall net costs of 'childcare services' for two-earner couple families and single-parent families are relatively high (compared to other OECD member states).

The ECEC workforce in school-based provision consists of graduate teachers, and assistants. For non-school services, the regulatory framework requires that centres have at least one degree-qualified teacher (predominantly ISCED[4] level 6), half of staff holding or working towards at least a short-cycle tertiary qualification (at least ISCED level 5), and half of staff holding or working towards at least the minimum requirement for all workers, a post-secondary qualification (ISCED level 4). In 2021, 92.9 per cent of paid contact staff in childcare centres had an ECEC-related qualification: 12.4 per cent had a bachelor's degree (ISCED level 6) or above; 47.5 per cent had an Advanced Diploma or Diploma in an ECEC-related field (ISCED level 5); and 33.2 per cent had a Certificate III or IV (ISCED level 4) in an ECEC-related field. The average gross weekly earnings for workers in these centres are above the national minimum wage, but well below average weekly earnings.

The Labor government elected in 2022 stated that early childhood is a policy priority, particularly 'affordable childcare'. In November 2022 it passed legislation to increase the Child Care Subsidy to parents; it has also tasked the Productivity Commission[5] to conduct an inquiry, to report in June 2024, into Australia's early childhood education and care system, 'focused on delivering our two key goals – removing barriers to workforce participation for parents and providing a foundation for our children's future wellbeing and success'.[6] A draft report published in November 2023 recommended that 'Up to 30 hours or three days a week of quality ECEC should be available to all children aged 0–5 years'(Australian Productivity Commission, 2023: 2). Two state governments (New South Wales and Victoria) announced plans in June 2022 to introduce an extra year of free early childhood education, from 2030 and 2025 respectively.

Canada

Canada has a population of 38 million, with an indigenous minority of under 5 per cent, and an ethnically diverse majority; it includes a substantial Francophone community (nearly a quarter of the total population), 85 per cent of whom live in the province of Québec. It is a federal state, with a federal government, 10 provinces and three territories, and many municipal or local authorities. Individual provinces and territories have responsibility for and control over their early childhood services; municipalities have little involvement with ECEC services except in the most populous province of Ontario, where the provincial government has delegated most of its powers to municipalities, except for regulation. The federal government has no education department, but has provided a series of funding initiatives for ECEC services, including a recent and major Canada-wide Early Learning and Child Care Plan, announced in 2021 and involving Can$30 billion of funding over five years; a newly formed Federal Secretariat on Early Learning and Child Care, located within Employment and Social Development Canada, is responsible for this strategy. Ministries of education are responsible for ECEC in all provinces and territories except Alberta. Education ministers work together on pan-Canadian initiatives through the Council of Ministers of Education,

The 13 provinces and territories have responsibility for parenting leave regulations, though payment is made by the federal Employment Insurance programme, and administered by Employment and Social Development Canada, except for the province of Québec, which has its own benefit programme and distinctive parenting leave policy. The distinctive leave policy in this majority Francophone province reflects the fact that Québec's point of reference for many social policy areas is 'not Canada or the United States but Europe – Scandinavia for work–life balance and France for family policy' (Doucet, McKay and Tremblay, 2009: 40).

Canada offers 50 weeks of parenting leave, none of which is well paid, with the exception of Québec which offers 50 weeks of which 30 are well paid; Québec also offers some flexibility in how parenting leave can be taken, with a shorter period of leave paid at a higher rate or a longer period paid at a lower rate. Compulsory school age is 6 years. All provinces and territories offer an entitlement to early childhood education for 5-year-olds, mostly for a full school day, and most now offer, or are phasing in, an entitlement for all 4-year-olds; attendance for 5-year-olds is compulsory in three provinces. This 'kindergarten' is nearly always provided in school-based provision.

There is no OECD data on ECEC attendance.[7] ECEC is provided in both school-based and non-school-based provision. School-based ECEC provision is mainly available in kindergarten or pre-kindergarten classes for 4- and 5-year-olds ('*maternelle*' in Québec). Most children attending ECEC services go to non-school provision, in variously named centres and with 'family day carers' ('*Service de garde en milieu familial reconnu*' in Québec), which provide for children from a few months to 5 years old and sometimes older. The official English term for ECEC services is 'early learning and childcare', though 'childcare' is widely used to describe non-school services. Schools are mostly provided by local school boards (or school divisions), which usually have primary responsibility for the operation of elementary schools, including kindergarten classes, although in a few provinces some religious schools are also publicly funded. Most non-school services are run by not-for-profit private providers; this sector accounts for nearly two-thirds of centre-based provision, with the remainder run by for-profit businesses and a very few that are publicly run.

Provinces and territories are responsible for regulating ECEC services and for developing curriculum frameworks. Almost all have a framework in place, with the exceptions of Nunavut and Yukon, where it is in development, and Newfoundland and Labrador and the Northwest Territories, where draft frameworks are being piloted (as at 2022). Most provinces have a curriculum framework covering children aged 0 to 5 years in all settings; New Brunswick has a dual curriculum system in place, with distinct frameworks for the English and French ECEC sectors. There are no national statutory assessment requirements.

There is no OECD data on public funding of ECEC services in Canada. School-based services are directly publicly funded; so are non-school services that offer the early childhood education entitlement. Other ECEC services are mainly funded by parental fees. But all provinces and territories provide some operational funding (direct payments to services), which sometimes takes the form of wage grants, and a growing number of provinces combine operational funding with setting province-wide parent fees in some or most of their regulated childcare services. All provinces and territories (except Québec) subsidise low-income families' use of the services by covering some or all of the fees on the parents' behalf, paying the subsidy directly to the service provider. Parent fee subsidies are administered by provincial or territorial governments, except in Ontario, where local (municipal or regional) governments are mandated to manage the administration of provincial childcare funding, including fee subsidies.

Québec does not use fee subsidy, but funds the majority of its services for children from 0 to 12 years operationally. Any parent of a child aged 0–4 or 5–12 years (in school) is eligible for a 'reduced contribution' (subsidised) space if one is available, paying only the provincially determined flat fee (Can$8.85 in 2023) regardless of parental employment status or income; 'childcare centres' and family day care, including some for-profit centres, are publicly funded in this way. In addition, there are unfunded for-profit centres for which parents receive a tax credit that reimburses between 26 per cent and 75 per cent of eligible fees paid, depending on parental income.

Substantial changes in funding, however, are underway across Canada, via the federal government's Early Learning and Child Care Plan, and the major new funding it is offering. In April 2021, the federal government announced the provision of Can$30 billion over five years for this strategy and committed to continue spending at the rate of Can$9.2 billion after 2026 (including Indigenous early learning). The strategy works through the federal government and the provincial and territorial governments' negotiation of agreements for its implementation, with federal money allocated according to the projected population of children from 0 to 12 years in each province or territory. In most cases agreements include the following provisions: reduction of 'childcare' fees by half by the end of 2022 and to an average of Can$10 a day by 2025–6; developing a plan for workforce reform and improvements, including a publicly funded wage grid; expanding spaces towards the goal of 59 per cent utilisation, with expansion to occur in the public and non-profit sectors only; commitment to evidence-based quality frameworks and data collection; improved training and wages for 'early childhood educators' (working in non-school settings); collaboration with and planning for Indigenous services; and improved access for vulnerable children and diverse populations.

Of particular significance is the challenge the strategy poses to the process of privatisation, as it envisages a publicly managed system with funding and tools to implement it; if this system is implemented, it will see the expansion of services under the strategy focused on the public and non-profit sectors only: funding will not go to for-profit services. We will return to consider the significance of this policy in Chapter 8, when we address whether and how the Anglosphere might be able to de-marketise and de-privatise its ECEC services. Overall, the strategy is intended to improve affordability, enhance quality, increase access and support inclusion. Before the onset of this strategy, OECD data showed the overall net costs of 'childcare services' for two-earner couple families to be above the OECD average, but well below, and very low, for single-parent families.

The ECEC workforce in school-based provision consists of graduate teachers and assistants, though the requirement for a specialised qualification in early childhood education varies across provinces and territories. Workers in non-school services are called 'early childhood educators' and are generally not graduate teachers. Qualifications for early childhood educators vary across the country; some provinces require some of this group to hold a two-year post-secondary early childhood diploma (ISCED level 4), while in others it is a one-year qualification. It is, however, proving so hard to recruit qualified staff that many centres operate without their required complement of such staff, a derogation sanctioned by governments; the major reasons for the lack of qualified staff in non-school settings are low wages, poor benefits and lack of recognition, along with low job satisfaction and educators moving to better-paid jobs in schools. The pay of early childhood educators and assistants is not competitive with other occupations that require a college education; in 2019, workers in childcare centres were making Can$19.97 per hour, 28 per cent less than workers in all other occupations, and this gap has persisted over time.

England

England has a population of 56.5 million, with no indigenous minority, though it has a substantial and growing minority ethnic presence. It is one of four countries that constitute the United Kingdom, but does not have its own devolved government or parliament. It is a unitary state, and though there are local authorities, in ECEC they play a secondary role to national government, supporting and promoting services (for example, distributing public funding to ECEC services that provide entitlements, and ensuring there is 'sufficient childcare for working parents, as far as is practicable', through managing the market), but rarely providing services themselves (they should not provide places unless there are no private providers willing to do so). At national level, responsibility for the early childhood system is split between the Department for Education (for ECEC services) and the Department for Business and Trade (for parenting leave); the former has responsibility for ECEC in England, the latter for parenting leave across the whole United Kingdom. In addition, the UK government's tax authority (His Majesty's Revenue and Customs) is responsible for administering the childcare subsidy paid to parents (see below).

The UK offers 14 months of parenting leave, though only six weeks is well paid. Compulsory school age in England is 5 years, though most children enter the first class of primary education ('reception class') when they are 4 years old. All 3- and 4-year-olds are entitled to 570 hours of free 'early education or childcare' a year, which is often taken to be 15 hours each week for 38 weeks of the year; this has been extended to 30 hours' free childcare for 38 weeks a year, but only for children whose parents are employed and meet certain earnings conditions. Some 2-year-olds are eligible for 15 hours' free 'education and childcare' if they meet certain conditions, for example, their parents are on benefits, or they are looked-after children or children with disabilities. Periods of free attendance can be taken in school-based or non-school-based provision, if the provider is approved and follows the curriculum.

According to OECD data for 2018 for the UK (not provided separately for the UK's four nations), 45 per cent of children under 3 years attended ECEC services, for an average of 19.5 hours a week, and 100 per cent of children aged 3 to 5 years. ECEC is in both school-based and non-school-based provision. School-based ECEC provision is mainly available in primary schools, in nursery classes for 3- and 4-year-olds and (for rather more than half of children) in 'reception classes' for 4- and 5-year-olds, though these are actually the first class of primary education. In addition, there are a relatively small number of nursery schools, separate schools that are dedicated to the education of 3- and 4-year-olds; these are under threat from financial cuts. Most children attending ECEC services go to non-school provision, mainly in 'nurseries', but also with 'childminders' (family day carers), from a few months old; there are also sessional 'pre-schools' (from 2 years) and Children's Centres; these Centres, intended to provide a wide range of services for children and parents, sometimes including education and 'childcare', will be described and discussed further in Chapter 6, and have been much reduced in number and capacity in recent years by financial cuts. Though not the official term, 'childcare' is widely used to describe non-school services, as well as the 30 hours' free entitlement in school-based services. Schools are either overseen and funded by local authorities ('maintained' schools), or are independent publicly funded schools run by not-for-profit trusts and accountable to central government ('academies' and 'free schools', which accounted for 39 per cent of primary school pupils in 2021). Except for Children's Centres, non-school services are nearly all privately owned, with most nurseries run as for-profit businesses.

All ECEC services are regulated by Ofsted (the Office for Standards in Education, Children's Services and Skills), a non-ministerial department of central government. Ofsted is responsible for registering and inspecting all ECEC services, as well as all schools and most other children's services. A single curriculum framework, the early years foundation stage (EYFS), specifies the standards that 'school and childcare providers must meet for the learning, development and care of children from birth to 5' and is 53 pages long; it has sections on overarching principles, learning and development requirements (including 17 'early learning goals'), assessment, and welfare and safeguarding requirements. There are two statutory assessments for reception-class children: the 'reception baseline assessment' of children when they enter reception class (i.e., at 4 years), covering language, communication and literacy, and mathematics; and the 'early years foundation stage profile', focused on children's attainment at the end of the EYFS (i.e., at 5 years) in relation to the 17 early learning goals.

According to OECD data, public funding of ECEC in the UK overall is low, below the OECD average. School-based services are directly publicly funded; so too are non-school services that offer the early education and childcare entitlement. For the remainder, parents pay fees but these are subsidised in two ways, both paid to parents: Tax-Free Childcare (a 20 per cent contribution towards 'childcare' fees for working families earning above minimum and below maximum thresholds), and Universal Credit (up to 85 per cent of 'childcare' costs for eligible low-income families). Both subsidies are the responsibility of the UK government and apply across all four UK countries. According to OECD data, the net cost of 'childcare services' for two-earner couple families and single-parent families is relatively high.

The ECEC workforce in school-based provision consists of graduate teachers and assistants. Staff working in other provision have lower qualifications; managers need only hold a NVQ level 3 qualification (ISCED level 4) and half of remaining staff must hold an NVQ level 2 qualification (ISCED level 3). Only 11 per cent are graduates, and over half of graduates have an Early Years degree rather than a teaching qualification. Overall, most staff are qualified at NVQ level 3 or lower, with a recent survey suggesting that the proportion with this level 3 qualification has actually decreased in recent years. Pay is low in non-school provision, with workers earning two-thirds the hourly rate of school-based workers and 24 per cent earning at or below the national minimum wage; an earlier study found 44.5 per cent claimed welfare benefits because of low pay. Turnover is high and increasing and recruitment is a problem.

Proposed changes in the March 2023 budget include the extension of free 'childcare' for 30 hours a week and 38 weeks a year to children from 9 months of age who have employed parents who meet certain earnings and working hours conditions, or approximately 22 funded hours a week if parents spread their entitlement out over the year. This will be phased in during 2024 and 2025.

Republic of Ireland

The Republic of Ireland (referred to as 'Ireland' below) has a population of 5 million, with a growing minority ethnic presence; Irish Travellers were officially recognised as an indigenous ethnic minority in March 2017. It is a unitary state, and though there are local authorities, they play a minor role in ECEC services compared to the national government. At national level, responsibility for the early childhood system is split three ways between the Department of Children, Equality, Disability, Integration and Youth and the Department for Education (for ECEC services) and the Department of Justice and Equality (for parenting leave).

Ireland offers 24 months of parenting leave, though none is well paid. Compulsory school age is 6 years. All children from 2 years and 8 months old are offered a two-year period of free 'early learning and care' for three hours per day, five days a week for 38 weeks per year under the Early Childhood Care and Education (ECCE) programme, but this is dependent on families securing a place in a service providing this offer: it is not, at present, a legal entitlement. This programme is delivered by non-school services.

According to OECD data for 2020, 36 per cent of children under 3 years attended ECEC services, for an average of 29.4 hours a week, and 100 per cent of children aged 3 to 5 years. ECEC services are in both school-based and non-school-based provision. School-based ECEC provision is mainly available from 4 years, when children may be enrolled in infant classes in primary schools, which are formally regarded as primary education; roughly half of 4-year-olds enter these classes, and the remaining children enter when they are 5 years old. There is also an Early Start Programme, a one-year intervention scheme offered in 40 selected schools in designated disadvantaged areas for children between 3.2 and 4.7 years. Most children attending ECEC services go to non-school provision, mainly in 'early learning and care' (ELC) centres, but also to 'childminders' (family day carers), from a few months old, and in sessional 'pre-schools' (from 2 years). Though it is not the official term, 'childcare' is widely used to describe these non-school services. Primary schools are state-funded but privately owned, 95 per cent by religious denominations (largely Catholic), while non-school services are all privately owned, with most ELC centres run as for-profit businesses.

Three organisations are involved in regulating ECEC services:

• Tusla (Child and Family Agency), a government agency that registers and inspects all non-school services;

- the Department of Education Inspectorate, which, apart from inspecting schools, conducts education-focused inspections of the ECCE programme; and
- Pobal, another government-funded agency, which monitors administrative and financial information.

A single curriculum framework, *Aistear* (National Council for Curriculum and Assessment (Ireland), 2009), covers all children from birth to 6 years in non-school settings and is 59 pages long, with sections on principles of early learning and development and on aims and learning goals for four themes; the framework is accompanied by guidelines to support ECEC centres and parents in its implementation and an online practice guide. Children under 6 years in primary schools are mainly covered by the primary education curriculum, although *Aistear* informs the primary curriculum and pedagogical approaches for this age group. There are no statutory assessment requirements.

According to OECD data, public funding of ECEC is low, well below the OECD average. School-based services are directly publicly funded; so are non-school services that offer the ECCE programme. For the remainder, parents pay fees, but these are subsidised for parents with children over 6 months who are using 'childcare' services, through a National Childcare Scheme that provides two types of subsidy: a universal subsidy and a means-tested subsidy. Parents apply for these subsidies, which are paid to the service provider, and the provider reduces the parents' bill accordingly. These two sources of public funding have recently been augmented by a third, Core Funding, paid direct to non-school services that sign an agreement with the government (90 per cent had in September 2022), and intended to improve affordability and quality through bettering staff pay and qualifications; this funding supports payment of a minimum wage for staff while maintaining fees in 2022/3 at September 2021 rates. According to OECD data, the net cost of 'childcare services' for two-earner couple families is relatively high, but much lower for single-parent families.

The ECEC workforce in school-based provision consists of graduate primary school teachers and assistants. Staff working in other provision, called 'early childhood educators', must have an ISCED level 4 qualification and room leaders ISCED level 5; in 2021, 34 per cent had a graduate-level qualification (ISCED level 6) or higher, up from 12 per cent in 2012. Average pay for workers in non-school settings has been low, in 2021 on average about 24 per cent above the national minimum wage, and turnover high. The new Core Funding scheme sets minimum pay rates for the 'childcare' workforce in services that have signed agreements, bringing an increase for 70 per cent of the workforce, though the minimum rate for 'early childhood educators' is still only 24 per cent above the minimum wage and only slightly above the living wage.[8]

Proposed changes include extending regulation and public funding to childminders by 2024, and a legal entitlement to early childhood education from 2028. A workforce plan, published in 2021, proposes improvements in education and qualifications for staff in ELC centres by 2028, including a graduate-led workforce, 85 per cent of early years educators to have at least ISCED 5, and a national programme of CPD opportunities (Government of Ireland, 2021: 15). In 2019, Ireland introduced a new form of parenting leave, parent's leave, in addition to parental leave; unlike the latter, the former is paid, but at a low flat rate; it has been extended from an initial two weeks to seven weeks (2023), rising to nine weeks in due course.

Scotland

Scotland has a population of 5.5 million, with no indigenous minority, though it has a growing minority ethnic presence. It is one of four countries that constitute the United Kingdom, and a wide range of matters are devolved from the UK government to the Scottish government and the Scottish parliament, including most, but not all, aspects of the early childhood system. There are also local authorities, which have responsibility for providing education and for ensuring that there are sufficient places for the early learning entitlement. At national level, responsibility for the early childhood system is split between the Scottish government's Early Learning and Childcare Directorate (for ECEC services) and the UK government's Department for Business, Industry and Industrial Strategy (for parenting leave). In addition, the UK government's tax authority (His Majesty's Revenue and Customs) is responsible for administering the childcare subsidy paid to parents (see below).

The UK offers 14 months of parenting leave, though only six weeks is well paid. Compulsory school age in Scotland is 5 years, and children actually start primary school when they are aged between 4.5 and 5.5 years old, depending when their fifth birthday is. All 3- and 4-year-olds are entitled to 1140 hours per year of free 'early learning and childcare' (ELC), the official term used for ECEC services; patterns of attendance for this entitlement are flexible, for example 30 hours a week during term-time or fewer hours spread out over the whole year. Some 2-year-olds are entitled to this provision if they meet certain eligibility conditions, for example looked-after children and children whose families receive a qualifying benefit, who comprise around a quarter of the 2-year-old population. The ELC entitlement can be taken in school-based or non-school-based provision, if the provider is willing to enter into a contract with its local authority (which dispenses funding) and follow the National Standard for Early Learning and Childcare, which consists of criteria across 10 areas.

According to OECD data for 2018 for the UK (not provided separately for the UK's four nations), 45 per cent of children under 3 years attended ECEC services, for an average of 19.5 hours a week, and 100 per cent of children aged 3 to 5 years. ECEC services are in both school-based and non-school-based provision. School-based ECEC provision is mainly available in primary schools as nursery classes for 3- and 4-year-olds; in addition, there are a relatively small number of nursery schools, schools that are dedicated to the education of 3- and 4-year-olds. Most children attending ECEC services go to non-school provision, mainly in 'nurseries' but also with 'childminders' (family day carers), available from a few months old to primary school age; there are also sessional 'pre-schools' (from 2 years), and Children and Family Centres, sometimes called community nurseries, which usually prioritise the children with the greatest needs and provide full-day ELC for children aged 0 to 5 years and a range of support services for families. Though it is not the official term, 'childcare' is widely used to describe these services. Schools are provided by local authorities ('maintained' schools). Except for Children and Family Centres, most of which are provided by local authorities, non-school services are mostly private, divided between those run as businesses for profit and those run not for profit.

Two bodies are responsible for the regulation of ECEC services: Education Scotland and Social Care and Social Work Improvement Scotland (SCSWIS), known as the Care Inspectorate. There is a national curriculum – Curriculum for Excellence – that covers the 3 to 18 years age range. Overlapping with the curriculum there is *Realising the Ambition: Being me* (Education Scotland, 2020), which provides practice guidance from birth to 6 years old; it is 116 pages long and includes sections on what I (the young child) need to grow and develop, the importance of play, early childhood curriculum and pedagogical leadership, putting pedagogy into practice, and critically reflective practice. In addition, there is the National Standard for Early Learning and Childcare, whose criteria must be met by services providing the early education and childcare entitlement.

According to OECD data, public funding of ECEC in the UK overall is low, below the OECD average. School-based services are directly publicly funded; so are non-school services that offer the ELC entitlement. For the remainder, parents pay fees, but these are subsidised in two ways (both paid to parents): Tax-Free Childcare (a 20 per cent contribution towards childcare fees for working families earning above minimum and below maximum thresholds), and Universal Credit (up to 85 per cent of childcare costs for eligible low-income families). Both subsidies are the responsibility of the UK government and apply across all four UK countries. According to OECD data, in the UK overall the net cost of 'childcare services' for two-earner couple families and single-parent families is relatively high.

Although there is no separate data on the Scottish workforce in EC services, it is likely they are similar to England, with school-based services staffed by graduate primary school teachers and assistants, and non-school services staffed by workers with lower qualifications and low levels of pay.

United States

The United States has a population of 331.9 million, by far the largest in the Anglosphere, with an indigenous minority of under 2 per cent, and a very ethnically diverse majority including substantial Hispanic, African American and Asian minorities; in 2019, for the first time, more than half of the nation's population under age 16 identified as a racial or ethnic minority. It is a federal state, with a federal (national) government, 50 states, a federal district, five major self-governing territories (including Puerto Rico and Guam) and several island possessions with no permanent inhabitants; there are also local authorities, counties and municipalities, nearly 14,000 public school districts, and 326 Indian reservations, areas governed by federally recognised Native American tribal nations. With so many different public entities, responsibility for the early childhood system is complex. The federal government provides various funding streams to support ECEC services, including:

- to enable states to improve ECEC coordination, quality and access;
- to support local education authorities or schools with large concentrations of children from low-income families;
- to support families with their childcare costs;
- to support early childhood services for at-risk children; and
- to provide services (the Head Start programme) to support the development of 3- and 4-year-old children from low-income families.

Individual states have responsibility for and control over their systems, with responsibility often further devolved to local authorities; local school boards administer most publicly funded schools. At federal level, responsibility for the early childhood system is split between the Department of Education and the Department of Health and Human Services (ECEC services) and the Department of Labor (parenting leave), while multiple state agencies (human services, state education, health, etc.) and local school districts administer ECEC services.

The US has no paid parenting leave, only 12 weeks' unpaid leave available for a variety of family and health reasons including childbirth. Compulsory school age varies across states from 5 to 8 years, with 6 years the most common. There is no national entitlement to ECEC services, though one year of publicly funded kindergarten is available (mainly for 5-year-olds) in all states; in 2020, a third of 4-year-olds attended publicly funded pre-kindergarten education, and levels of attendance varied considerably, from none at all in some states to universal provision in others. Kindergarten is provided in schools, but pre-kindergarten can be in school-based or non-school-based provision.

According to OECD data for 2018, 66 per cent of children aged 3 to 5 years attended ECEC services, well below the average for OECD member states; there is no OECD information on attendance for children under 3 years. ECEC services are in both school-based and non-school-based provision. School-based ECEC provision is mainly available in pre-kindergarten and kindergarten classes in primary schools, mostly for 4- and 5-year-olds respectively. Most children attending ECEC go to non-school provision, in various kinds of centres or with family day carers. Though not the official terms, 'childcare' and 'day care' are widely used to describe these services. Schools are mostly provided by local school boards, but an increasing proportion are independent publicly funded schools run by private organisations with a contract with state governments or school boards ('charter schools', which accounted for 7 per cent of school pupils in 2021). Over 80 per cent of non-school services are privately owned, divided between those run as businesses for profit and those run not for profit.

Responsibility for regulation is generally at the state level, but the Head Start programme is governed by federal regulations. There is no national curriculum, though Head Start centres follow a federally mandated curriculum the goal of which is to promote school readiness among at-risk children. Individual states have early childhood curriculum standards or curriculum guidance.

According to OECD data, public funding of ECEC in the United States is very low, well below the OECD average. School-based services are directly publicly funded. The funding of other ECEC services is complex, ranging from centres that are entirely privately funded to services supported to varying degrees by local, state or federal funds. Parents who pay fees are subsidised in two ways through the tax system, both of them via payment to parents: the Child and Dependent Care Tax Credit and the Exclusion for Employer-provided Child Care. In addition, the federal Child Care and Development Fund provides financial assistance to low-income families to access childcare so that parents can attend work, training or education, and also funds to improve the quality of childcare services. Again, according to OECD data, in the United States overall the net cost of 'childcare services' for two-earner couple families and single-parent families is relatively high.

School-based services are staffed by graduate teachers. Non-school services are mostly staffed by workers with lower qualifications and low levels of pay; in the majority of states, pay is below the living wage for a single adult.

Having set out the basic details of the early childhood systems in these seven Anglophone countries, we turn now to an analysis, offering one interpretation or reading of these descriptive accounts.

Notes

1   The OECD, or Organisation for Economic Cooperation and Development, is an intergovernmental economic organisation with 38 member countries, the majority of which have high-income economies, including all the Anglophone countries covered in this book. Founded in 1961 to stimulate economic progress and world trade, it has extended its reach into areas of social policy, including family policy and education. The OECD data used includes 'childcare costs' for parents. The section (PF3.4) of the OECD Family Database that covers 'Childcare support' includes estimates of 'gross childcare fees' and 'net childcare costs' for families. The former does not take account of government subsidies to parents using 'childcare' services; the latter 'takes into account gross childcare fees', plus 'childcare-specific supports designed to reduce the costs faced by parents, and the interaction between childcare[-]specific policies and any other tax and benefit policies'. Our reference to 'childcare' costs in this chapter is to 'net childcare costs'.
2   Although 26 weeks of 'Primary Carer's leave' is paid at 100 per cent of earnings, a ceiling is placed on payments that is below the national minimum wage, which means the actual level of payment is always low.
3   The exception is Te Kura, formerly known as the Correspondence School, which is the only state-run provision. It offers distance education programmes, including free early childhood programmes for children aged 2 to 6 years.
4   ISCED is the International Standard Classification of Education, in which level 3 is 'upper secondary education', level 4 is 'post-secondary non-tertiary education', level 5 is 'short-cycle tertiary education, and level 6 is 'bachelor's degree or equivalent tertiary education level'.

5   Australia's Productivity Commission describes itself as 'the Australian Government's independent research and advisory body on a range of economic, social and environmental issues affecting the welfare of Australians' (https://www.pc.gov.au/about; accessed 4 October 2023).

6   Chambers et al., 2023.

7   National statistics for children under 6 years in 'regulated or unregulated child care' are published by Statistics Canada, but do not include children attending kindergarten (Statistics Canada, 2021). These national statistics are therefore not comparable with comparative data published in the OECD Family Database, which has no data for Canada.

8   A national living wage will replace the national minimum wage from 2026. The living wage will be set at 60 per cent of the median wage in any given year. The national minimum wage will remain in place until the 60 per cent living wage is fully phased in.

3
Early childhood systems in the Anglosphere: similar features, similar failings

Early childhood systems: the Anglosphere model

The national summaries in the previous chapter provide a welter of detail, with a jumble of differing terminologies, initials and numbers; faced by such copious detail, it can be all too easy to miss the wood for the trees. But stand back a bit and the wood does emerge, defined by the features that the seven Anglosphere countries covered in this book have in common. In this section, we identify these features, which give the early childhood systems in these countries not only a similar identity, but an identity that is distinctly different from many other countries. This distinct identity is what we term the 'Anglosphere model'. We also consider some of the common consequences of this model, in particular the failings to which it gives rise.

The term 'model' highlights similarities across the seven countries. But a word of caution should be added. These similarities do not mean that the early childhood systems in these countries are identical. There are differences in how similar features manifest in each country, for example the differing proportion of private (for-profit) providers in what are mainly non-publicly provided services, or the differing proportion of places provided by educational institutions such as schools or kindergartens in what are childcare-dominated systems.

Split childcare-dominant system

As we noted in Chapter 1, early childhood services in all countries start out split, 'split between services that have a predominantly employment or welfare function (providing "childcare for working mothers" and support for poor or otherwise disadvantaged families), and others that have a predominantly educational function'. And despite an education role now being widely applied to all ECEC services, a split still runs through today's services. What do we mean by 'split'?

Building on an earlier study for UNESCO of integration of ECEC services (Kaga et al., 2010), seven structural dimensions can be identified, and services in any country can be defined as split or integrated for each dimension:

- Policy making and administration
- Regulation
- Curriculum or similar pedagogical guidelines
- Access to services
- Funding (including who pays and how payment is made)
- Workforce (including structure, education and pay)
- Type of provision

In a 2019 report, Eurydice, an EU network 'whose task is to explain how education systems are organised in Europe and how they work' (https://eurydice.eacea.ec.europa.eu/), lists four 'core dimensions of ECEC policy for an integrated system from birth to the start of primary education' (Eurydice, 2019: 12). They are similar to four of the dimensions listed above, namely, setting (type of provision), ministry (policy making and administration), staff (workforce) and curriculum; regulation, access and funding are not included by Eurydice. We shall, however, continue to include them in our discussion of structural integration.

Rather than a simple binary – split or integrated – it is more accurate and useful to think of ECEC services in any country as being on a continuum, running from totally split (not integrated on any of the seven dimensions) to totally integrated (integrated on all seven dimensions). As can be seen in Table 3.1, which includes the seven Anglosphere nations, as well as France and Sweden, which feature in Chapter 5, no country is fully integrated; the nearest, by a long way, to achieving this is Sweden, followed by Aotearoa New Zealand. In some cases (Ireland, Scotland), ECEC services are only integrated on one dimension; France is not integrated on any.

To say that ECEC services in the Anglosphere, except for Aotearoa New Zealand, are still split on most dimensions is not to say they are unusual in any way; that is how these services are in most countries. What distinguishes them is *how* they are split. The split in ECEC services has often been described as being between 'care' (or 'childcare') and

Table 3.1 Extent of integration of ECEC services and of these services with parenting leave for Anglosphere countries and France and Sweden

	Policy making & administration	Regulation	Curriculum	Access to services	Funding	Workforce	Type of provision	Integration ECEC and parenting leave	Public spending on ECEC as per cent GDP (2019)
Australia	✓✓	✓	✓	×	×	×	×	×	0.6 per cent
Canada	Ø✓	✓	✓	×	×	×	×	×	NI
England	✓	✓	✓	×	×	×	×	×	0.5 per cent
Ireland	×	×	×	×	×	×	×	×	0.3 per cent
N. Zealand	✓	✓	✓	×	×	✓	×	×	0.9 per cent
Scotland	✓	×	×	×	×	×	×	×	0.5 per cent
USA	×?	?	?	×	×	×	×	×	0.3 per cent
France	×	×	×	×	×	×	×	×	1.3 per cent
Sweden	✓	✓	✓	✓	×	✓	✓	✓	1.6 per cent

Sources: Koslowski et al., 2022; OECD Family Database, Chart PF3.1.A

Notes

✓ integrated; × not integrated

Policy making and administration: in federal nations, the first symbol refers to federal government, the second to state, provincial or territorial governments. ? indicates that there is variation between the states or provinces. Ø for Canada denotes that there is no federal ministry with responsibility for ECEC.

Integration ECEC and parenting leave: whether these two policy areas are integrated, i.e. if there is a gap between the end of well-paid parenting leave and the start of an entitlement to ECEC services

Public spending on ECEC as per cent of GDP: the figure for England and Scotland is the overall figure for the UK.

For countries where children enter school at age 5 (such as Australia, Aotearoa New Zealand and the United Kingdom), pre-primary expenditure data is adjusted by adding in the expenditure corresponding to children aged 5 who are enrolled in primary school.

'education', but this needs redefining today when, in many countries, all services are meant to have an educational function; for example, most Anglosphere countries have a 'curriculum' or similar document covering all services, 'childcare' or school-based or kindergarten. More relevant is the deep-seated fault line that runs between services that are school-based or kindergartens and services that are not school-based or kindergartens, and which are often identified, officially or in public parlance, as 'care' services, being referred to, for example, as 'childcare' or 'day care' services.

What distinguishes the split in the Anglosphere is that these 'care' services predominate, accounting for the majority of places in ECEC services and therefore for most of the children attending. In other countries, as we shall see in Chapter 5, it is school-based and kindergarten services that are predominant. Where they exist in the Anglosphere, school-based and kindergarten services are mostly attended by children for only one or two years, while other ECEC services take children for a longer period, from a few months old right up to school age. Outside the Anglosphere, in a few cases children are in school-based or kindergarten services throughout the early childhood period, but far more frequently all children enter school or kindergarten at around 3 years of age and remain there for three years. Put simply, school or kindergarten has a secondary role in the Anglosphere.

The predominance of 'care' services in the Anglosphere's split ECEC provision is not just a matter of the distribution of places and children between different services. It is also a matter of how people think and talk about early childhood services, and here we can say that there is a powerful 'childcare' discourse, apparent in daily conversations, media reports and official pronouncements. Whether parents, media, policy makers or politicians, people in the Anglosphere simply cannot stop talking about 'childcare', to the extent that it often dominates discussion about early childhood services; as we put it in Chapter 1, 'childcare' seems a preoccupation, almost an obsession, in the Anglosphere, and in the process constantly reinforces split structures; indeed, split thinking goes along with split structures. Here are just a few examples of this interminable 'childcare discourse'.

- In England, there are constant media reports about the high 'childcare' costs faced by parents, and in July 2022 the government announced, in a press release headed 'Drive to reduce the cost of childcare for parents', a 'childcare regulatory changes consultation' on plans to increase 'the number of children that can be looked after by each staff member in early years settings' (https://www. gov.uk/government/news/drive-to-reduce-the-cost-of-childcare-for-parents). The government funds what it terms '30 hours free childcare' a week, in both 'childcare' services and school-based provision, a benefit restricted to 3- and 4-year-olds with employed parents (but to be extended to children from 9 months of age); it also offers free provision to 2-year-olds whose families meet certain eligibility conditions, the heading on the official website describing this at first as 'Free education and childcare for 2-year-olds', before settling in subsequent text for just 'childcare' (https://www.gov. uk/help-with-childcare-costs/free-childcare-2-year-olds). This 30 hours' 'free childcare' for some children has been added to an existing universal entitlement to 15 hours per week which was originally introduced as 'early education', but which now appears on the official website with the heading '15 hours free childcare for 3 and 4-year-olds', before a later reference to 'free early education and childcare' (https://www.gov.uk/help-with-childcare-costs/ free-childcare-and-education-for-2-to-4-year-olds).

- Both the Irish and Scottish governments refer officially to ECEC services as 'early learning and (child)care' (see also Canada below) – which is easy to consider unexceptional until you remember that neither would refer to 'primary learning and (child)care'. Audit Scotland, an independent public body responsible for auditing most of Scotland's public organisations, provides a guide for parents and carers 'to answer some frequently asked questions about funded ELC', but the webpage for this guide is headed 'Childcare in Scotland – a parents' guide' (https://www.audit-scotland.gov.uk/reports/e-hubs/childcare-in-scotland-a-parents-guide). The Irish government has a 'National Childcare Scheme', described as providing 'financial support to help parents to meet the costs of childcare', and there are 'City and County Childcare Committees' that 'support and assist families and early learning and care and school-age childcare providers[1] with childcare matters at local county level' (Department of Children, Equality, Disability, Integration and Youth (Ireland), 2023). Citizens Information, the national agency responsible for supporting the provision of information, advice and advocacy on social services, has a webpage headed 'Your childcare options' (Citizens Information, 2023).

- The Australian federal government provides what it terms a Child Care Subsidy, describing it as 'the main way the Australian

Government helps families with child care fees' (Department of Education (Australia), 2023); the Labor government that took power in 2022 has increased the Child Care Subsidy level and has, according to the minister responsible for early years, 'the "aspiration" of fully universal childcare' (Butler, 2022). At state level, in June 2022 the New South Wales government announced plans to extend early education ('pre-kindergarten') to all 4-year-olds from 2030, to be provided in 'pre-schools', while at the same time announcing plans to spend A$10 billion over the next 10 years on the 'childcare' sector, giving subsidies to private childcare providers, with the intention of lowering fees and increasing women's labour force participation (Raper, 2022a, 2022b).

- The federal government in the US has an Office of Child Care that 'supports low-income working families through child care financial assistance' (https://www.acf.hhs.gov/occ) and recently put forward proposals intended to provide 'support to families to ensure that low- and middle-income families spend no more than seven percent of their income on child care, and that the child care they access is of high-quality [*sic*]' (https://www.whitehouse.gov/briefing-room/statements-releases/2021/04/28/fact-sheet-the-american-families-plan/). The Build Back Better Bill, proposed by the Biden administration in 2021, offered universal and free pre-school education for all 3- and 4-year-olds alongside a large investment in 'child care ..., saving most American families more than half of their spending on child care' (White House, 2021); the Bill failed to gain approval in Congress.

- Aotearoa New Zealand, as we shall see in Chapter 7, has a strong discourse of 'early childhood education', but a 'childcare discourse' is still present, for example in the terminology of 'education and care services', and funding streams titled 'childcare subsidy', 'flexible childcare assistance' and 'guaranteed childcare assistance payment'. The National Party, elected to government with two coalition partners in October 2023, has proposed a 'Family Boost childcare tax credit', a tax rebate for 'childcare' costs (New Zealand National Party, 2023).

- Perhaps most striking is the example of Canada. As we have seen in the national summary in the preceding chapter, the federal government has announced a major initiative involving large new sums of money for ECEC services, with some ambitious goals. Introducing this 'Canada-wide Early Learning and Child Care Plan' in the 2021 budget, the federal government described its goal as to build a Canada-wide, community-based system of quality child care. … Just as public school provides children with quality education in their neighbourhoods, the government's goal is to ensure that all families have access to high-quality, affordable, and flexible early learning and child care no matter where they live. The government will also ensure that families in Canada are no longer burdened by high child care costs – with the goal of bringing fees for regulated child care down to $10 per day on average within the next five years. (Government of Canada, 2021) But what the new strategy does not do, as this excerpt shows clearly, is contest the split system and the predominant childcare discourse; the aim is not to extend the existing free public education for 4- and 5-year-olds to younger children while increasing the hours available, but to widen access to 'early learning and child care' by reducing 'high child care costs'. Split thinking continues into implementation, with a new Federal Secretariat on Early Learning and Child Care, whose job is 'to build capacity within the government and engage stakeholders to provide child care policy analysis to support a Canada-wide Early Learning and Child Care (ELCC) system' (Government of Canada, 2022). This same childcare discourse is apparent in how news about the federal initiative has been presented. For instance, in March 2022 an education charity in Ontario headed a short news item, about that province signing an agreement with the federal government to obtain an allocation of the new federal funding, with 'Ontario joins the rest of Canada with new child care agreement'. The agreement, the item continues, 'provides funding for 71,000 new licensed child care spaces', and 'Only licensed child care operators are eligible for the program, including both child care centres and licensed home child care agencies' (People for Education, 2022). A local newspaper in the same province runs a story headed 'Child care costs set to come down to $10-per-day by 2025 for parents of young children: Here's what you need to know'; the article refers to 'early learning' twice, compared to 11 times for 'child care' (J. Mitchell, 2022). As a final example of media coverage, a national Canadian newspaper heads an item on the federal initiative 'How much parents benefit from the national child-care plans depends on where they live' (McGinn, 2022). The same emphasis on childcare is apparent in public discussions of the new Plan. For instance, a 'two-day policy symposium that gathered over 60 researchers, Indigenous experts, advocates, policy makers and child care sector stakeholders from across Canada' in Ottawa in June 2022 was titled 'What now for child care?' And although the event's purpose was 'to take stock of how far early learning and child care policy has come on the path to a quality, inclusive early learning and child care (ELCC) system for all', the programme for Day 1 was headed 'Child care challenges ahead' and for Day 2 'Child care policy refresh' (Childcare Resource and Research Unit, 2022). Like other Anglosphere countries, Canada acknowledges the importance of education in its early childhood system (or rather 'learning', a term we will question in the final chapter), yet it cannot get beyond being fixated with 'childcare'. So, despite the appearance of 'learning' with 'care' in its ambitious Plan, 'childcare' has come to dominate the way this initiative is conceptualised and presented.

To problematise, as we are doing here, the prominence given to 'childcare' or 'day care' services in the Anglosphere model of ECEC services, and the endless talk of 'childcare', is not to suggest that the needs of employed or studying parents should be ignored. We agree with what Loris Malaguzzi[2] said back in 1975 about early childhood services in Reggio Emilia: 'schools [for young children] must adapt to factory hours, progressively opening up to workers' children with improved responses to family needs, while maintaining as far as possible the opportunity for parents to collect children at different times' (Malaguzzi, cited in Cagliari, Castagnetti et al., 2016: 212). Yet while Malaguzzi took it as self-evident that employed parents should be supported through the opening hours that early childhood services offered, he never thought that this important but mundane organisational matter should define these services or distract from their main purpose: for him, as for us, these services are 'schools' (or 'kindergartens', or some similar education-based term), not 'childcare services', and their main (but *not* their only) purpose is education provided as a right of children.

Nor do we problematise the prominence given to 'childcare' or 'day care' services in the Anglosphere model in order to deny or devalue the place of 'care' in early childhood services, or, indeed, in any other services for children and adults. We think 'care' is essential, and indeed would argue that 'care' should be central to *all* human services, including all sectors of education. But we mean 'care' understood as an ethic that guides how we should relate to each other, what has been called an 'ethics of care', and not 'care' used as a descriptor or definition of certain services separately provided for particular groups of children or adults or viewed as a commodity that these services sell to parents. We will return to this important distinction and the place of care in early childhood services in Chapter 8.

Early childhood services mainly privately provided and fully marketised

Public provision of ECEC services by local or provincial or central government is limited in the Anglosphere, in marked contrast (as we shall see in Chapter 5) to France and Sweden (and many other countries). This is partly because of the minority role of school-based or kindergarten services, which are often provided by public bodies, though even where these services exist they may be provided by private organisations (for example kindergarten associations, faith groups, free or charter schools), albeit with public funding. But it is also because most non-school or non-kindergarten services ('childcare' or 'day care' centres, family day care), which, as we have seen, offer the majority of places in the Anglosphere, are rarely provided publicly, depending instead to a great extent on a variety of community-based and private providers. Some of these providers are various types of non-profit organisations (for example community groups, cooperatives, charitable bodies) – 'community-based services'. But a substantial and growing role in the Anglosphere is played by private providers – for-profit businesses supplying and selling ECEC services. The contribution of these for-profit providers varies somewhat between countries – it is lowest in Canada, highest in England – but is substantial overall.

The majority of private for-profit providers are proprietors delivering one or two centres (in addition, there are family day carers, often operating as essentially very small businesses). However, larger players are emerging and expanding. Although they still account for a minority of provision, the 'market share' of these businesses is growing, mainly through mergers and acquisitions. The market in childcare is consolidating in most Anglosphere countries, and behind this process and the corporate consolidators is what has been termed 'financialisation'.

Financialisation, described as a key feature of the 'neoliberal experiment' (Stiglitz, 2019a), is 'a process involving the increasing role of financial motives, financial markets, financial actors and financial institutions in the operation of the domestic and international economies'

(Blakeley and Quilter-Pinner, 2019: 5). Features of this process in early childhood services include: business 'growth' generated by mergers and acquisitions, rather than the opening of new centres; the key role of both national and international private investors to finance this expansion, including investment banks, pension funds and, in particular, private equity; and recourse to borrowing to finance this growth strategy. Antonia Simon and her colleagues, in their study of private childcare provision in England, tellingly titled *Acquisitions, Mergers and Debt: The new language of childcare*, found that

> private-for-profit companies in the ECEC sector are heavily indebted, and they have very complex financial structures involving foreign investors and shareholders. They have necessarily adopted a shareholder model of corporate governance. We also identified that a considerable amount of money is being extracted for debt repayment. For example, … two of the largest private-for-profit [nursery] chains we examined were heavy borrowers, with leverage ratios of debt to total assets of between 51 per cent and 101 per cent. (Simon et al., 2022: 10)

This process of financialisation, and attendant corporatisation, can be exemplified from two perspectives. The first is the perspective of a company that describes itself as the 'UK's leading healthcare and childcare broker', offering market information and facilitating the sale and purchase of childcare services, part of a growing business sector servicing the burgeoning 'childcare market'. Here is an excerpt from the company's bullish annual review, 'Childcare and Education Market: 2022', published in January 2022:

> 2021 was an exceptional year for mergers and acquisitions in the early years space with total transaction values estimated to exceed £500,000,000 with heightened activity in all levels of the market. As we enter 2022 the outlook for M&A [Markets and Acquisitions] in the market has never been more positive and we believe we are entering a golden window of opportunity. As such, we forecast the following for 2022:
>
> •   Accelerated level of consolidation within the early years sector, split as follows

- Private Equity backed childcare groups delivering their scale-up plans, increasing EBITDA [earnings before interest, taxes, depreciation and amortisation] growth through strategic acquisitions.
- 'Bulge Bracket' transactions – record multiples paid to acquire childcare groups who own 50+ settings.
- European diversifications – additional European/Global entrants to acquire UK based operators.
- Local to Regional – Sub 5 setting groups utilising their local knowledge to acquire new settings, thus expanding their geographical base.
- Some UK Based Groups expanding into overseas markets in Europe and further afield.

The report continues by highlighting how the 'UK Childcare sector [i.e., private nurseries] remains highly fragmented', with thousands of single-site nurseries, and how finance is readily available for companies hoping to expand, including by snapping up these individual operators.

Private Equity – In recent years, an increasing number of Private Equity backed groups have entered the early years market. Generally, the smaller, private equity-backed operators are scaling at a much faster rate in comparison to the market-leading Childcare Corporate Operators (such as Busy Bees and Bright Horizons). Recently a number of private equity investors have exited the market selling on to large private equity houses. This will provide added stimulus as new investors seek to deliver their own growth plans.

Funding Markets – The appetite to fund childcare acquisitions is strong with liquid funding markets opening up an array of opportunities: – i.e., for smaller operators to expand, for small groups to scale up to become regional operators and for regional operators to challenge the large-scale providers. The availability of relatively low-price debt is supporting the PE-backed consolidators as they take advantage of strategic acquisition opportunities with funding plentiful. The recent acquisition of a major shareholding in Kids Planet Day Nurseries by investment firm Fremman Capital represents the latest significant transaction in the early years market and provides fresh capital to deliver further expansion for the Kids Planet business.

International Entrants – European operators have diversified their strategies in recent years with platform acquisitions in the UK market. In 2019, French-based operator LMB acquired Old Station Nursery group, who have since completed multiple acquisitions.

(Redwoods Dowling Kerr, 2022)

These references to 'international entrants' and 'European operators' point to another trend in the business of 'childcare': the spread of multinational corporations, building up their operations across countries and continents. Just as some overseas operators are moving into the UK, so some UK operators are moving overseas. This provides a second example of financialisation and corporatisation, this time from the perspective of Busy Bees, the largest nursery provider in the UK and also a global corporation, currently with over 400 nurseries in Europe and over 850 sites globally – and 'always looking for new sites' (Busy Bees, 2024). Its overseas acquisition and financing record between 2015 and 2021 is set out below, using news reports appearing in *Nursery World*, a leading trade magazine covering nurseries in the UK.

Busy Bees expands into South-East Asia with acquisition of 60m nurseries (2015)

Busy Bees, the UK's largest childcare provider, has acquired its first international nurseries, buying 60 settings in Singapore and Malaysia. ... The nurseries, which in total provide more than 6,500 childcare places, and the college, were previously owned by Knowledge Universe. In 2013, Knowledge Universe, Busy Bees' largest majority shareholder, sold its share of the business to Teachers' Private Capital, the investment arm of the Ontario Teachers' Pensions Fund. (*Nursery World*, 2 February 2015)

Busy Bees gains major shareholder (2017)

Temasek [Singapore's sovereign wealth fund] will acquire a strategic minority stake in the UK's largest nursery group from majority shareholder Ontario Teachers' Pension Plan. The Canadian company, which manages the pensions of more than 300,000 Canadian teachers, invested in Busy Bees Nurseries in 2013 and will remain the majority shareholder .... State-owned holding company Temasek owns and manages a portfolio worth £158 billion as at 31 March 2017, covering areas including financial services, telecommunications, media and technology, transportation, energy and resources. ...

The UK's biggest childcare provider made its first international purchase in 2015 with the acquisition of 60 nurseries across Singapore, Malaysia and Singapore's Asian International College. Busy Bees continued its international expansion earlier this year when it acquired Calgary-based BrightPath Early Learning, Canada's only publicly-traded childcare chain, which cares for 8,950 pre-school children in 78 settings across Ontario, Alberta and British Columbia. (*Nursery World*, 2017)

Busy Bees expanding in China (2018)

The UK's largest childcare provider Busy Bees is to open 32 nurseries in China over the next five years. The nursery group, which already has a 200-place setting in the country, will open a further five settings in China this year, followed by another 27 by 2023, in partnership with its Chinese stakeholder – Oriental Cambridge Education Group (OCEG). (*Nursery World*, 2018)

Busy Bees Childcare buys Irish nursery group (2019, 2021)

Established in 1995, Park Academy Childcare operates eight settings across South Dublin and North Wicklow, providing 700 places. With the deal, Busy Bees now operates 650 sites globally, caring for more than 55,000 children across the UK, Ireland, Jersey, Singapore, Malaysia, Canada, Australia, North America, and Italy. This is the nursery group's second acquisition in Ireland after purchasing Giraffe Childcare in 2019. (Morton, 2021a)

Busy Bees Childcare moves into New Zealand (2021)

Busy Bees has bought the New Zealand-based Provincial Education group, which operates 75 settings, providing more than 5,500 places across the North and South Islands. The acquisition of Provincial Education, the third largest early childcare education provider in New Zealand, from majority shareholder Waterman Private Capital, Ascentro Capital and its founders, is expected to complete at the end of this month (October). ... Busy Bees Childcare has also taken over the Think Childcare Group of 71 sites and more than 7,100 places in Australia. ... Together the deals mean the nursery group will operate 222 settings across Australia and New Zealand. This is in addition to 417 sites in Europe, 127 in North America and 83 in Asia. ... Busy Bees Group chief executive Simon Irons added, 'Busy Bees intends to become the leading early years educator in Australia and New Zealand.' (Morton, 2021b)

Busy Bees' rapid expansion has come at a price. In December 2022, it was reported in *The Sunday Times* that the company owed over £790 million to its parent company and banks and has a mounting backlog of interest payments:

> Busy Bees had revenues of £589 million last year [2021], but its financing costs added up to £112 million. Stripping out property rental from its financing costs, 15p in every pound that parents paid in fees were incurred by interest expenses. Those costs are not currently paid out in cash to its owner, but the debt is rolled over to be repaid when the business is sold or refinanced in future years. ... [Professor Atul Shah], who works at City, University of London, added: 'Busy Bees has an aggressive way of structuring ownership typical of private equity. Parents paying for the cost of childcare in its nurseries are also unwittingly funding Busy Bees' ambitious global expansion trail. UK childcare has become a lucrative strategy for Canadian teachers' pensions.' (L. Tobin, 2022)

These examples (Redwoods Dowling Kerr and Busy Bees) are of companies based in England, though Busy Bees operates across the rich world. But the same process of financialisation and corporatisation, wheeling and dealing in ECEC services that are treated as assets and commodities, is to be found elsewhere in the Anglosphere. Chapter 7 includes examples from Aotearoa New Zealand, while Australia is another hotspot for such commerce. Here, two-thirds of 'long day care services' are run for profit (United Workers Union, 2021: 3), with a concentration of private service ownership by 'publicly listed commercial companies and Australian real estate investment trusts' (Hill and Wade, 2018: 27).[3]

In a situation where '[s]tock market investors and foreign investment funds are now key players' (United Workers Union, 2021: 3), the financial press is full of reports of Australian 'childcare' providers being bought and sold and advice to potential investors. As an example, in June 2021 we find a financial expert recommending 'two ways to play the childcare sector on the ASX' (the Australian Securities Exchange).

It pays to follow what the smart money is buying and selling. Quadrant Private Equity last week bought Affinity Education from Anchorage Capital Partners, another private equity firm. Affinity is one of the largest early-learning groups with more than 150 centres nationwide, covering childcare, kindergartens[,] preschools and Outside-School-Hour-Care (OSHC). Private equity firms trading assets among each other is nothing new. But the deal, reportedly worth [A]$650 million [US$440 million], says much about the growth prospects of the childcare sector, particularly now after the effects of Covid on centre enrolments. ...

So why is Quadrant, a top private equity firm, making such a big bet on childcare now? Like many industries, childcare has had a strong recovery after Covid. After halving at the peak of the pandemic last year, operator occupancy has mostly returned to pre-Covid levels and there has been no structural change to childcare demand as [a] result of the pandemic, said Charter Hall Social Infrastructure REIT during its interim-results presentation in late March. ...

[One of the longer-term factors driving investment] is higher government assistance for childcare. Business forecaster IBISWorld says pressure for further childcare funding reforms 'will likely continue to mount' during and after Covid, as more parents seek more flexible childcare options amid a changing workforce landscape. Greater emphasis on individualised childcare options will feature. Private equity firms might be betting on the government increasing childcare assistance (it introduced temporary free childcare during the peak of the Covid crisis) in response to growing public pressure. Industry bodies want an increase in subsidies to improve childcare affordability for parents. ...

Quadrant's acquisition is timely. It follows a bidding war this year between Busy Bees Early Learning and Alceon Private Equity for the ASX-listed Think Childcare Group. (Busy Bees prevailed). Again, the deal reinforced the renewed interest in childcare assets. (Featherstone, 2021)

Note here the reduction of early childhood services to 'assets', the constant reference to 'childcare' (the word gets 13 mentions in this short extract of 'childcare' discourse), and the lure for private investors of profit to be made from public funding ('government assistance', 'subsidies'). We will return in the final chapter to how public funding might be used in reverse order, to help *de*-privatise the Anglosphere's early childhood system.

A second example, from *Property Australia*, the digital newsletter of the Property Council of Australia, is headed 'Government investment drives interest in childcare assets', and once again we can sense the feeding frenzy among financial institutions at the prospect of accessing public money:

> Investment from governments at all levels are [*sic*] pouring into childcare to make it more accessible and affordable, and this strong pipeline has created a hotbed of investor activity in childcare assets. The two big ASX players, ARENA REIT and Charter Hall own just 7.5 per cent of the market, with childcare assets typically being own [*sic*] by high-net-worth individuals. As an extension of its strong focus on social infrastructure, Australian Unity opened a childcare fund towards the end of last year, with 11 properties, valued at [A]$60.5 million [US$41 million] alongside a further 6 in due diligence. Mark Delaney, Fund Manager – Australian Unity Childcare Property Fund said interest from the wealth fund manager followed on from the group's catch cry of 'making people thrive' and how it can empower women to go back to the workforce. ...
>
> Australian Unity is currently in its third capital raise for the childcare fund, which will close on 30 November 2022. Capital raised from [*sic*] will add to the existing [A]$52 million [US$35 million] it has raised, earmarked to fund future acquisitions. Mr Delaney said ... 'We're seeing a flight to a defensive asset class from the wider economy because of the support that childcare offers, typically long weighted average lease expiries (WALEs), 15 years at fixed annual increases, and the unique government support that other sectors don't have.'
>
> According to Ray White [an Australian real estate group], total sales of childcare assets grew 99.96 per cent through 2021 to [A]$279.77 million [US$189 million], with the average price in regional NSW [New South Wales] sitting at [A]$2.3 million, while metroplitan [*sic*] assets secured [A]$5.2 million on average. ...
>
> In its first full year of operation Australian Unity's childcare fund witnessed a return of 4.15 per cent to investors with an average WALE of 14.3 years, 100 per cent occupancy and the lowest annual review rental increase of 3 per cent per annum. In a quarterly update, Australian Unity said it expects yields within the childcare sector to remain steady in the 4.5–5.5 per cent range for premium

assets. Australian Unity said recent lease agreements around Victoria, rates have increased from the 2021 Victorian average of [A]$3,265 per place to an average of [A]$3,620 per place across a variety of regional, urban expansion, and inner-city locales. (Property Council of Australia, 2022)

As well as the turgid and impenetrable financial vocabulary and the recurring reference to 'childcare' (10 times), we see here again early childhood services in Australia being treated as assets, and in particular as property assets. In 2021 REITs accounted for 'around seven per cent of the total [childcare] market, with private investors, syndicates, funds and owner-operators controlling the rest of the investable universe', a market for 'child care real estate in Australia … projected to be worth more than [A]$28 billion' (Prka, 2021).

As we have said, this spread of big business still accounts for only a minority of ECEC services in the Anglosphere, albeit an expanding minority. But it is an increasingly significant part of the larger picture of a sector dominated by community-based and private providers. Just as the Anglosphere discourse of 'childcare' goes largely unremarked and unquestioned, so too does the discourse of privatisation of early childhood services. Many (including policy makers and politicians) seem to take it for granted that these services can and should be treated both as private commodities themselves, to be bought and sold in the 'childcare and education market', and as private businesses selling commodities ('childcare', education) to parent-consumers, just another way of making money and expanding opportunities for profit, much of it coming from the public purse. Taking these things for granted, many see nothing problematic about the spread of financialisation and corporatisation into early childhood systems, as part of a wider trend towards the commodification of early childhood services.

But not everyone. Some dissenting voices can be heard (see, for example, Roberts-Holmes and Moss, 2021; Vandenbroeck et al., 2022). We include our voices in this dissenting view when we return to the subject of privatisation of early childhood services in Chapter 8. We will argue there that a transformed early childhood system should be a public system providing a public good, with no place for profit.

Or indeed for markets: privatisation of early childhood services in the Anglosphere has been accompanied by marketisation, a process described as 'government measures that authorise, support or enforce the introduction of markets, the creation of relationships between buyers and sellers and the use of market mechanisms to allocate care' (Brennan et al., 2012: 379) – or any other commodity. Brennan and her colleagues remind us that marketisation has extended beyond childcare when they conclude:

> The use of markets and market mechanisms to deliver [childcare and eldercare] is one of the most significant and contentious ways in which welfare states have been transformed. … In the last quarter of the 20th century, enthusiasm for neo-liberal ideas about competition and choice, together with increasing pressures on public finances, have led many governments to adopt policies that foster markets in care and encourage for-profit providers. (Brennan et al., 2012: 377–8)

And, of course, the onward march of marketisation has occurred in many other areas, including health and all sectors of education (Deeming, 2017).

Marketisation of early childhood education and care takes two forms: markets in which 'providers' of early childhood services compete with each other to sell their 'commodities' to 'customers'; and markets in which providers themselves are bought and sold as assets, examples of which we set out earlier in this chapter. Markets are often associated with private services, but under neoliberalism publicly provided services, such as schools, have in some cases (England being a clear example) been marketised, made to compete for custom with each other and with private providers. Certain values are central to marketisation: competition, individual and informed choice, and calculation of costs and benefits; they are meant to drive effective markets that enhance consumer preference, value for money and customer-responsive innovation. Just as privatisation and commodification have been widely accepted as natural and unexceptional in early childhood services, so too has marketisation. We will in due course extend our dissent to marketisation, contesting its values and arguing for a transformed early childhood system inscribed with very different values, including democracy and cooperation.

Weak parenting leave

In addition to ECEC services that are split, childcare-dominated, marketised and extensively privatised, the early childhood systems in the Anglosphere contain a further split, the result of modest – if any

– entitlements to early childhood services and weak parenting leave. The latter is weak in several ways.

First is the very limited amount of well-paid leave (and to be widely used by parents, leave has to be well paid); the UK has just six weeks, five countries have no well-paid leave, and the United States is exceptional among higher-income countries who are members of the Organisation for Economic Cooperation and Development (OECD) in having no paid statutory leave at all. Québec stands out with 30 well-paid weeks, but the rest of Canada has none.[4]

Second, no Anglosphere country has designed parenting leave to promote more equal sharing between mothers and fathers; as a consequence take-up by fathers of leave (apart from short periods of paternity leave, where it exists) is low.

Third, there is a large gap between the end of well-paid leave and the start of any universal entitlement for children to attend ECEC services – or else there is either no well-paid leave at all or no entitlement to ECEC services or (as in the US) neither. Over the last 25 years there has been some movement towards such ECEC entitlements among the Anglosphere countries, but they are still not found in every country and where they do exist the earliest is from 3 years of age. This offers another example of yet to be achieved integration in the Anglosphere's early childhood systems, though this is not, as we shall see, unique to the Anglosphere.

Finally, parenting leave is weakened in a number of Anglosphere countries by the imposition of conditions that lower the proportion of parents actually eligible to benefit. In Canada (but excepting Québec), many part-time and non-standard (contract) workers are not eligible for leave payments: as a consequence, 'a large proportion of Canadian parents are excluded from government-sponsored benefits …, and these exclusions are both class-, and, by extension, racially-based' (Doucet, McKay and Mathieu, 2019: 341); in Québec, with a more inclusive system, 89 per cent of mothers received leave benefits in 2017, compared to 65 per cent in the other nine provinces (Mathieu et al., 2020: Figure 1). Among European countries, ineligibility for leave is high in Ireland and the United Kingdom, with exclusions for self-employed and recently employed workers. By contrast, coverage is virtually universal in Sweden, whose parenting leave is discussed in Chapter 5 (EIGE, 2020).

Though the Anglosphere is not, as we have noted, unique among higher-income countries in having weak parenting leave, taken overall its parenting leave is the weakest.

And low public expenditure

The final feature of the early childhood system in the Anglosphere is the relatively low level of public expenditure on early childhood systems. Table 3.1 compares public expenditure on ECEC services, using information in the OECD's Family Database. Overall, expenditure is particularly low in Ireland and the US, and just below the OECD and EU averages for Australia and the UK. This reflects the minority position of school-based services, which are usually universally available, free of charge and fully tax-funded, and the majority position of other, 'childcare', services, which are normally at least part-funded by parents and generally have a low-paid workforce.

This overall picture needs to be qualified. First, there is no information for Canada, a reflection of this federal country having no national Ministry for Education to supply national-level data to the OECD. Second, Aotearoa New Zealand is an exception, with public expenditure above the average for OECD member states; the reason for this, linked to the country's radical reform of its workforce, will become apparent in Chapter 7. Third, most Anglosphere nations have recently increased their expenditure or have plans to do so, possibly moving them closer to the OECD average; as they started late and low, there is a process of catch-up going on.

The way public expenditure on ECEC services is provided is also significant. Some goes in the form of direct funding to services, mostly to schools or kindergartens but also to 'childcare' services where they provide early education entitlements; this is 'supply-side' funding. But another part takes the form of 'demand-side' funding, that is, payments tied to individual parents, often means-tested, to subsidise their individual costs when using 'childcare' services; these payments may be made direct to parents (as in England and Scotland) or to the services that parents use (as in Australia, Ireland and Aotearoa New Zealand). This form of funding is a means of supporting marketisation, by increasing the purchasing power of individual parents, and so improving their ability to be active consumers in the market of services.

Finally, public expenditure on parenting leave should be added to that on ECEC services to get the full picture of public expenditure on early childhood systems. The OECD Family Database has information on 'public expenditure on maternity and parental leaves per live birth', but as this is presented on a different basis from information on 'public spending on childcare and early education' (shown in Table 3.1), the two sets of data cannot be simply aggregated to give an overall figure for public expenditure on early childhood systems. The general picture, however, is consistent and underwhelming. In 2019, the US spent nothing on parenting leave, and all the remaining Anglosphere countries spent below the OECD average; only Canada is close to this average (at 76 per cent), with the remaining four countries (Scotland and England are subsumed within the UK figure) lagging far behind: Australia and the UK (34 per cent), Ireland (28 per cent), and Aotearoa New Zealand (27 per cent).

The Anglosphere model: changes afoot

At the time of writing (spring 2023), there have been recent proposals for change in most countries in the Anglosphere, either agreed or under consideration. In Canada, the federal government's Early Learning and Child Care Plan, outlined in the national summary in Chapter 2, is being implemented through agreements made between the federal government and each province and territory. Involving a large injection of federal funds into provincial ECEC services, this initiative is intended to increase services, reduce costs to parents and improve the position of the workforce; the aim is to have a system of childcare services across the country whereby full-day childcare is available at $10 a day.

In England, a substantial increase in funding was announced in the March 2023 budget, for implementation in 2024 and 2025. This will extend the existing scheme offering '30 hours free childcare' for 3- and 4-year-olds to children from 9 months of age, in effect 1140 hours per year, since the 30 hours per week is for 38 weeks per year. This extension will be confined as before to children with employed parents who meet certain working-hours and income conditions. Because of the government's focus on employed parents, it has been estimated that this expansion of the free entitlement will directly benefit just over half of parents with a child aged 9 months to 2 years old (Gaunt, 2023). Scotland, by contrast, in 2021 introduced 1140 hours per year of free provision for all 3- and 4-year-olds and some 2-year-olds, not only those with employed parents, but has so far made no announcement about extending this universal entitlement to younger children.

In Australia, the federal government's Plan for Cheaper Child Care has gained parliamentary approval, and has delivered 'more affordable child care, including by increasing Child Care Subsidy rates from July 2023' (*Local News Plus*, 2023). This demand-side subsidy, for individual parents but paid direct to providers, is passed on to parents through a reduction in fees. The additional cost to public funds will be A$4.7 billion.

Two other sets of national proposals are noted in Chapter 2; both include measures to improve the qualifications and pay of the workforce in ECEC services and both are likely to progress. Ireland aims to introduce a legal entitlement to access early childhood education and to continue the improvement of education and qualifications for Early Years Educators in non-school services, including achieving a graduate-led workforce, and 85 per cent of staff having qualifications at ISCED 5 or higher by 2028, and to extend regulation and public funding to childminders by 2024. Following the recommendations of an Expert Group on a New Funding Model for Early Learning and Care and School-Age Childcare, it has also recently introduced 'Core Funding', direct funding for those ECEC services that sign contracts with government, 'committing to working in partnership with the State for the public good, and to a fee freeze on parental fees' (Department of Children, Equality, Disability, Integration and Youth (Ireland), 2022). This new form of funding is intended to 'improve quality, affordability, accessibility and sustainability', including through increased pay and support for employing graduate staff, while freezing parental fees. Lastly, Ireland has been gradually introducing a paid period of parental leave, albeit with a low flat-rate payment and (confusingly) called 'parent's leave', running alongside the original and still unpaid 'parental leave'.

Aotearoa New Zealand, which already has a majority graduate workforce of early childhood teachers in its ECEC services, plans to regulate for 80 per cent qualified teachers and is taking steps (from February 2023) to move towards parity of pay for staff in non-kindergarten teacher-led settings (for example 'education and care centres') with staff working in kindergartens, which will also mean parity with primary school teachers. The government further proposes to introduce 'network planning' to ensure a coherent approach to provision of ECEC services, attempting some regulation of the market in the interests of a more equitable distribution of services. We will return to these proposed changes in Chapter 7.

Finally, the United States federal government has proposed substantial developments in the country's early childhood system. The administration's 2021 Build Back Better Act proposed six-year funding to enable:

- universal and free pre-school for all 3- and 4-year-olds;
- families on lower and medium incomes to pay no more than 7 per cent of their income on childcare and states to expand access to high-quality, affordable childcare to about 20 million children a year;
- 12 weeks' paid 'family and medical leave' for all workers.

In his State of the Union speech in March 2022, President Biden urged Congress to support this legislation:

> If you live in a major city in America you pay up to $14,000 a year for childcare per child. … But middle-class and working folks shouldn't have to pay more than 7 percent of their income to care for their young children. My plan would cut the cost of childcare in half for most families and help parents, including millions of women who left the workforce during the pandemic because they couldn't afford childcare, to be able to get back to work, generating economic growth. My plan doesn't stop there. It also includes home and long-term care. More affordable housing. Pre-K for three- and four-year-olds. All of these will lower costs to families. (Biden, 2022: 52:30)

Note the continuing framing of policy in terms of 'child care' and the separation of 'child care' and 'pre-K'. However, such criticism is immaterial, as the Act failed to get Congressional approval, being replaced by the Inflation Reduction Act, focused on climate and health measures, with support for early childhood services and paid leave dropped.

These developments demonstrate a continuing and growing government policy interest in early childhood systems – at least in the service part if not in parenting leave – which finds expression in increased public funds for 'childcare' services, to reduce the cost to parents and encourage expansion in provision. This is often accompanied by support for improvements in the 'childcare' workforce, including in qualifications and pay. The general picture is more of the same with more money, and no apparent appetite for systemic transformation as opposed to adjusting the existing system.

Typically, there is no systemic and critical analysis of that system. Canadian commentators worry that in 'the rush to cobble together a Canadian national ECEC system primarily on budgetary terms, … thinking succumbed to pressure for a rapid signing of bilateral agreements between the Federal government and provincial and territorial jurisdictions' (I. Berger et al., 2022: 8). The recent announcement of an extension of 'free' attendance in England is cast in terms of 'childcare'; it confirms government's turn away from universal educational provision, as the right of all children, to providing employment support, a targeted benefit for some parents. It brings with it no consideration, let alone reform of provision, providers or workforce.

Funding reforms in Ireland were not so rushed and were based on the work of an Expert Group that met over a 24-month period (Partnership for the Public Good, 2021). Similarly, recent reforms on staffing implemented or proposed in Ireland have been based on careful analysis, leading to the production of 'Nurturing Skills', a workforce plan for early learning and care and school-age childcare (Government of Ireland, 2021). But neither has been extended to include a significant sector of the early childhood system, namely infant classes in primary schools, so reinforcing the split system. When 'Nurturing Skills' refers to '[a]dopting an integrated approach', this involves 'bringing together the workforces in ELC and SAC, both centre-based and home-based' (p. 7), with no consideration of teachers working in schools with young children; they are not part of this workforce plan. The introduction of 'Core Funding' based on the Expert Group's recommendations has added to the complexity of the Irish system, split between school-based and non-school-based provision, increasing the number of funding streams for early childhood services from four to five.

In Australia, the federal government announced in February 2023 an inquiry by the Productivity Commission into the country's early childhood education and care system which should 'make recommendations that will support affordable, accessible, equitable and high-quality ECEC that reduces barriers to workforce participation and supports children's learning and development, including considering a universal 90 per cent child care subsidy rate' (Australian Productivity Commission, 2023: iv). The inquiry published a draft report in November 2023; a final report is due in mid-2024. The Commission emphasised in its draft report that 'Without diminishing the importance of female labour force participation, this inquiry centres children in ECEC policy' (Australian Productivity Commission, 2023: 4). Among its recommendations were: that 'Up to 30 hours or three days a week of quality ECEC should be available to all children aged 0–5 years'; prioritising the 'workforce challenges facing the sector'; and some changes to the funding of the Child Care Subsidy to help lower-income families (Australian Productivity Commission, 2023: 2). As with recent developments in other Anglosphere countries, the existing system for ECEC is not questioned; nor are changes to parenting leave considered alongside reform of early childhood services.

The reforms for Aotearoa New Zealand largely build on earlier transformative changes to that country's early childhood workforce. The proposal to move to 'network planning' is, though, a first step to reining in unbridled marketisation, without, as yet, instituting a wider government inquiry into the twin issues of marketisation and privatisation. However, a new coalition government, elected in October 2023, may adversely affect the progression of these reforms (discussed further at the end of Chapter 7).

The Anglosphere model: a qualification

Before turning to consider some of the consequences of what we have called the 'Anglosphere model' of early childhood systems, we should qualify the use of 'Anglosphere'. We use it in this book to indicate that countries in the Anglosphere, our focus of interest, have rather similar systems. But this model is not exclusive to early childhood systems in the Anglosphere; it can also be found elsewhere.

Japan and Korea, for example, also have split systems in which 'childcare' services dominate, taking children from birth to 6 years, and providing more places than kindergartens, which take 3- to 6-year-olds; in both countries public services are in a minority compared with private and community-based services. They differ from Anglosphere countries (with the exception of Aotearoa New Zealand) in having longer periods of well-paid parenting leave and rather higher levels of public expenditure on ECEC services. Beyond the confines of this book, therefore, the 'Anglosphere model' would need renaming.

The Anglosphere model: some consequences

A 2021 report on the early childhood system in England concludes, 'Despite significant investment, there is no national coherent vision for early childhood education and care. ... The system accordingly is confused and fragmented' (Archer and Oppenheim, 2021: 3). The absence of a 'coherent national vision' would seem to apply across the Anglosphere, epitomised by its split nature, while all systems merit the description of 'confused and fragmented'. But the Anglosphere's early childhood systems are more than just split (both between services and between services and parenting leave); they are also dominated by non-school or 'childcare' services, and reliant on marketised and privatised provision. This is not only a recipe for confusion and fragmentation, but also for inequality, divisiveness and incoherence. Here are four examples.

First, in addition to a confusing mix of different types of services and myriad providers, and as well as profuse funding streams, *the split childcare-dominated system sends confusing messages about what early childhood services are for*. This confusion was the subject of a 2022 BBC radio documentary titled (and this is itself significant and symptomatic of the confusion) 'What is childcare for?' The presenter, who had a 2-year-old daughter attending a private nursery at considerable cost, introduced the programme as examining the issue of childcare, and more specifically, ... asking what's childcare actually for. When parents like me pay our nursery fees, are we spending that money on ourselves so we can go to work, or are we spending the money on our children, to enable them to socialise and introduce them to education? For many, I guess the answer is both, but when it comes to government support what I've discovered is an unhappy friction between these two goals, where it's arguable that neither is really being fulfilled. (C. McDonald, 2022: 1:00)

Despite a few references to 'education', 'learning' and 'development', it is the language of 'childcare' that recurs most frequently during the 30-minute programme, culminating in a discussion of what 'a universal, free childcare system' would look like and cost and the presenter concluding with a reprise of her original question:

What do we want our system to be? Do we want to focus on making sure children have the best start in life, or do we need to provide a far more flexible system to look after children while their parents work? Or, as is likely the case, do we want it all and build a system that can do both properly? (C. McDonald, 2022: 27:24)

We can see here how the continuing dominance of 'childcare' – in discourse, in policy, in provision – muddies the early childhood waters in a most unhelpful way, leading to this sort of confusion about purpose. In our view, the primary purpose of early childhood services is education for young children, though, as discussed at some length in the final chapter, it is by no means the only purpose; supporting employed parents is one of potentially numerous subsidiary purposes. We would not ask 'What is childcare for?' when it comes to services for older children, namely schools, so why are we fixated on this question when it comes to services for younger children?

Of course, 'childcare' services in the Anglosphere have increasingly acquired the trappings of education (curricula, learning goals, and their workers often being defined as 'educators' and their role as 'readying' children for school). Yet the dominant Anglosphere discourse of 'childcare' leaves these services stranded in no-man's land, stuck in an indeterminate position, with some of the trappings of education yet confined and defined by the carapace of 'childcare'. Lacking parity with schools and teachers, childcare services and childcare workers are consigned to an inferior and subservient role in an educational hierarchy, and constantly reminded by politicians, policy makers and parents that their main task is 'childcare'.

Moreover, just as the constant talk about 'childcare', along with the delineation of some early years services as 'childcare' provision, distracts from what is, in our view, the primary role of early childhood services, education, it does no favours for 'care'. It supports and sustains a simplistic and narrow understanding of 'care' as a saleable commodity required specifically by some parents to enable them to go to work, rather than promoting the understanding of 'care' as a complex and vital form of relationship – an ethics of care – that should suffuse *all* services for *all* children (and *all* adults). Similarly, the introduction in most countries of some free education or an entitlement to education from the age of 3 or 4 years supports and sustains a simplistic and narrow understanding of 'education' as something that starts then, rather than being a right for *all* children from birth (cf. UN Committee on the Rights of the Child, 2006: para. 28).

Second, the Anglosphere's *childcare-dominated split systems have division and exclusion baked into them*; they combine a minority of places in schools or kindergartens, services mostly associated with universal entitlement and access, with a majority of places in 'childcare' services, mostly associated with providing a selective service for some but not all children, either those with employed parents who choose that their children go to 'childcare for working parents' and can afford the costs (so generally higher-income families), or, far less often, those referred by welfare agencies as being in need of special support. The split also militates against taking a broad and inclusive view of the system, with an increasing focus over time on 'childcare for working parents', at the expense of considering what sort of system could meet the needs of all children and all families.

Third, the Anglosphere's *childcare-dominated split systems generate higher costs for parents*. Schools are not only universal in orientation but usually provided free of charge, while 'childcare' services are, as just noted, selective in entry and also usually based on parents paying fees. It is the case today that in all Anglosphere countries some parents receive public subsidies to cover part of their 'childcare' costs, while some period of attendance at ECEC services for children over 3 years is often available free. But while parental fees in 'childcare' services may be mitigated by such public subsidies, the default position of most of these services is reliance on parents paying some part of the costs. Given the dominant position of 'childcare' services and the relatively low level of public expenditure in most parts of the Anglosphere, it is not surprising that (in the words of the OECD):

> Centre-based care is most expensive for the two-earner couple in the English-speaking OECD countries (Australia, Canada, Ireland, New Zealand, the United Kingdom and the United States), plus also the Czech Republic, the Netherlands and Switzerland. In all of these countries, the net cost of childcare for the two-earner couple works out [as] at least 18% of average earnings, rising to around 35% in Switzerland, and as much as 38% in New Zealand. (https://www.oecd.org/els/soc/PF3-4-Childcare-support.pdf: 3)

The costs for a single parent are also above the OECD average for Aotearoa New Zealand, Australia, the UK and the USA. In short, a childcare-dominated system is also oriented towards being costly for users.

Fourth, the Anglosphere's *childcare-dominated split system is bad for the workforce*. Staffing of schools and kindergartens is based on teachers, who have degree-level qualifications and relatively good pay and other working conditions; they are supported by assistants, less well qualified and paid, but still usually benefitting from relatively good employment conditions. By contrast, the workforce in non-school and usually private or community-based 'childcare' settings (both childcare centres and family day care) for the most part have qualifications well below those of teachers and have poor pay and other employment conditions. One of the most striking features of the Anglosphere countries is the recurring reports of the lamentable employment conditions of the 'childcare' workforce. An excerpt from a recent report on ECEC services in England is typical:

> Findings from several studies suggest that pay is a significant factor in practitioners' propensity to leave their employer and/or the sector altogether. The average wage in the early childhood education and care workforce is £7.42 an hour, compared to £11.37 an hour across the female workforce (Social Mobility Commission 2020). This is underscored by Bonetti (2019), who found that 44.5% of childcare workers were claiming state benefits or tax credits.

> Recruitment continues to be a significant challenge for early childhood education and care providers. According to Ceeda (2019), in 2018 32% of settings had vacant posts compared to the wider labour market where 20% of employers had vacancies (Winterbotham et al. 2018).

Turnover of the early years workforce appears to be increasing, rising from 13% in England in 2013 (DfE 2014) to 24% in 2018 (NDNA 2019b), with many staff leaving for better paid retail jobs, further exacerbating the recruitment challenge. (Archer and Oppenheim, 2021: 23)

An article from Australia, whose author describes herself as 'an early education and care (childcare) policy nerd', makes the same point more forcefully:

> It is no exaggeration to say that our childcare system is on the verge of collapse, with services are [*sic*] unable to recruit the educators they need. ... [I]f I was the minister, I would be funding education and services so they could increase the wages of their staff. The workforce crisis can't wait for inquiries or reports. The main reason we have a crisis is that educators and early childhood teachers are paid shit wages. If we fund services to increase wages, more people will want to join or stay in the sector. (Bryant, 2022)

Given the major role of 'childcare' services in the Anglosphere's early childhood systems and the poor employment conditions of most workers in these services, it is clear that the systems have an inherent problem: they are premised on a low-cost employment model intended to get as many places as possible for as little expense as possible. (The same is true for the even larger numbers working in other 'care' services in the Anglosphere, most obviously those for elderly people.) This model is problematic, to put it mildly. It is exploitative; it militates against gender equality in employment, given that more than 95 per cent of 'childcare' workers are women; it negates the importance and the complexity of work in early childhood services; and it is unsustainable, as women are increasingly opting for better-paid employment.

Evidence of this unsustainability crops up in reports from around the Anglosphere of problems with recruitment and retention and, consequently, of chronic shortages of 'childcare' workers. In England, the national inspection agency (Ofsted) reports:

> Many providers have faced ongoing challenges in recruiting and retaining qualified staff. Nurseries had problems retaining high-quality, qualified and experienced staff before the pandemic and this is getting worse. The early years sector is competing with, and

losing out to, higher paid or more flexible employment. (Ofsted, 2022a: para. 2.8)

In Canada, while every province and territory has signed up for the federal government's Canada-wide Early Learning and Child Care Plan,

> an increasingly critical worker shortage threatens to derail the program. StatsCan reports that Canada's childcare workforce shrank by 21 per cent during the pandemic. According to Jim Stanford of the Centre for Future Work, that shortfall and the anticipated expansion of demand under [Can]$10-a-day childcare means an additional 200,000 childcare workers will be needed over the next decade, almost double the current number. ... Rachel Vickerson, executive director of the Association of Early Childhood Educators of Ontario, says better compensation and working conditions are key to solving the problem. (Helenchilde, 2022)

On the other side of the world, in Australia, the same story plays out.

> Labor [the federal government] has announced a [A]$4.7bn policy to further subsidise childcare from July 2023 as part of its plan to improve women's participation in the workforce. But John Cherry from Goodstart Early Learning said the country would need to employ an additional 9,000 childcare workers and fill the 7,000 vacancies the sector already faced to meet the rise in enrolments. Early childhood education centres are already struggling to keep up. At Goodstart, between 80 and 100 centres have capped enrolments due to staff shortages. ... Low pay, burnout and lack of professional recognition are the main forces driving the mass exodus. 'Lots of people are telling us they could earn more stacking shelves at Coles or Bunnings – and they absolutely can,' he said. (Australian Associated Press, 2022)

In the United States, we read that 'Staff shortages are crippling childcare centers across the U.S., and that's only the beginning of the problem'.

> [M]any parents are scrambling to find childcare to comply with in-office mandates [returning to workplaces after home-working during Covid]. But many are running into long waiting lists and limited options. Seven in 10 childcare centers don't have as many open slots as they'd like right now. The primary reason? They

can't find enough staff. That's according to a new survey of over 13,000 U.S. childcare workers released Tuesday by the National Association for the Education of Young Children (NAEYC). 'There is limited supply because there is limited staff,' Michelle Kang, NAEYC CEO, said in a statement. ...The staffing crisis is creating a domino effect, leading to more burnout and more childcare workers leaving the industry for jobs at places like Target and Amazon where employees can make more than [US]$20 per hour as a starting wage. (Leonhardt, 2022)

The low-cost employment model is premised on a preponderance of childcare workers, as opposed to teachers or other graduate professionals, in the Anglosphere's early childhood system. But it is worsened by another feature of the system: privatisation. For this employment model to work, at least to its fullest extent, it depends on a high level of privatised services. A common feature of services in the Anglosphere is that the workforce in private ECEC services has lower pay and poorer conditions than those in public services; the former are also less likely to be unionised, and so are in a weaker bargaining position. Of course, public subsidies can be increased and private providers required to improve pay as a condition of receipt, but the more public money handed over to private providers, and the more conditions attached that require close monitoring, the more questions are likely to be asked about relying on private provision for delivering a public good; why should increasing amounts of public money be given to private providers, an increasing number of which are large businesses? And what is the point of a competitive market of providers if it is increasingly regulated by tight conditions to ensure the proper use of public funds?

Privatisation is problematic in other respects. Private providers tend to be less accessible to children with disabilities or any kind of special need that involves extra expenditure (Penn, 2019a). They are also less accountable, at least to parents and communities, since

[b]usiness control of the company rests with the owners or shareholders. In a large nursery chain, which owns several hundred nurseries, major decisions may be made at the head-office level, which is distant from the daily work of the nursery, or might even be located in another country. ... The model of cooperative childcare and democratic decision-making in which staff have a role, and local authorities have oversight and act as co-ordinators and support networks, a model put forward by many childcare advocates, is very far from the reality of most childcare businesses. (Penn, 2019a: [6])

Furthermore, there is consistent evidence, from Canada (Cleveland et al., 2008), Aotearoa New Zealand (L. Mitchell, 2012), the UK (Mathers et al., 2007) and the US (Sosinsky, 2012), that it matters who provides early childhood services. Quite simply, services from for-profit private providers perform less well. As Lloyd and Penn (2014: 390) conclude, 'within childcare markets the quality of private-for-profit providers tends to be worse than that in public and not-for-profit services'. Helen Penn, arguing that the financial priorities of nurseries run as private businesses ultimately override the interests of children and families, has recently been even more forthright:

> No doubt there are good private nurseries with conscientious owners and inspired leaders who provide a considerate, loving and imaginative service for young children and their families. But in general, a privatized system means that they will always be the exception rather than the rule ... in a demoralizing situation where pay, prospects and job conditions are poor, parents struggle to afford the fees, and vulnerable children receive little, if any, extra support. (Penn, 2019b: 108)

Beach and Ferns, drawing on Canadian experience, agree:

> Research has borne out child care advocates' claims that for-profit child care is less likely to provide high quality care than are public or non-profit auspices. But understanding the market's influence on quality goes beyond this to consider the way that the market limits quality and confines our thinking about the possibilities of quality. In a child care market we may see some excellent examples of individual programs, but individual solutions and competition dominate at the expense of improving programs overall. (Beach and Ferns, 2015: 58)

Then there are the consequences of marketisation, an intrinsic feature of the Anglosphere model, accepted by governments (like privatised services) as self-evidently desirable – so self-evident indeed that not one Anglosphere government has thought it necessary to research and evaluate marketisation, or indeed privatised provision. Reliance on these twin pillars is therefore very much an article of faith, and one that does not hold up well to scrutiny. For those who have studied how marketisation works in practice have come to the conclusion that it does not work very well.

One problem is inequality. Deborah Brennan and her colleagues conclude in their article on 'The marketisation of care', which spans elder- as well as childcare, that 'Markets almost inevitably therefore lead to increasing inequality in the quality of care' (Brennan et al., 2012: 380). Inequality of care is matched by inequality of access. A recent report concludes that the 'childcare market [in England is] failing to deliver on quality or access[.] … Too many families are unable to access the childcare they need, while children in low-income households are accessing lower quality care than their better off peers' (Statham et al., 2022: 6). Another recent report, this time from Australia, points to how and why the market leads to unequal distribution of services:

> market dynamics encourage more supply in socioeconomically advantaged areas and major cities, where parents and guardians generally have greater ability and willingness to pay.
>
> Decisions by providers to offer childcare services in a particular area are influenced by their expected viability, which in turn is driven by an area's relative advantage, workforce participation, demographics and geographic location. The occupancy level of a childcare service is a key driver of revenues and profits. …
>
> Remote communities, and locations with a higher proportion of lower income households have fewer childcare services and are relatively under-served. Areas located in the lowest three socioeconomic deciles have a greater proportion of not-for-profit providers compared to more advantaged areas. (Australian Competition and Consumer Authority, 2023)

This should not, of course, come as a surprise; whatever the supposed virtues of markets, delivering equality is not one of them.

A second major problem is that choice and competition in these markets, mechanisms intended to ensure that consumers get their first preference at the lowest cost, are inherently defective, in part because leading actors – parents – do not seem to know how to perform their prescribed role as fully informed consumer. These and other problematic consequences of marketisation are summed up by the economist Gillian Paull, who writes:

> Childcare is not a typical good or service. Its inherent nature contains a number of characteristics which create problems in the functioning of the market and means that the market outcomes may

not meet parents' preferences at minimum cost. … [T]hese problems fall into five main categories. First, parents may not make the best choices. … Second, there is considerable variation in the quality of care. …Third, competitive pressures to provide what parents want may be reduced by parental reluctance to express dissatisfaction or to switch between providers. … Fourth, competitive pressures may also be reduced by high entrance costs for new providers. … Fifth, it may be difficult for providers to obtain a highly qualified workforce. … The first two problems affect the ability of parents to make the best choices or express their preferences over childcare options; while the last three reduce competitive pressures for providers to produce the best mixture of type and quality, to produce at minimum cost. (Paull, 2012: 229, 230, 231)

In their overview of the commodification of ECEC services, which they define as 'the processes of privatisation and marketisation as well as other ways in which education in general and ECEC in particular are turned into a commodity', Michel Vandenbroeck et al. (2022: 21) develop Paull's critique further, concluding that

economists as early as the 1990s have empirically demonstrated that childcare is a quite imperfect market, that parents do not behave as consumers, and that private childcare markets do not evolve towards an optimal price/quality ratio, whatever that may mean (Blau, 1991). Over the last few decades, scholars have repeatedly shown that the assumptions of rational parental choice, higher quality, or better adaptation of supply and demand are flawed and that very often commodification has resulted in lower wages and staff qualifications, changing images of children with a stronger focus on schoolification, precarious overall quality, and increased inequalities (e.g. Mocan, 2007; Moss, 2009; Sosinsky, Lord and Zigler, 2007). In the presence of a growing body of robust empirical evidence demonstrating that the assumptions underlying the childcare market are false, the continuing belief in commodification by policy makers cannot be understood other than as an ideological choice that must be debated and confronted with alternative visions for competent childcare systems.

In the next chapter, we look further into the question of motivation, including the ideology that has led so many policy makers to choose marketisation and privatisation, despite an absence of supportive evidence that it is in the best interests of children or families, or indeed that markets in ECEC services work as markets are supposed to.

One other potential consequence of marketisation and privatisation should be noted. They produce a great diversity of providers and services, all competing with each other; they also depend on a low-cost employment model, based on low qualifications and pay, which 'limits quality'. At the same time, governments have increased public funding, in the expectation that early childhood services will deliver high returns on this investment by society, and, as we shall discuss further in the next chapter, today those anticipated returns include 'readying' young children for compulsory schooling. How do we resolve this conundrum of getting high returns on investment from such services, most of which are run privately?

One answer is strong governing of children and services by the imposition of various managerial technologies, including the specification of performance standards (for example prescriptive curricula and learning goals, or other prespecified outcomes), the creation of centralised inspection systems, and the introduction of measures of performance (for example standardised assessments of services or children). As well as enabling stronger governing to ensure early childhood services deliver what governments expect in return for public funds, these technologies can be justified as improving the workings of the market, and providing information to enable consumers (i.e., parents) to calculate the best choices available to them from the different options on offer.

Anglosphere countries vary in how far they have imposed such managerial technologies. For example, as we shall see in Chapter 7, Aotearoa New Zealand has resisted a prescriptive curriculum and standardised assessments, leaving far more autonomy to its well-qualified workforce. At the other extreme are Australia, England and the US.

Kristen Cameron and Deron Boyles describe the spread of standardised assessments of childcare services in the US.

One way in which neoliberal ideology has taken hold in early childhood education in the United States is the rapid proliferation of Quality Rating and Improvement Systems (QRIS). As of January 2017, every state in the United States (except Mississippi) was in some stage of creating a QRIS, a system intended to identify and encourage the development of specific factors associated with the concept of 'quality'.... QRIS are built on a foundation of program evaluation data, which are used to issue rewards, ratings, and reports that purport to inform parents which centers offer the highest quality care and education. For an increasing number of early childhood educators, the concept of 'high-quality' as a state-mandated aspirational goal is unquestioned, as are the metrics used to determine and designate quality.

Similarly, there is an assuredness to the stories that are told and the research that is presented about the 'return on investment' of childcare, another concept rooted in neoliberalism, which holds sway in early childhood education in the United States. (Cameron and Boyles, 2022: 102)

They go on to describe the application of QRIS to their home state of Georgia, where

the QRIS is known as Quality Rated (QR). 'Similar to rating systems for other service-related industries, Quality Rated assigns a quality rating (one star, two stars, or three stars) to early education and school-age care centers that meet a set of defined program standards' (Department of Early Care and Learning, n.d.c). …

The year-long QR process includes the creation of a program portfolio, a series of classroom observations, program evaluations (using the ECERS/ITERS[5]), and state-approved professional development plans for all educators. At the end of the QR assessment period, the early childhood education center is awarded a number of stars, based on an overall score, ranging from one-, two-, or three-stars; one-star indicates the lowest quality. These ratings are made available to anyone seeking childcare through Georgia's childcare database. (Cameron and Boyles, 2022: 103)

Australia is another federal state, but here a single national standard has been constructed, albeit applied by state governments. The Australian Children's Education and Care Quality Authority (ACECQA) is 'an independent national authority … guided by a governing Board whose members are nominated by each state and territory and the Commonwealth [the federal government]. … The Board is accountable to Education Ministers' (https://www.acecqa.gov.au/about-us; accessed 7 October 2023). The Authority assists state 'governments in administering the National Quality Framework (NQF) for children's education and care', the NQF including a National Quality Standard that sets 'a high national benchmark for early childhood education and care and outside school hours care services in Australia' (Australian Children's Education & Care

Quality Authority, 2018). It does this through defining standards in seven 'quality areas', each area being broken down into a number of 'standards', and each 'standard' broken down into a number of 'elements'. Services are rated by state regulatory authorities and 'given a rating for each of the 7 quality areas and an overall rating based on these results'; there are five overall ratings ranging from 'significant improvement required' to 'excellent', and all services must display their rating.

In addition, there is a national curriculum for children from birth to 5 years, the National Approved Learning Framework titled *Belonging, Being and Becoming: The Early Years Learning Framework for Australia* (EYLF). This is described as 'extend[ing] and enrich[ing] children's learning from birth to five years' (Council of Australian Governments, 2020: 5). The EYLF, a 51-page document, 'comprises three inter-related elements: Principles, Practice and Learning Outcomes', with five broad outcomes specified, each broken down into 'key components' (Council of Australian Governments, 2020: 22).

England has gone furthest in its governing of early childhood services, just as it has gone furthest with marketisation and privatisation. All early childhood services, whether in schools or childcare services, are inspected by a national governmental agency, Ofsted (Office for Standards in Education, Children's Services and Skills), and given a rating of 'Outstanding', 'Good', 'Requires improvement' or 'Inadequate'; Ofsted reports and ratings are available online. There is a national curriculum for young children, the 'Statutory framework for the early years foundation stage' (EYFS), a 53-page document that includes the specification of 17 'early learning goals' (ELGs), which define 'the level of development children should be expected to attain by the end of the EYFS' (p. 11) (that is, the end of the first class in primary school, at 5 years old), though each goal includes a number of 'sub-goals': for example, the early learning goal for 'Word Reading' specifies that

Children at the expected level of development will:

- Say a sound for each letter in the alphabet and at least 10 digraphs;
- Read words consistent with their phonic knowledge by sound-blending;
- Read aloud simple sentences and books that are consistent with their phonic knowledge, including some common exception words.

(Department for Education (England), 2023a: 26)

Finally, and exceptionally, comes testing. Towards the end of the EYFS, English children are subject to two national assessment measures. Teachers apply the Reception Baseline Assessment to children at the start of reception class (i.e., at 4 years old), comprising two areas of learning: mathematics (covering 'early calculation', 'mathematical 'language' and 'early understanding of pattern'), and literacy, communication and language (LCL), covering 'early vocabulary', 'phonological awareness', 'early reading' and 'early comprehension'. They use an online scoring system 'to maximise the manageability of the administrative tasks, enabling quick, easy and automated recording'. Then, at the end of reception class (when the children are 5 years old), teachers apply the early years foundation stage profile to assess children on the basis of observations and 'best-fit' judgements against prescribed criteria for their performance on the 17 ELGs. For each ELG,

> teachers must assess whether a child is meeting the level of development expected at the end of the EYFS, or if they are not yet reaching this level and should be assessed as 'emerging'. The Profile is intended to provide a reliable and accurate summative assessment of each child's development at the end of the EYFS in order to support children's successful transitions to year 1. (Department for Education (England), 2023a: 5)

The deployment of such technologies, intended to normalise performance and outcomes, brings with it certain risks. By focusing attention on predetermined and standardised criteria, it can lead to overlooking and underestimating learning among diverse cohorts of children: 'In busy ECEC environments, young children's more ephemeral and subtle signs of learning may all too easily be overlooked or dismissed, rather than observed and documented in ways that value the diverse contributions and capacities of *all* learners' (Cowan and Flewitt, 2020: 121, original emphasis). Loris Malaguzzi was highly critical of this approach, which he called 'American' or 'Anglo-Saxon testology', for being a reductive and distorting process 'where it is enough to do some tests on an individual and immediately the individual has been defined and measured in some way', the result being 'a ridiculous simplification of knowledge, and a robbing of meaning from individual histories' (cited in Cagliari Castagnetti et al., 2016: 331, 378). Cameron and Boyles point to a similar problem for early childhood services in their article subtitled 'The tensions of engaging in Froebelian-informed pedagogy while encountering quality standards'. Commenting on the experience of one service in the US state of Georgia with a specific pedagogical identity, they conclude: 'Piagetian developmentalism and neoliberal-oriented values are inherent to QR visions of children and teaching. At The Neighborhood Nursery School, maintaining a Froebelian-inspired approach to early childhood education while undergoing the QR process has been challenging' (Cameron and Boyles, 2022: 105).

There are other risks. The ends may lead to dubious means, as teachers and other early childhood workers strive to achieve the specified outcomes. In England, 'ability grouping' of young children, from as early as 3 years old, dividing them up on the basis of predictions of current and future performance in different subjects, has become widespread; this has spread as a calculated strategy and 'necessary evil' to achieve required outcomes for Early Learning Goals and the 'phonics screening check', a national assessment of 6-year-olds. In a national survey, ability grouping of children aged between 3 and 5 years old was found to be most common in Phonics (76 per cent), Maths (62 per cent), Reading (57 per cent) and Literacy (54 per cent) (Roberts-Holmes, 2018). Stephen Ball (2003) has coined the chilling phrase 'terrors of performativity' for an assemblage of negative effects on adults and children that can arise in a neoliberal regime that privileges competition, accountability and management.

We have focused on the consequences of the 'Anglosphere model' for the services side of early childhood systems, with its split between schools or kindergartens and 'childcare' services, and its embrace of marketisation and privatisation. But there is, as we have shown, a further split in the system, whose consequences merit attention: that between parenting leave and ECEC services, or, to be more precise, a split or gap between the end of well-paid parenting leave and the start of any entitlement to ECEC services. Such a gap is indeed common and not just in Anglosphere countries, although the US, the largest and wealthiest country in the Anglosphere, stands out as the only high-income country with no entitlement at all to paid leave of any kind. But the situation is particularly bad in the Anglosphere, with most countries offering little or no well-paid leave and ECEC entitlements also underdeveloped. The lack of policy synergy is not helped by different government ministries having responsibility for parenting leave and ECEC services, a separation that sustains the lack of coherence between these policy areas. As a consequence of this institutional and policy incoherence, children and parents in the Anglosphere face a long period when early childhood systems guarantee neither well-paid leave nor an ECEC service, with all the difficulties and stress that this incoherence can bring. As we shall see in Chapter 5, when we consider the case of Sweden, it does not have to be like this.

We can sum up by saying that the Anglosphere's model of early childhood is not successful. The splits that run deep through it cause dysfunction, which is perhaps hardly surprising given that the policies and services have so often been spawned in a haphazard and piecemeal way. The combination of privatisation and marketisation, adding up to the commodification of ECEC services, a hallmark of the Anglosphere, does not work well in its own terms and is totally inappropriate for an early childhood system committed to democracy and equality, inclusiveness and solidarity. The latter would be our political choice, as we set out in more detail in Chapter 8. If it has any good consequences, these are confined to the money men who profit from financing and running the flourishing world of 'Childcare Corporate Operators', and it is men in the main, for unlike the early childhood workforce in nurseries and other services, 'at senior-management level most childcare companies are run by men, predominantly from a finance or business background' (Penn, 2019a: [6]).

But if, as we contend, the Anglosphere countries have similar profiles and similar failings, how can we account for this? What causes might explain the common adoption of a distinctive early childhood system? We turn now to consider these questions.

Notes

1   This reference to 'school-age childcare' is a reminder that 'care' services and a 'childcare' discourse continue once children start school, with the Anglosphere referring to school-age (child)care services, providing for children before and after school hours.
2   Loris Malaguzzi (1920–94) was one of the greatest educational thinkers and practitioners of the twentieth century, and played a leading role in developing the world-famous early childhood education system in the Italian city of Reggio Emilia that includes children under and over three years of age.
3   Real estate investment trusts (REITs) are described by the Australian Securities Exchange as 'listed investment vehicles that provide exposure to property assets such as office towers, shopping malls, industrial buildings – even hotels and cinemas. ... [They] are pooled investments overseen by a professional manager. ... [Y]ou can buy and sell them through your broker, in the same way as shares' (ASX, n.d.).
4   Québec operates its own parenting leave policy, which includes the option of five weeks' paternity leave paid at 70 per cent of earnings up to a high ceiling and another option of 25 weeks' parental leave at 75 per cent of earnings; Québec has a majority of French speakers and so is in effect a Francophone province in an Anglosphere country. The rest of Canada has a more generous system of parental leave than other Anglosphere countries, with up to 35 weeks' leave paid at 55 per cent of earnings, but the ceiling applied to payments is significantly lower than Québec and eligibility conditions are more restrictive.
5   ECERS, the Early Childhood Environment Rating Scale®, is an assessment tool developed in the United States and first published in 1980; it is an observation schedule comprising 37 individual items, with the scores from subsets of these items aggregated to provide seven scale

scores. According to the Frank Porter Graham Child Development Institute at the University of North Carolina at Chapel Hill, the ECERS is 'the most widely used early childhood environment quality assessment instrument in the United States and worldwide – used in more than 20 countries and formally published in 16 of those countries, with additional translations currently underway' (https://ers.fpg.unc.edu/development-ecers-3; accessed 7 October 2023). ITERS, the Infant/Toddler Environment Rating Scale, has been developed for use in services for children under 3 years.

4
The Anglosphere model: looking for causes

We have argued that early childhood systems in the Anglosphere are characterised by certain features, including a childcare-dominated split, marketisation and privatisation, weak parenting leave and low public expenditure. So what might be the causes? What's behind it all? In this chapter we offer a number of possible reasons.

The starting point is the weak representation in the Anglosphere countries of dedicated early childhood education services, whether in schools specifically for young children, such as we shall see in the next chapter when discussing France and Sweden, or in kindergartens. This is not to say there has been no experience of such educational provision in these countries. There have been and still are some important examples. One is nursery schools in England, with their innovative pioneers, including Margaret and Rachel MacMillan and Susan Isaacs. Another is the kindergarten movement in Aotearoa New Zealand, which dates back to the late nineteenth century; the New Zealand Free Kindergarten Union, established in 1926, was strongly committed to the importance of well- and appropriately qualified teachers. But these have been exceptions. Moreover, such schools and kindergartens are usually only attended for two years, and nursery schools in England, as already noted, are few in number and under threat today from financial cuts.

Overall, therefore, what has been missing in the Anglosphere is the development of a substantial and autonomous early childhood education sector. Where school-based provision for young children does exist, it has often been subsumed within primary schools, such as 'nursery classes' (England, Scotland), 'kindergarten' and 'pre-kindergarten classes' (Canada and the US) or 'infant classes' (Ireland). Given these conditions, as the need for more ECEC services has grown, both for children and for parents, it has mostly been met by non-school-based provision, such as playgroups, nurseries and other childcare services.

But there is far more to the Anglosphere model than this, especially if we stand back and take a wider view of social policies. If we look at comparative studies of welfare states, some researchers have argued that the countries of the Anglosphere all fall into the same category or type, what the Danish sociologist Gøsta Esping-Andersen calls a 'liberal' welfare regime. Esping-Andersen argues that there are three core elements that characterise such liberal welfare states:

> It is, firstly, residual in the sense that social guarantees are typically *restricted* to 'bad risks'. ... [It] is, secondly, residual in the sense that it adheres to a *narrow* conception of what risks should be considered 'social'. ... The third characteristic of liberalism is its encouragement of the *market*. (Esping-Andersen, 1999: 75, 76; emphasis added)

This liberal welfare regime manifests itself in flat-rate means-tested benefits, an expectation that the majority will make their own welfare arrangements, and a strong tendency to rely on private provision and the promotion of market solutions. This is in marked contrast to other types of welfare regime, especially the 'Nordic' or 'social democratic' regime, an example of which is Sweden, discussed in the next chapter. Viewed in this way, the Anglosphere's ECEC services and parenting leave policies are not surprising, but simply embody these liberal welfare regime traits: targeted or residual public support, reliance on self-help, and encouragement of marketisation and privatisation. But there is more, what we might call the intensification of the liberal welfare state under a powerful and pervasive influence: neoliberalism.

The neoliberal era and its imaginaries

The Anglosphere's liberal welfare regime has been ramped up, one might say turbocharged, by a development we introduced in the first chapter: the growing political and economic influence of neoliberalism. Variously described as 'a thought collective and political movement combined' (Mirowski, 2014: 2), a 'political ideology, a set of ideas that offer a coherent view about how society should be ordered' (Tronto, 2017: 29), and a successful narrative or story (Monbiot, 2016; Raworth, 2017) that 'like many successful political narratives, provides not only a set of economic or political ideas, but also an account of who we are and how we behave' (Monbiot, 2017: 30), neoliberalism began to make its influence felt in the 1970s, as the post-war economic order entered into crisis. 'Stagflation', with its combination of high inflation and low growth, brought an end to a period of sustained economic recovery, accompanied by the expansion of welfare states, what the French called *Les Trente Glorieuses* – the glorious 30 years.

But, as the economist Kate Raworth (2017: 59) puts it, neoliberalism's

> big time came at last in 1980 when Margaret Thatcher [Prime Minister of the United Kingdom from 1979 to 1990] and Ronald Reagan [President of the US from 1981 to 1989] teamed up to bring the neoliberal script to the international stage. ... [T]he neoliberal show has been playing ever since, powerfully framing the economic debate of the past 30 years.

It has framed not just the economic debate, but also the debate and policy making in many other fields, including education, where neoliberalism's 'Global Education Reform Movement' has spread across countries and sectors with its symptoms of market logic, standardisation, focus on a few core subjects, business management models, and test-based accountability.

As we discussed in Chapter 1, the main plotline in the neoliberal script is the economisation of everything. Indeed, 'Part of the reason for the neoliberal takeover was the striking simplicity of its core message: everything has a price and, if markets are freed to determine that price, prosperity and social harmony will follow' (Fortunato, 2022). This economisation shows itself in several ways, including the spread of marketisation and privatisation into every field and the importance attached to calculation and individual choice exercised by the autonomous subject acting as *homo economicus*; every relationship, every thing, every decision becomes transactional, reduced to determining what or who offers the greatest return, the best value for money. In this way, we have all been taught over many years to live our lives – and indeed to think of ourselves – as consumers rather than citizens; this being so, neoliberalism has produced us.

But equally important has been the effect of economisation on how we perceive and think about the world. Neoliberalism has produced a powerful set of economised images or understandings that, 50 years ago, before neoliberalism's ascendancy, would have seemed strange, shocking or laughable, but which today are simply taken for granted, part of a new normal.

Before looking at the images neoliberalism has produced in the field of early childhood, we want to explain very clearly what we mean by 'images'. We use 'images' to refer to the idea that 'the world and our knowledge of it are seen as *socially constructed* and all of us, as human beings, are active participants in this process' (Berger and Luckmann, 1966; original emphasis), 'engaged in relationship with others in meaning making rather than truth finding' (Dahlberg et al., 2013: 24). Images are our constructs: how we imagine people and things to be, the meanings we give to them. This could be considered a philosophical position, about how we create knowledge, indeed what knowledge is: a process of social construction or meaning making. But it also receives some important support from the field of neuroscience. Anil Seth, a leading researcher in the field of consciousness science, has described perception of the outside world as

> an active, action-oriented construction, rather than as a passive registration of an objective external reality. Our perceived worlds are both less than and more than whatever this objective external reality might be. Our brains create our worlds through processes of Bayesian best guessing in which sensory signals serve primarily to rein in our continually evolving perceptual hypotheses. We live within a controlled hallucination which evolution has designed not for accuracy but for utility. (Seth, 2021: 273)

Or, to put it in a nutshell, the brain is a 'prediction machine' that is constantly generating best-guess causes of its sensory inputs. Seth argues, 'We never experience sensory signals themselves, we only ever experience interpretations of them', through a process of 'continuous making and remaking of perceptual best guesses [by the brain]', so that all our experiences 'are always and everywhere grounded in a projection of perceptual expectations onto and into our sensory environment' (Seth, 2021: 83, 124).

Loris Malaguzzi argues not only that all of us have images, but that these 'perceptual expectations' have significance for our actions, our behaviours, and our relations with others, in this case children.

> Each one of you has inside yourself an image of the child that directs you as you begin to relate to a child. This theory within you pushes you to behave in certain ways; it orients you as you talk to the child, listen to the child, observe the child. It is very difficult for you to act contrary to this internal image. (Malaguzzi, 1994: 1)

Our argument is that neoliberalism, with its powerful will to economise, shapes the way we understand or construct objective external reality, how we interpret what is 'out there', including in the early childhood field. It plays a major role in forming the 'perceptual expectations' we project onto our 'sensory environment'. Put another way, neoliberalism forms our ways of seeing, or our images, and these images are strongly imbued with economic interpretations.

So, for example, as illustrated in Chapter 3, early childhood services are today widely understood as businesses, selling commodities ('childcare' and 'learning') in markets, competing with similar businesses for market share, and widely understood as commodities themselves that can be bought and sold, becoming the subject of mergers and acquisitions and of financialisation and corporatisation. Such images are saturated by the economic and the calculating, and fashioned through the application of the language of the market and finance to early childhood services, including the use, and normalisation, of terms such as 'mergers and acquisitions', 'transaction values', 'bulge-bracket transactions', 'private equity', 'childcare corporate operators', 'funding markets', 'platform acquisitions' and 'deal multiples'. As we saw in Chapter 3, this type of vocabulary is common parlance today, without being widely questioned or attracting opprobrium; it is highly productive.

But economised images are not confined to services. Neoliberalism has produced an image of the parent as a private commodity-purchasing customer, a supposedly informed and savvy consumer calculating the early childhood service that is the best buy for her or him, weighing up cost, preference and purchasing power: *homo economicus* incarnate. It has produced an image of the early childhood worker as a businesswoman, managing her assets and seeking to grow her business; but also as a technician, whose job in the business it is to apply proven technologies to deliver the commodities for sale, ensuring that children achieve predetermined and externally specified outcomes: the standard against which her performance and that of the business will be assessed.

But most of all, neoliberalism's economisation has produced potent and consequential images of the young child, in particular as a vessel of potential human capital, a vessel that needs careful preparation or readying to ensure future realisation of this potential. What do we mean by 'human capital'? And why does it matter?

The allure of human capital and the dominance of an economic rationale

Human capital theory (HCT), first articulated in the 1950s, has become enormously influential today, not least in education, including early childhood education and care. It has 'developed into one of the most powerful theories in modern economics. … [It] lays considerable stress on the education of individuals as the key means by which both the individual accrues material advantage and by which the economy as a whole progresses' (Gillies, 2011: 224, 225). It is closely related to neoliberalism, and its economisation of everything. One of HCT's initial proponents, the Nobel prize-winning economist Gary Becker, was part of the original post-war group of neoliberal thinkers and advocates, the Mont Pelerin Society, named after a Swiss resort where a group of free market economists met in 1947, subsequently developing into a closed, members-only debating society, backed by businesses and billionaires (Stedman Jones, 2012).

Becker himself has described the essence of HCT and its importance in the contemporary world.

> Human capital refers to the knowledge, information, ideas, skills, and health of individuals. This is the 'age of human capital' in the sense that human capital is by far the most important form of capital in modern economies. The economic successes of individuals, and also of whole economies, depend on how extensively and effectively people invest in themselves. (Becker, 2002: 3)

Human capital, which as well as competencies and attributes includes qualities such as reliability, self-reliance and individual responsibility, adds up therefore to 'marketable skills that will generate higher income' acquired through investment in education, including occupational training (Bernheim and Whinston, 2008: 359–60). The focus, then, of HCT is on the capacities needed by individuals for economic success, and by employers and by national economies in a highly competitive and globalised market economy. Investment in education – by parents, by the state and by the self – is the main way to fully realise this essential economic resource.

Under the sway of neoliberalism and HCT, the overriding purpose of education, from the early years upwards, has become economised. Education in the past has often had an economic purpose, to better equip children and young people to enter the labour force, but other purposes

– social, cultural, ethical, democratic – have usually been recognised as important too. But today, under neoliberalism, education has been increasingly framed as having a primarily or even exclusively economic rationale, with the production of human capital at the core of this rationale. Fazal Rizvi and Bob Lingard write:

> [as a result of the] almost universal shift from social democratic to neoliberal orientations … educational purposes have been redefined in terms of a narrower set of concerns about human capital development, and the role education must play to meet the needs of the global economy and to ensure the competitiveness of the national economy. (Rizvi and Lingard, 2009: 3)

David Labaree makes the same argument in blunter terms:

> From the global education reform movement [GERM] to its policy apparatus in the Organisation for Economic Co-operation and Development (OECD) and its policy police in the Programme for International Student Assessment (PISA) testing program, we have seen one goal trump the others. Nowadays, the uniform message is human capital *uber* [sic] *alles*. (Labaree, 2017: 281)[1]

This economised argument for education has now spread to early childhood, which it is argued provides the essential foundation for human capital production, and as such promises the best returns on educational investment. Margaret Stuart, in her 2011 doctoral thesis, subtitled 'Human capital theory and early childhood education in New Zealand', argues that HCT 'has influenced the direction of ECE policy and practice since the beginning of the twenty-first century', so that the 'value of ECE, as with education in general, is discussed in terms of cost-benefit investment returns to both the individual and the state' (Stuart, 2011: viii).

This intensified economisation of education, including early childhood education, has gained momentum from the work of another Nobel prize-winning economist and HCT proponent, James Heckman, like Becker from the Chicago School of Economics. In recent years, Heckman has wielded great influence over policy makers across the world. Stuart explains:

> Heckman's arguments … suggest that improved social skills learned at ECE are traits that will make for efficient and effective future workers. Social rather than academic skills are essential workers'

traits, Heckman suggests. Early targeted investments build the attitudes and dispositions required by compliant workers in the twenty-first century. ... *Thus early intervention spending makes good economic sense, as 'early investment produces the greatest return in human capital'.* (Stuart, 2011: 93–4; emphasis added)

On his own website, Heckman has claimed that

A critical time to shape productivity is from birth to age five, when the brain develops rapidly to build the foundation of cognitive and character skills necessary for success in school, health, career and life. Early childhood education fosters cognitive skills along with attentiveness, motivation, self-control and sociability – the character skills that turn knowledge into know-how and people into productive citizens. ...

Our economic future depends on providing the tools for upward mobility and building a highly educated, skilled workforce. Early childhood education is the most efficient way to accomplish these goals. (Heckman, 2022a: [1])

Such economistic rationales have been spread far and wide by international organisations. To quote from a webpage of the influential Organisation for Economic Cooperation and Development headed 'Investing in high-quality early childhood education and care':

Economists such as Nobel prize-winner James Heckman have shown how early learning is a good investment because it provides the foundation for later learning. The big insight from these economists is that a dollar, euro or yen spent on pre-school programmes generates a higher return on investment than the same spending on schooling. (OECD, 2011: 1)

A recent World Bank report has the title 'Better jobs and brighter futures: Investing in childcare to build human capital'. The authors write:

Investing in more and better quality childcare is an important strategy for countries seeking to build human capital and could bring transformational change to many government priority areas. The expansion of quality childcare presents an incredible opportunity to deliver better jobs and brighter futures by improving women's employment and productivity, child outcomes, family welfare, productivity, and overall economic development. (Devercelli and Beaton-Day, 2020: 10)

Michel Vandenbroeck (2020: 188) has described the 'Heckmanization' of early childhood education and care as 'the reduction of meaning of early childhood education to its econometric dimensions'. Alongside this reduction of meaning for early childhood education, young children have been intensively economised, imagined as 'investments for future economic productivity' and as impending human capital, positioning them as at the starting point of a trajectory that will lead via a continuous educational progression to full realisation as productive, flexible and market-ready workers. This hyper-economic image of the young child – what we might call 'neoliberalism's child' – is entangled with an earlier image of the young child as a reproducer of knowledge, identity and culture, starting life with and from nothing, who must be made '"ready to learn" and "ready for school" by the age of compulsory schooling' (Dahlberg et al., 2013 : 48). The readying role of early childhood now clearly stretches beyond primary schooling, right through to readying for an adult future, since 'the highest rate of economic returns comes from the earliest investments in children' (Heckman, 2022b), a future that is preordained, following preordained stages, each with its preordained outcomes.

What has been called the 'neoliberal school readiness discourse' (Cameron and Boyles, 2022: 103) not only contributes to an economic image of the young child, but also helps construct an image of a young child who is lacking, deficient, in need, an image that Malaguzzi has called the 'poor' child.

> The concept of early childhood as a *foundation* for lifelong learning or the view that the early childhood institution contributes to children being *ready to learn* by the time they start school, produces a 'poor' child in need of preparation before they can be expected to learn, rather than a 'rich' child capable of learning from birth. (Dahlberg et al., 2013: 83; original emphasis)

Last but not least, a third image emerges, the image of the young child as becoming, but a predictable becoming following known stages to a predetermined fate: the image of the young child as *foretold becoming*.

This economic rationale for early childhood services, as the essential first stage in human capital formation and the child's foretold becoming, has been augmented by two further essentially economic arguments. First, and again drawing on HCT, the parent (which, in practice, usually means the mother) is seen not only as a consumer but also as a stock of achieved human capital, accumulated through her own education and other experience; she must ensure that this asset can be effectively maintained and put to use, in her and the economy's interest. For parents of younger children this is presented as the need to access 'childcare', as a way of delegating caring responsibilities through purchasing services in the marketplace. Without such access, not only will the parent's achieved 'human capital' go unused, it may well waste away, since 'The stock of human capital in the economy depends not only on initial education and training, but also on work experience via on-the-job training and learning by doing' (Joshi and Davies, 1993: 50); a parent's time away from the job, to care for a child, is a wasted opportunity to increase 'human capital'. The conclusion, from a human capital perspective, is clear:

> Better childcare could enable the economy to utilise and conserve the stock of human capital embodied in women who become parents. ... Childcare is an investment in human capital. ... Particularly if daycare continues while children are at primary school, the earnings gained represent conservation of this human capital. For the woman of middle-level skills, whom we have considered, about 20 per cent–30 per cent of the earnings gained arose from wage conservation. For the increasing number of women with higher skill levels, there is more to conserve. (Joshi and Davies, 1993: 51, 59)

Note here the language not only of 'human capital', but also of 'childcare' and 'day care'.

The second economic argument is that early childhood services can not only enhance and maintain human capital, but in addition represent a cheap way to mitigate a wide and diverse range of social problems, such as those listed in the UK government report quoted in Chapter 6 (Department for Education and Skills (England) et al., 2002). This further bolsters the appealing economic rationale for early childhood services: that they represent a good investment of public funds as they generate high rates of return, provided they adopt the correct technologies; that is, they must be of good 'quality' and deploy effective programmes. This bullish economic approach is summed up by the OECD (2011: 1): 'Looking at ECEC as an investment makes sense because the costs today generate many benefits in the future. And the benefits are not only economic: benefits can be in the form of social well-being for individuals and for society as a whole.'

It is not our intention here to critique the soundness of these economistic arguments for early childhood services, whether they do in fact deliver the promised returns (for a general critique, see Moss, 2013; for a critical analysis of studies which attempt to assess long-term economic outcomes of centre-based early childhood interventions, see Penn et al., 2006). Rather, our intention is to emphasise the extent to which the rationale for early childhood services (and to an extent parenting leave) has been engulfed by these economic arguments as part of a wider process of the economisation not only of education, but of parenthood and childhood.

Images are productive

It is easy to ignore or dismiss all this stuff about images as rather esoteric, far removed from the supposedly evidence-based process of policy making and the everyday reality of early childhood services and what goes on inside them. But this would be a big mistake, for images do matter, and in a big way. It is through images that neoliberalism, as Stephen Ball puts it, 'structures our experience of the world – how we understand the way the world works, how we understand ourselves and others, and how we relate to ourselves and others' (Ball, 2020: xv). Images, how we perceive ourselves, others and the world, therefore, have consequences. One of the leading sociologists of childhood, Berry Mayall, summed this up very concisely when she wrote that 'children's lives are lived through childhoods constructed for them by adult understandings of childhood and what children are and should be' (Mayall, 1996: 1).

More specifically, if the images we see when viewing the world through a neoliberal lens are the way policy makers, practitioners and parents see and understand young children and early childhood services, then those images will be productive of policy, provision and practice. Policy makers, for instance, may use the rhetoric of 'evidence', 'what works' and 'research tells us' to suggest an objective and dispassionate approach to their choices, but it will be neoliberal images, subjective images, that determine to a large extent what evidence they consider (and what, conversely, they dismiss) and how they make meaning of that evidence, what ends and means they assume to be natural and self-evident, as well as what possibilities they would never consider, as being beyond the pale.

So, if your image of the early childhood centre is as a business selling a commodity and kept on its toes by the discipline of market competition, enabling private services will be a default position and marketisation will seem an obvious and preferential way to order provision. If you are focused on maximising the use of already achieved human capital by enabling parents to be in the labour market, 'childcare' will seem a natural way to talk about some early childhood services, and having some services only for children of employed parents – 'childcare' provision – will seem self-evident. If your image of the young child is future human capital, needing firm foundations for a lifetime of readying, the young child as a foretold becoming, then it will shape the approach you think should be taken to pedagogy and pedagogical practice. It will be an approach that values predetermined outcomes and predictable progression, standardised measures to check performance, everything spelt out and categorised in a comprehensive manual for development and well-being. As Vasco d'Agnese puts it, this is an educational ontology

> in which learning is delivered and benchmarked as any other commodity or goods[,] … in which teachers act as providers of what is to be delivered, thus taking no real responsibility for what they teach … [and which] ossifies the way in which human beings dwell in the world by reducing such a dwelling, such a belonging to the earth to facing predetermined challenges through predetermined skills. (d'Agnese, 2018: 64–5, 76)

This leads to what Loris Malaguzzi (cited in Cagliari, Castagnetti et al., 2016: 421) called 'prophetic pedagogy', the partner of 'Anglo-Saxon testology', a pedagogy which 'knows everything beforehand, knows everything that will happen, knows everything, does not have one uncertainty, is absolutely imperturbable', which knows the answer to every question asked. The neoliberal world and the young child's place in it are fixed and pre-established, leaving no place, if returns are to be earned on investments, for imagination or creativity, for uncertainty or surprise, for displacing the boundaries of the given or allowing the new to enter the child's experience (d'Agnese, 2018).

A matter of timing

The Anglosphere, particularly the UK and the USA, has been at the epicentre of neoliberalism, adopting the neoliberal script from an early stage as offering the answer to everything, with its story lines about the virtues of competition and markets, individual choice and calculation, commodification and privatisation. In such conditions, it has been easy to adopt and take for granted the economisation of ECEC services. This is economisation in terms of:

- imaginaries (the images of the early childhood centre as marketised business, the worker as businesswoman and technician, the parent as consumer, and the young child as future human capital);
- rationales (for children the start of their preparation for becoming human capital, for adults their productive deployment as achieved human capital); and
- policies (commodification, marketisation, privatisation of early childhood services, standardisation and control of pedagogical performance, and the pervasive 'childcare' discourse).

At the same time, parenting leave, at least as a universal statutory right, has been adopted belatedly and without much conviction, and very much on the cheap. To neoliberals it smacks of unwelcome external regulation of the labour market and seems to be at odds with a belief in the primacy of the market; the preferred neoliberal approach to parenting leave would be to leave it to individual employers to offer it as an incentive to recruit and retain employees, and not to regard it as a universal right of employment or citizenship.

What has been critical here is timing. Policy interest in ECEC services in the Anglosphere grew from the 1980s, in response to rapid changes in women's education, employment and expectations and to the labour market's growing demand for female workers. This growing demand for and interest in ECEC services in the Anglosphere have, therefore, occurred at the same time as neoliberalism has moved centre stage in its constituent countries, along with its educational fellow traveller, the Global Education Reform Movement. In such conditions, with existing liberal welfare states overlaid by neoliberalism, it is not surprising to see the Anglosphere's expansion of ECEC services relying heavily on private provision and markets, led by the rapid expansion of 'childcare for working parents' conceptualised as a commodity for sale to parent-consumers, and accompanied by the hesitant adoption of weak parenting leave. 'Childcare', as we have seen, has also acquired an educational veneer, in recognition of its contribution to the formation of human capital, with persuasive voices claiming that research shows that investment in children's education should start young, when it will secure the best returns.

These economistic arguments largely account for the increased policy attention and public funding for early childhood systems in the Anglosphere in recent years, but also contribute to a situation in which this has been accompanied by so little systemic change: more interest, more money, more of the same. If you want to boost human capital and get young children readied for later schooling, focus on a rapid increase in places through opening up the market to private providers; if you want to make better use of adult (female) human capital, go for more 'childcare'; if you want to do all this on the cheap, to maximise returns, subsidise the use of private 'childcare' providers that adopt a low-cost employment model. But, at the same time, attempt to control performance with a strong regulatory regime.

The one addition to the existing mix has been some targeted intervention programmes, usually with 'Start' in the title, for example Early Start (Ireland; Victoria, Australia), Head Start (US), StrongStart (British Columbia, Canada), Sure Start (England). These have been exercises in delivering 'evidence-based' intervention programmes for children and parents (in effect, mothers) defined as 'problematic'; the investment has seemed very attractive to policy makers because it holds out the prospect of more high returns, while avoiding the need to address deep-rooted causes, notably the major structural inequalities, insecurities and injustices that have thrived in neoliberal societies. But these have been exercises in wishful thinking. In the sceptical words of Ed Zigler, one of the founders of the US Head Start programme, writing 40 years on from its inception:

> There is no magical, permanent cure for the problems associated with poverty. This does not mean that early intervention is not worth doing. The data merely suggest that we become realistic and temper our hopes. Generally speaking, children whose families are poor do not match the academic achievement of children from more advantaged homes. The point of school readiness programs like Head Start and public Pre-Kindergartens is to narrow this gap. Expecting the achievement gap to be eliminated, however, is relying too much on the fairy godmother. Poor children simply have too much of an environmental handicap to be competitive with age-mates from homes characterized by good incomes and a multitude of advantages. …
>
> Are we sure there is no magic potion that will push poor children into the ranks of the middle class? Only if the potion contains health care, child care, good housing, sufficient income for every family, child rearing environments free of drugs and violence, support for parents in their roles, and equal education for all students in

all schools. Without these necessities, only magic will make that happen. (Zigler, 2003: 10)

Magical thinking and the prospect of economic success have offered a simple but compelling rationale to politicians for spending more on early childhood services, while a mix of more of the same, augmented by neoliberalism's recipe of marketisation, privatisation and tighter management, has offered a simple but compelling strategy.

One other consequence of neoliberalism's fixation on economy, management and returns has been the marginalisation of politics. As we have already noted, to the neoliberal it is axiomatic that 'there is no alternative', that neoliberalism provides an infallible guide to how life should be. With the ends fixed, the only choices left are to select the most effective means: answers to that snappy technical question, 'What works?', answers that will determine the most effective 'human technologies' to apply in human services, including early childhood. The expansion of early childhood systems in the Anglosphere has therefore been marked by forays into the field of technical practice, seeking evidence of effective procedures (or 'programmes', as they are often called), but rarely into the more complex field of early childhood politics, with its political questions and political choices that would lead back into and disrupt the closed world of ends. What are ECEC services for? What values and what ethics do they espouse? What image of the young child, the early childhood worker, the early childhood centre, do they project? What do we mean by 'education' and 'care'? What do we want for our children?

It is possible, therefore, to understand the causation of the Anglosphere's distinctive model of early childhood services and policies as owing much to the interplay of policy interest with a particular historical and political context. The importance of timing will become even clearer in the next chapter when we consider two countries, France and Sweden, that have very different early childhood systems, developed with very different historical and political timetables. It would, though, be a mistake to reduce this model to a historically inevitable process, beyond human agency, to conclude that there was or is no alternative. There were and are alternatives, but (with one exception, Aotearoa New Zealand) these have yet to be considered and acted upon.

What is striking is the failure of Anglosphere countries, when faced with increasing demand for more, better and more accessible ECEC services, to react with curiosity or to think critically: to think about the problems associated with what they already have; to think about the varied rationales and purposes; to think what they need and what options they might have; to be curious about experiences in other countries and to use thought and curiosity to question assumptions and ways of doing things; and then to think about the direction in which they might want to go and how to get to their destination. Without such healthy doses of curiosity and reflection, without the application of critical thinking, without introducing politics into the equation, the response to increasing demand has been to 'remain within the same mode of thought' (Foucault, 1988: 155). The inevitable result has been more of the same, variations on an existing theme, with long-standing problems unresolved and indeed becoming more problematic over time: 'reformist tinkering' (Unger, 2004: lviii) not systemic transformation.

For those who question whether such critical thought and human agency are possible as a basis for transformational policy making, we will present examples of where it has happened and to good effect – in Sweden (Chapter 5) and in Aotearoa New Zealand (Chapter 7). Chapter 6, about England, will provide examples of what happens where it has started to happen, only to falter.

Note

1   PISA is an international large-scale assessment (ILSA) study which began in the year 2000 and is conducted by the Organisation for Economic Cooperation and Development. It aims to evaluate education systems worldwide by testing the skills and knowledge of 15-year-old students in participating countries/economies. Every three years, a randomly selected group of 15-year-olds take tests in key subjects – reading, mathematics and science – with focus given to one subject in each year of assessment. The number of countries participating in PISA has increased from 32 in 2000 to 85 in 2022.

5
Early childhood systems beyond the Anglosphere: two different models

We take a break now from our focus on the Anglosphere, to offer some comparisons from beyond this group of countries, introducing two different types of early childhood system and exemplifying each by the case of a particular country. The value of a comparative approach such as this is argued by Joe Tobin, a leading exponent of international comparative research into early childhood education using ethnographic methods, in an article in which he describes effective strategies for conducting this type of research and explains his rationale for doing so. We have already quoted from this article at the start of Chapter 1, but do so here at greater length because his rationale for looking beyond our own national experiences is so compelling.

> International comparative studies of early childhood education are difficult to conduct but, when done well, worth the effort …. Practice as well as scholarship in early childhood education (as in other subdisciplines of education) suffers from provincialism. This is perhaps particularly (but by no means uniquely) true of the United States, with its long and continuing belief in American exceptionalism and its tendency to conflate knowledge produced by its citizens and based on U.S. educational settings with universal truths. Comparative international studies can push back against this provincialism by challenging taken-for-granted assumptions, expanding the menu of the possible, and illuminating the processes of global circulation of early childhood education policies and practices. (J. Tobin, 2022: 297, 298)

Provincialism, we might say, is global in its presence; all of us are prone to it and for understandable reasons. Yet it comes at a price for the sufferers (all of us potentially), and sometimes the price is compounded if the provincial subject comes to believe that her or his particular viewpoint is really the truth – displaying the exceptionalism that, as Tobin warns us, confuses the particular with the universal. In the world of early childhood services, where research and policy solutions are so dominated by the Anglosphere and its English language, provincialism can easily become insouciant imperialism.

By juxtaposing two systems, and two countries, France and Sweden, that differ substantially from the countries of the Anglosphere, we aim to contribute to the cause of eroding provincialism when it comes to early childhood systems. By doing so, we hope to make more visible some of the Anglosphere's particularities and the assumptions that lie behind them. Furthermore, by 'expanding the menu of the possible', and including an instance of a system that we think has achieved transformation, we open up for the second part of our book, which explores the theme of transformation in the Anglosphere, what directions it might take and why and how it might occur. As it should be with comparisons, our aim is not replication, 'policy exporting', but rather stimulation of the curiosity and thought we wrote of in the previous chapter. Our hope is that the encounter with difference will provide an opportunity not only for questioning what exists but also for envisaging and critically exploring different possibilities.

The chapter is divided between France and Sweden, and we include detailed national profiles for both countries in Annex A, alongside the seven Anglosphere countries. We start the section on each country with a summary that outlines the salient features of its early childhood system, based on the national profile in Annex A, before discussing the evolution and present status of each system. We note, too, how the system in each country – France's 'school-dominant split' system and Sweden's 'integrated, education-based' system – is replicated elsewhere, the former more widely than the latter.

School-dominant split system: France

National summary

France has a population of 68 million, with no indigenous minority (except in some overseas territories such as French Guiana), but with a substantial minority ethnic presence. It is a unitary state with (in metropolitan France) 13 regions, 96 *départements*, and nearly 35,000 local authorities (*communes*). *Départements* are responsible for regulating some ECEC services (crèches and family day carers), while *communes* provide many services for children under 3 years and their parents, support the increasing private sector and have extensive responsibilities for school-based services. At national level, responsibility for the early childhood system is split three ways between the Ministry of Solidarity, Autonomy and People with Disabilities and the Ministry of National Education, Youth and Sports for ECEC services, and the Ministry of Labour, Employment and Economic Inclusion for parenting leave.

France offers 36 months of parenting leave, though only 4 months is well paid. Compulsory school age used to be 6 years, but since 2019 education has been compulsory for children from 3 years; parents may choose to educate their children at home, but the great majority receive education in schools. Two-year-olds from disadvantaged areas are also entitled to attend schools, but there are insufficient places for them and geographical disparities, with more places in the North and West.

According to OECD data for 2018, 60.5 per cent of children under 3 years attended ECEC, for an average of 31.6 hours a week, and 100 per cent of children aged 3 to 5 years. ECEC is in both school-based and non-school-based provision. Most children attending ECEC services go to school-based ECEC provision, *écoles maternelles*, which are schools dedicated to the education of 3- to 5-year-olds, with some 2-year-olds also attending; children mostly attend for a full school day. Non-school provision is for children under 3 years old who are not yet at school, with most children at family day carers (*assistantes maternelles*), and the remainder in full-time or sessional centres (crèches and *haltes-garderies*) or at home with nannies. School-based services are jointly provided by national government (responsible for the curriculum and teachers' salaries) and local government (responsible for buildings, cleaning, salaries of classroom assistants and leisure-time staff), and local government also provides many crèches and some family day carers. However, many family day carers are private providers; private for-profit crèches have developed since 2004, when ECEC services were opened up to them, and are rapidly growing in number, while for a number of years, the number of private *écoles maternelles* has also been increasing.

Several organisations are involved in regulating ECEC services: *Protection maternelle et infantile* (PMI) services in *départements* authorise and control non-school-based services; *inspecteurs de l'éducation nationale* (inspectors of national education) are responsible for the inspection of teachers in *écoles maternelles*, though not of the head teacher. The *inspection générale de l'éducation nationale* (IGEN; general inspectorate of national education) and the *inspection générale de l'administration de l'éducation nationale et de la recherche* (IGAENR; general inspectorate of educational administration and research) are two inspectorates of the Ministry of Education; they are responsible for implementation of curricula, interventions in initial and in-service training, and making reports on various topics. For children under 3 years in non-school services, the recent *Charte nationale pour l'accueil du jeune enfant* (2021) promotes 10 principles for sustaining educational projects and coherence in this sector. There is a national school curriculum for 2- to 5-year-olds, the *apprentissages premiers* or first stage of the education system; the *école maternelle* was integrated with primary schooling during the early 1990s; successive cycles of learning provide continuity and teachers are qualified to work with 2- to 12-year-olds.

According to OECD data, public funding of ECEC is relatively high, above the OECD average. School-based services are directly publicly funded; crèches receive substantial direct public funding from *communes* and also from *Caisses d'allocations familiales* (Cafs; family allowance funds), which are financed by contributions from employers and employees. For the remainder, parents pay income-related fees and those using family day carers can receive subsidies from Cafs. According to OECD data, the net costs of 'childcare services' for a two-parent family are around the OECD average and relatively low for a single-parent family.

The ECEC workforce has a multiplicity of occupations and qualifications. The staffing of school-based provision consists of graduate teachers (*professeurs des écoles*), who are employed by national government and have a master's degree (ISCED 7) that qualifies them to work in both *écoles maternelles* and *écoles élémentaires* (primary schools), and *agents territoriaux spécialisés des écoles maternelles* (ATSEM; assistants), who are employed by *communes* and normally have a two-year certificate from a vocational secondary school (ISCED 3). Municipal staff also clean schools, supervise during lunchtimes and work in leisure-time centres out of school hours, which includes Wednesday afternoons (when schools are closed) and during holiday periods; many children attend these centres, which are generally within school buildings and staffed by *animateurs*, who have one month of training (or rather longer for heads of leisure-time centres).

Staff working in non-school provision include: paediatric nurses (*puéricultrices/puériculteurs*), who work in any kind of crèche, generally as a head, and have a bachelor's degree-level qualification (ISCED 6); early childhood educators (*éducatrices/éducateurs de jeunes enfants*), who also work in any kind of crèche, often as heads, and whose qualification has been changed from a post-secondary qualification to a bachelor's degree (ISCED 6); and auxiliary paediatric nurses (*auxiliaires de puériculture*) and educational support workers (*accompagnant éducatif/ accompagnante éducative petite enfance*, AEPE), who are the main workers in direct contact with children and have an ISCED 3 qualification. This non-school workforce is low-paid, particularly the staff at the bottom of the hierarchy, and, unlike teachers in the school sector, do not enjoy long holidays and have only a few opportunities for career advancement. For those working as family day carers, 160 hours of training is required.

Emergence of a stable system

France has a long and proud tradition of ECEC services, which have been supported by the state from an early date. The first school for young children, the antecedent of today's *école maternelle* but then called a *salles d'asile* (literally, room of asylum or shelter), was opened in 1826 in Paris by Émilie Mallet, the wife of a Protestant banker, and Jean-Denys Cochin, a wealthy Catholic notable and mayor of the 12th arrondissement. One of the influences on these pioneers was the school opened at New Lanark in Scotland in 1816 by Robert Owen. *Salles d'asiles* developed rapidly in a number of cities; 260, attended by 30,000 young children, were open in 1837, under the supervision of *comités des dames*, and receiving private donations and municipal subsidies. From 1836, the Ministry of Public Instruction had increasing influence on these philanthropic services, introducing the first regulations and, from 1847, female inspectors and a training centre (Luc, 2010).

From the beginning, 'the founders of the *salles d'asiles* and the administrators of [the Ministry of] Public Instruction give them a dual mission: care and education' (Luc, 2010: 9,[1] authors' translation). By the start of the 1880s, there were 5,000 *salles d'asiles* providing for 650,000 children, around 20 per cent of 2- to 6-year olds. Three-quarters of these institutions were directed by nuns. A further 20 per cent of this age group were attending schools for older children, often run by religious orders. In 1881, with the introduction in France of free and secular primary schools, these *salles d'asile* were incorporated into the state education system, becoming known as *écoles maternelles*. Two famous inspectors, Marie Pape-Carpentier (1815–78) and Pauline Kergomard (1838–1925), resisted the model of the elementary school and promoted a specific education for children under 6 years.

For a long time, only older children from modest backgrounds attended *écoles maternelles*, which were concentrated in urban areas. But from 1945 attendance increased significantly, extending to the whole of society, as the educational role of these schools was progressively recognised by middle-class families. By the 1990s, 35 per cent of 2-year-olds attended them; their attendance was accompanied by debates and research on whether this age group should be in schools or non-school services. Finally, during the presidency of François Mitterrand (1981–95), the Ministry of Education decided to give priority to 2-year-olds in *écoles maternelles* situated in disadvantaged areas. But from 2000 the proportion attending fell, because of the increasing birth rate, a lack of political will, and a shortage of civil servants; although the place of 2-year-olds in *écoles maternelles* was reaffirmed in 2013, the proportion attending nowadays has dropped to 11 per cent.

Non-school services followed a different course, despite also originating in charity initiatives (Bouve, 2010). They first appeared in 1844, established by Firmin Marbeau, deputy mayor of the 1st arrondissement of Paris, after which they rapidly increased in number during the 1840s, and were intended for children from a few weeks to 3 years old whose mothers 'went out to work and were of good behaviour'. From 1862, approved crèches could receive state subsidies, with a later decree (1897) emphasising provision of 'hygienic and moral care; by 1902, there were 408 crèches, mainly in and around Paris. Unlike *écoles maternelles*, for a long time crèches were considered to be primarily welfare institutions, concerned in particular with health and hygiene; especially from 1945, they were associated with the creation of the PMI, and paediatric nurses and paediatric auxiliary nurses played a leading role.

However, there have been some significant changes in non-school services in more recent years, especially from the 1980s and led by a number of reports and commissions. Terminology changed from *mode de garde* to *mode d'accueil* (from supervision to welcoming), and the change was accompanied by a more educational orientation. *Éducateurs/trices* entered crèches during the 1960s, and although they continue to be a minority of the staff from 2000 they could become heads. A decree in 2000 required an 'educational project' in each crèche, though there was no curriculum until 2021, when the *Charte nationale d'accueil du jeune enfant* was introduced. Collaboration with the Ministry of Culture has supported bringing art into services for young children.

This history has left France with a totally split early childhood system (see Table 3.1), in which school provision is dominant: the *écoles maternelles*, and not 'childcare' services, are central to this system. Non-school provision is confined to children under 3 years, at which point, and in some cases earlier, children enter the school system; *écoles maternelles* may share premises with primary schools[2] and follow the same opening hours, traditionally eight hours a day from 8.30 to 16.30 (except Wednesdays, when schools close in the afternoon), providing virtually all children with full-time education for three years before primary school begins. Indeed today, attendance at this early childhood service is compulsory from 3 years of age, and in this respect France is following a number of other countries in making some period of early childhood education obligatory (for example Argentina, Austria, Bulgaria, Croatia, Cyprus, the Czech Republic, Hungary, Luxembourg and Mexico). Schools also take some 2-year-olds.

Unlike in the Anglosphere, in France school-based provision is often in separate schools for young children rather than in classes attached to primary schools.[3] France also differs from the Anglosphere in that public authorities, both national and local, play a major role in providing ECEC services, though with a growing presence of private providers in non-school services. But, as in the Anglosphere, the workforce in school-based and non-school-based ECEC services is split and different, with teachers qualified to master's level and less qualified assistants in the former, and a mix of different types of workers (though no teachers), some graduates but others less qualified, in the latter.

The model of a 'school-dominant split' early childhood system is widespread in Europe and beyond, though in some countries it is the kindergarten, rather than the school, that is dominant. To name just a few examples, this model can be found in Argentina, Austria, Belgium, Brazil, Hungary, Italy, Mexico, Poland, Portugal, Russia, Spain, Switzerland and Turkey. In some of these cases, unlike in France, first steps have been taken towards a more integrated system, involving ministerial responsibility, regulation and curriculum, but the more profound divisions – in funding, access, workforce and, above all, type of provision – remain. Countries like France, which have a school-dominant split early childhood system, also mostly share with each other, and indeed with the Anglosphere, a substantial disjuncture between parenting leave and ECEC services, with a long period of time between the end of well-paid leave and the start of an entitlement to attend an ECEC service. The gap in France is slightly less pronounced than in the Anglosphere, because the full period of maternity leave is well paid, but it is still substantial.

The split in France between school and non-school services is a significant problem. To take a few examples: while attendance at ECEC services for children from 3 years is universal, indeed compulsory, attendance at services for children under 3 years is much lower overall and very unequal, varying by area and being much lower for children from low-income families; children who do attend these services have to move at age 3 to settings and environments unlike the ones they are used to, including marked differences in staffing, orientations and relations with parents; crèches for children under 3 years remain 'a context still strongly marked by medical power' (Verba, 2014: 175), sometimes leaving educators (*éducatrices*) feeling isolated. While teachers in the *écoles maternelles* are highly qualified, with a master's degree, they are not specialised in working with young children, and need more knowledge of early childhood, of appropriate practices for working with young children, their parents and professionals in the care sector, and of coping with diversity (Garnier, 2016).

Despite these and other problems, and despite some municipalities attempting projects to 'bridge' the whole early childhood period from birth to 6 years (Péralès et al., 2021), the French split system is deeply embedded and resistant to change, with *écoles maternelles* closer to primary schools than to crèches. There have, of course, been policy changes, but within the confines of the system and not to the system itself; transformation has not been attempted, let alone achieved. The stasis of the French system is epitomised by the continuing use over many years of the term *école maternelle*, literally 'motherly school'. This has clear similarities to *scuola materna,* the term originally adopted in Italy by the Catholic Church and the national government for their schools for 3- to 6-year-olds, intended to emphasise the 'motherly' qualities of these schools and their role of mother substitute. Today that term has been replaced by another, *scuola dell'infanzia,* 'school for young children', which emphasises their current aim of providing a distinctive environment for the education of young children This term was chosen in the 1960s and 1970s by those *comuni* (local authorities) in Italy that decided to provide their own schools for young children, adopting a very different view of young children and their education from that adopted by Church and State. That view and term eventually carried the day across Italy and all schools; Italy, too, has brought all ECEC services into the education system. The *école maternelle*, however, remains unmoved in France, as does the crèche under the continuing remit of a welfare, rather than education, ministry.

A fully integrated early childhood system: Sweden

We turn now to the second country featured in this chapter, a country where systemic transformation has been attempted and almost entirely achieved, showing that moving from a split to an integrated system is possible. Given our interest in the possibility of transformation in early childhood systems, which provides the focus of the next three chapters, we pay considerable attention here not only to *what* Sweden's transformed system looks like, but also to *how* it has come about.

National summary

Sweden has a population of 10.5 million, with a small indigenous minority (the Sami people), and a recent and growing minority ethnic presence. It is a unitary state with 21 regions and 290 local authorities (municipalities or *kommuner*). The latter play a major role in the early childhood system, having overall responsibility for local services and planning provision, and running most early childhood services themselves as well as funding private services. At national level, the Ministry of Education and Science is responsible for all ECEC services, while the Ministry of Social Affairs is responsible for parenting leave.

Sweden offers 18 months of parenting leave, with 13 months well paid; mothers and fathers are both entitled to three months of this well-paid leave, a quota that cannot be transferred to the other, and the remaining time is left for parents to divide between themselves. Compulsory school age is 6 years. All children are entitled to a place in an ECEC service from 12 months of age, with 525 hours per year (approximately 15 hours per week) of free attendance from the autumn term when they become 3 years old.

According to OECD data for Sweden, 46 per cent of children under 3 years attended ECEC in 2018,[4] for an average of 31.7 hours per week, and 94 per cent of children aged 3 to 5 years. Nearly all ECEC is one type of provision: centres for children from 1 to 6 years old called 'pre-schools' (*förskolor*), which are legally classed as a type of school. This leaves a small number of children (less than 3 per cent) who attend family day care (*familjedaghem*). Most pre-schools, 71 per cent in 2020, are run by local authorities; the remainder are publicly funded but either private or community-based, run for example by parent or staff cooperatives.

The Swedish Schools Inspectorate (*Skolinspektionen*) is responsible for the national inspection and evaluation of the school system (both pre-schools and schools) and ensures that all schools follow laws and regulations. Municipalities are expected to inspect and evaluate pre-schools on a continuous basis, through annual follow-up and evaluation measures. There is a national *Curriculum for the Preschool (Lpfö 18)* (Skolverket, 2018), which is 26 pages long (in the English-language translation) and consists of two parts: the fundamental values and tasks of the pre-school, and goals and guidelines.

According to OECD data, public funding of ECEC services is high, well above the OECD average. ECEC services are directly publicly funded, including the 525 hours a year free attendance for children aged 3 years and over. For the remainder parents pay fees, but there is a maximum charge (*maxtaxa*) capped at a low level, with exact payments depending on how many children parents have attending pre-schools and on parental income; the maximum payable is 1510 kr per month for a first child at pre-school, 1007 kr for a second child and 503 kr for a third child. According to OECD data, the net costs of 'childcare services' for a two-parent family and a single-parent family are relatively low.

Apart from the small number of family day carers, the ECEC workforce consists of graduate pre-school teachers (*Förskollärare*) (ISCED level 6), who account for just over 40 per cent of workers in pre-schools, and childcare assistants (*Barnskötare*) with an ISCED 3 qualification. Salaries are individually negotiated and, given the shortage of qualified pre-school teachers and assistants, there can be considerable variation; overall, they are slightly lower than for school teachers. There is a high level of trade union membership, most pre-school teachers being members of *Lärarförbundet* (the 'Teachers' Union'), the product of the amalgamation in 1991 of three previous unions for pre-school teachers, free-time pedagogues[5] and school teachers (except for most teachers at secondary and upper secondary level, who have their own separate trade union).

A system transformed

When faced by contemporary Sweden, with its modern cities, high standard of living, extensive welfare state, and its near fully integrated and universal early childhood system, it may be easy to assume that this is how the country has always been. But this transformation came about relatively recently. The country changed from a predominantly poor rural society to a modern urbanised and industrialised one from the late nineteenth century onwards, while the welfare state began its modern development in the 1930s under a long series of Social Democratic governments.

Like those of so many other countries, its ECEC services began split and continued so for many years. The first crèche was opened in 1854, for the children of poor working mothers, and subsequent crèches were mostly run for the poor by foundations and churches: 'They were open from seven in the morning until seven in the evening. ... The interior was spartan, they had large groups and the staff often had no training' (Martin Korpi, 2016: 10). Froebelian kindergartens reached Sweden from Germany in the 1890s, and were 'open three to four hours a day and were run for purely pedagogical purposes, often by private persons. ... [T]he children came from affluent, well-educated families. ... Those working in the kindergartens were liberal, radical women' (Martin Korpi, 2016: 13). In 1904 the Moberg sisters, who ran a Froebel training college for kindergarten workers, opened the first *Folkbarnträdgård* ('kindergarten for the children of the people') for children from 3 years upwards. These were 'intended for all children, including those of workers, either for a low fee or completely free ... to counteract the growing gaps in society, and create greater harmony between different social classes' (Martin Korpi, 2016: 13). With the backing of politicians, prominent philanthropists and medical doctors, these services were also imbued with a holistic view of care, health and pedagogy/education (Lenz Taguchi and Munkhammar, 2003).

This split system, with its separate roots in poor relief and in a particular pedagogical philosophy, eventually came together, organised around one type of provision, the pre-school. But it took a long time and was the result of much discussion over many years of the need for ECEC services, society's responsibility for its provision, and how this should be done. It is worth telling this transformative story in some detail as it has a bearing on the failings of Anglosphere early childhood systems and the possibilities for their transformation.

In 1932, Sweden entered a period of more than 40 years' unbroken rule by the Social Democratic party,[6] during which time the country's welfare state was built, based on universal and generous welfare benefits and services. The Social Democratic Prime Minister for most of the 1930s, Per Albin Hansson (1885–1946), introduced the metaphor of the 'People's Home' (*Folkhemmet*) to represent a concept of society as a community where everyone cares for each other and which is imbued with solidarity and equality. Also influential at this time were Alva Myrdal (1902–86) and her husband Gunnar Myrdal (1898–1987), both Social Democratic politicians, the former a sociologist and the latter an economist. Addressing a long-term decline in the Swedish birth rate, they argued that

> the problem for us is: depopulation or social reforms. And the programme will be: a new society characterised by social solidarity, where the whole nation to a greater extent will feel responsible

for the children who will become their next generation. (Myrdal and Myrdal, 1934; quoted in Chronholm, 2009: 229, Chronholm's translation)

The programme they advocated included universal child allowances, housing allowances for families with many children, free health care for children, free education with free school books and school meals – and free nurseries.

Alva Myrdal set out her thinking about what form this provision might take in greater detail in her book *Stadsbarn: En bok om deras fostran i storbarnkammare* ('Urban children: a book about their upbringing in bigger nurseries'), published in 1935, where she presented her ideas for a reformed Swedish early childhood system. Myrdal was highly critical of what existed, arguing that it was split and polarised between two extremes: 'poor relief' services for the less well-off, and services which prepared children from wealthier families for private schools. Seeking to combine and integrate these two extremes, she advocated the *storbarnkammare* ('bigger nursery'), a new institution at the very heart of the community, providing for all children, whether or not their mothers were employed, and which should have high standards including a well-educated workforce; the stigma of poverty that attached to crèches should, she argued, be done away with. Myrdal's vision for these nurseries was broad and ambitious; according to Lenz Taguchi and Munkhammar, it was

to help free the child from a home environment lacking in the spatial and material opportunities necessary for stimulating innate abilities to foster proper development and learning. At the same time she wanted to free mothers from the home and help them take responsibility for educating their children in a scientifically sound manner within an institution. Implicit in her vision, shared by other feminists, was another key argument for full-time pre-schooling, namely enabling women to take part in the public work force. The *Storbarnkammaren* was also conceived as a convenient local meeting place for parents, grandparents and neighbours, where children and grown-ups could mingle, play and talk at night after working hours. This was an important part of Myrdal's vision of equality, both between the sexes as well as between different social classes. (Lenz Taguchi and Munkhammar, 2003: 9)

Although only a few such nurseries were opened at the time, and many considered them necessary but not really desirable, Myrdal's ideas were to be important subsequently, contributing to the later adoption of a comprehensive early childhood system (Dahlberg, 2000a).

During the Second World War, when Sweden was neutral, increasing demand for women in the labour force led to a 1941 Population Commission that made proposals on the funding and regulation of ECEC services (both 'day care centres' and 'play schools' as crèches and kindergartens were then known) and for their expansion. State funding was allocated in 1943, under legislation stipulating that responsibility for developing and regulating pre-schooling would gradually shift from the state to the municipalities. These developments were not, however, uncontested, with widespread opposition to women's employment and 'day care centres', though not to 'play schools', which were never questioned. Then, 'after the war, it was as if the new attitudes concerning women's employment and the importance of the day care centre from the time before the war had never existed. ... The woman's place was at home and that was what she should go back to' (Martin Korpi, 2016: 18). Significantly for the future, there was also disagreement over whether ECEC services were more an educational or a social issue.

> The pioneers, backed mainly by liberal politicians, insisted that pre-schooling was an educational issue. The 1940s had already seen heated arguments over whether school or social authorities were best suited to supervise the institutions. The Ministry of Health and Social Affairs was given the responsibility, but the decision was far from unanimous. (Lenz Taguchi and Munkhammar, 2003: 8)

What precipitated the transformative change of course in Sweden's early childhood policy and system was the economic boom of the 1960s, and a renewed labour shortage, combined with increasingly vocal demands from women for employment and equality. Under Olof Palme (1927–86), a young Social Democratic Prime Minister (between 1969 and 1976 and 1982 and 1986) committed to gender equality, the government responded by building up new policies during a 'decade of commissions', through which, 'In the traditional Swedish manner, the issues were carefully examined, circulated for official comment and support was built up for decisions and reforms' (Martin Korpi, 2016: 27). It is important to note that these commissions were not the start of public debate about early childhood policies, for, as Martin Korpi observes, 'One of the main ingredients of the history of Swedish preschool is the lengthy period over which debates were held on the merits of public child care – its advantages and disadvantages, how and why – and society's responsibility for its provision' (Martin Korpi, 2016: 15). The earlier work of Myrdal and others, and the discussions they stimulated, were important precursors.

The national *Barnstugeutredning* ('commission on nursery provision') sat for four years, starting work in 1968. The government tasked this commission with presenting proposals on how a system that met social, educational and care needs might be developed in Sweden (Hammarström-Lewenhagen, 2013). It 'mobilised expertise from every corner of the country to assist them in their work' (Martin Korpi, 2016: 23). What emerged from this wide-ranging and open process was genuinely transformational, both organisationally and pedagogically, and decisively influenced the future direction of Swedish policy and services; it was to be the 'foundation, ideologically, pedagogically and organisationally for the full-scale expansion of child care in the municipalities' (Martin Korpi, 2016: 23), a foundation on which an integrated early childhood system was built. Care and education were to be merged in a completely new way, the Commission condemning an outdated view that 'supervision [care] was something you offered the poor while educational activities were for the stimulation of better-off children' (Skolverket, 2000: 18).

Some idea of the challenges faced by the Commission and of its bold response is given by Barbara Martin Korpi, a senior Swedish civil servant who was to play a leading role over many years in the evolution and integration of Swedish ECEC services and their eventual transfer (in 1996) into education from the social welfare system.

What did the day care centres look like at the time of [the] Commission on nursery provision? They were managed in an authoritarian way with staff hierarchies, and the children were divided into various groupings – infants, toddlers, intermediate and older children – based on the development psychology ruling at that time where a child's development was considered to proceed along definite stages. Food, rest, hygiene, and outdoor activities were all considered to be important. Getting a place in a day care centre was still very much based on needs assessment, many children had single mothers. The romantic spirit of Fröbel still remained in the play schools catering for children at home aged 5–6 [compulsory school age was then 7 years], often with elements of traditional handicrafts – sewing, cross-stitching, churning butter, spinning wool and working with wood handicrafts. The prevailing view then was that children start to become social beings at the age of four. The day care centre was still regarded by many as something of a necessary evil. …

Work teams, children in mixed age groups, integration and normalisation of children with functional disabilities, pedagogical dialogue, theme work, the importance of play, design of the premises, pedagogical material and co-operation with parents – all these areas were highlighted in the commission. The aim of this was to bring about a powerful democratisation of activities for children, and introduce a progressive pedagogy for creating equivalent conditions for growing up. (Martin Korpi, 2016: 23, 23–4)

We will not dwell here on the new pedagogical direction set by the Commission with its recommendations on 'pedagogical dialogue'. This was aimed at developing a two-way and more democratic relationship between pedagogues and children 'based on respect for the child, and treating the child as an individual, and having a belief in the child's ability, curiosity and desire to learn' (Martin Korpi, 2016: 24), taking inspiration from Paulo Freire's work (and later from Loris Malaguzzi and the schools for young children in Reggio Emilia). We will focus instead on the organisational reforms, which set Sweden on a course to an integrated system, moving beyond the decades-old split between childcare and kindergarten. For central to these reforms was the development of a new and universal type of provision for young children in Sweden, that could 'satisfy an ever-growing demand for childcare, expectations about gender equality, [and] children's civic education … under pedagogical guidance'[7] (Hammarström-Lewenhagen, 2013: 24).

This involved the merger of part-time and more educationally oriented kindergartens or play schools (lekskola) with full-time and more welfare-oriented day care centres (daghem) to form a single institution and concept, the pre-school (förskola), intended to combine the best of day care centres and play schools, integrating care with pedagogical activities, and intended for all children, including those with disabilities. No longer would there be split centre-based services; there would still be family day care, though the Commission regarded this type of provision as mainly a temporary measure during the expansion of pre-schools. A corollary of this reformed provision was to be a reformed workforce, bringing together the different workforces from day care centres and from kindergartens or play schools to form a new integrated profession: the pre-school teacher (*förskolelärare*). This reform brought its own challenges:

> Half-day and full-day services [play schools and day care centres] differed greatly in staff training and working practices. The integration of the two would be rather painful for many teachers in half-day services, since their professional experience was not valued equally with that of young pre-school teachers trained in the approaches recommended by the Commission. (Lenz Taguchi and Munkhammar, 2003: 11)

Underlying these reforms was a political commitment to ECEC services as a public responsibility, with the provision of pre-schools and *fritidshem* ('free-time services' or what the Anglosphere calls 'school-age childcare') being made a municipal (local authority) duty. National oversight and guidance was to be undertaken by the National Agency of Health and Welfare, which placed the new integrated ECEC services within the social welfare system, for which the Ministry of Social Affairs had overall responsibility.

One other commission in the 'decade of commissions' should be mentioned. The *Familjestödsutredningen* ('family support commission') was appointed in 1974 to investigate the pedagogical conditions for the youngest children in ECEC services. The Commission was also tasked with looking into parental leave. In 1975 Sweden had changed maternity leave to parental leave that fathers could also use, a world first, but as a result of the Commission's recommendations this leave was extended in 1978 to cover 12 months: nine months with earnings-related benefit payments similar to sickness benefit, and a further three months with benefits paid at a common flat rate; generous paid leave for the care of sick children was also introduced. Drawing on research, its own and others, the Commission was able to

> demonstrate that small children can have close relationships with people other than their mother, and that primary relationships with their parents were maintained even though the child was in a day care centre. The importance to children of their fathers was highlighted in a new and radical way. Small children also form social contacts with each other, and benefit from being together with other children. (Martin Korpi, 2016: 28)

Significantly, discussions about the length of parental leave and the appropriate age for children to enter pre-schools were joined up, so linking the two policy areas. All this work took place in a context of public debate about gender equality and gender roles. The Prime Minister, Olof Palme, made a speech in Washington, DC, about the importance of men's emancipation and introduced gender equality as a main political topic for the 1972 congress of the Social Democratic party: 'The term *jämställdhet* (gender equality) was now firmly established, not only in political debates but also as an important concept for future state policies' (Chronholm, 2009: 231).

The 1960s and 1970s, therefore, set the Swedish early childhood system on a new course, based on integrating ECEC services themselves and these services with parenting leave. With these measures, Sweden had become a European leader in ECEC and family policy. And though change was led by Social Democratic governments, there was wide-ranging cross-party agreement in the *Riksdag*, Sweden's parliament.

This course has been followed ever since. The number of places in pre-schools has been vastly increased (and places in family day care have greatly decreased): the number of children attending early childhood services rose more than tenfold between 1970 and 1998, from 71,000 to 720,000 (Lenz Taguchi and Munkhammar, 2003: 10); at the same time, there are now very few children under 12 months attending. Entitlement to an ECEC service has been extended until it is now universal: that is, it is irrespective of parental employment status, and it dovetails with well-paid parenting leave; the right of children not only to a pre-school place but to an early childhood education has been emphasised. The pre-school workforce has evolved so that today just under half are graduate pre-school teachers, qualified to work both in pre-schools and in pre-school classes in primary schools. These latter classes developed after the introduction in 1991 of a voluntary start at primary school of 6 years (while 7 years was retained as the start of compulsory schooling).

Outside observers, especially in the Anglosphere, continue to talk about Sweden (and other Nordic countries) as having 'childcare' systems. But this is wrong: they have early childhood education systems. In Sweden, the primarily educational identity and purpose of early childhood services have been confirmed by the transfer in 1996 of national responsibility for these services from the social welfare system to the education system and the Ministry of Education and Research, a move that had already taken place locally in many municipalities. This transfer brought about further changes: the introduction of a 'curriculum for the pre-school'; a universal entitlement to an ECEC service from 12 months of age, not dependent (as before) on parents being employed or studying; a new funding system that provided 525 hours a year of free attendance for children from 4 years old and set a cap or maximum fee (*maxtaxa*) on what parents pay for the remainder of pre-school; and the legal designation of pre-schools as 'schools' and their heads as *rektorer* (school heads). Early childhood provision is clearly now predominantly an education issue, though it retains a social function, not least in supporting employed parents through extended opening hours for pre-schools. (For a fuller discussion of the transfer of responsibility for early childhood services in Sweden to education, and its aftermath, and a comparison with the transfer of responsibility to education at around the same time in England and Scotland, see Cohen et al., 2004, 2018.)

One other development should be mentioned in this account of the evolving Swedish early childhood system. In 1995, the so-called 'father's month' was introduced into Swedish parenting leave. Previously the whole period of parenting leave could be divided between parents as they chose, with the result that leave was very largely used by mothers; experience in Sweden and elsewhere shows that such 'family months' of leave are invariably taken mostly or wholly by mothers. Now the 'father's month' established a new 'use it or lose it' principle: if the father did not take his month, it was lost for good to the family, a measure intended to incentivise fathers to use more leave. Subsequently, a second and then a third 'father's month' have been added, matched by a similar number of 'mother's months', and reducing the period of leave that parents can choose how to divide. These changes to parenting leave, which could be seen as integrating men more into the early childhood system, have not yet led to equality but have contributed to change in that direction:

> Almost all families use paid Parental leave in Sweden. ... In 2020, most Parental leave days were taken by women during the first year of the child's life, while men tended to take leave when the child was between the ages of one and three.[8] However, most leave days are taken before children reach the age of two; all children are entitled to an ECEC place from 12 months of age. While mothers still take more Parental leave, the proportion of total days used by men has slowly increased. In 2002, fathers took about 12 per cent of all Parental leave days used in that year; by 2021, it had increased to 30 per cent. The numbers are the same in 2022, indicating a stand still. On average women took 78 days and men took 39.5 days during 2022. The percentage of couples that are sharing Parental leave

equally (40 to 60 per cent) is very slowly increasing. For children born in 2019, 19.4 per cent of couples equally shared leave used during the child's first 24 months. (Duvander and Löfgren, 2023: 548)

After decades of debate, deliberation and development, Sweden has moved to an almost fully integrated early childhood system, as Table 3.1 shows clearly. There remains just one exception, one step still not taken: funding. Here there are still two principles and two methods at play. Parents pay towards the cost of pre-schools, though the amount is greatly reduced by the adoption of a cap, set at a low level, on such payments. At the same time most of the cost is paid by the state, with a certain amount of pre-school attendance for older children (525 hours a year for children from 3 to 5 years old) totally free to parents. Thus, a welfare principle (means-tested service contributions by users) sits uneasily beside an education principle (attendance free of charge at the time of use). This might have been resolved when ECEC services transferred into the education system in 1996, but it was not. Parents may not pay much, but taking the final step to universal free attendance, at least for a certain period each day, has so far proved a step too far.

A rider should be added to this brief recent history of the Swedish early childhood system. Despite the early and strong development of a generous welfare state and many years of Social Democratic government, Sweden has not escaped the powerful influence of neoliberalism. Since the 1990s,

> the public sector has undergone significant 'marketisation'. Healthcare and education have been to a substantial degree outsourced to private enterprise.
>
> Today Sweden is the only country in the world which has embraced the proposal by the conservative economist Milton Friedman for vouchers in schools[9] and has a large number of schools run by privately-owned companies, many quoted on the stock exchange. The gap between rich and poor has widened. (Bengtsson, 2022)

Sweden, therefore, 'stands out as one of the main proponents of marketization in education, along with Chile and New Zealand, and as a pioneer in privatization policies' (Westberg and Larsson, 2022: 705). Nor have the country's early childhood services been immune.

Under the influence of neoliberalism, a new discourse and new rationalities began to emerge in the late 1980s, a shift described by Gunilla Dahlberg:

> [T]he *market* and the *enterprise* now seem to have come to function as valid symbolic metaphors and practices. ... The language of the market and the enterprise signals a shift in early childhood pedagogy from a common good to a service for the customers. ...
>
> The preschool is seen as successful if it can promote *freedom of choice* while also promoting proliferation and differentiation. Efficiency is now increasingly related to the number of different profiles of preschools the local authorities can offer, as well as to how large a percentage are turned into private preschools during a fixed time interval. ...
>
> The market idea also implies competition, and preschools that do not have sufficient *customers* have to close down. The old idea of building the system on solidarity between preschools in the area, where staff connected to local authorities would support centers that were not functioning well, is in dissolution. (Dahlberg, 2000b: 211, 212; original emphasis)

In this changing ideological environment, early childhood services in Sweden have been subjected to marketisation. Governments have encouraged an increasing presence of non-public providers by extending public funding to them, starting under Social Democratic governments with non-profit, community-based providers in the 1980s, and extending under centre-right governments in the early 1990s to for-profit private providers. Following the introduction of a voucher system into the school system in 1991, a voucher system for pre-schools was introduced in 2009 (Westberg and Larsson, 2022). But despite these pressures, the majority of pre-schools are still run publicly, by local authorities, and early childhood services are still widely acknowledged as a public good. Sweden has maintained and deepened the main features of its early childhood system, with its emphasis on universal and educationally oriented early childhood services and its integration of these services with parenting leave. It has also maintained a high level of public expenditure on its early childhood system. Public spending on early childhood services is well over twice as much proportionately as in Anglosphere countries, except for Aotearoa New Zealand (see Table 3.1), and is used to fund services directly. On parenting leave, public spending is more than twice as much as in Canada, and more than five times as much as in the UK, Ireland, Australia and Aotearoa New Zealand.

The Swedish model: some consequences and causes

This model of a fully integrated, education-based early childhood system is not confined to Sweden: it is a common pattern across all five Nordic states, as well as a handful of other European countries, including Estonia and Slovenia. If we return to Sweden, some of the benefits of this model are apparent. It removes the discontinuities, divisions and inequalities of split systems, whether childcare-dominant or school-dominant, replacing them with a nearly seamless experience running over five years or so, from the end of well-paid parenting leave to the start of primary schooling. Early childhood becomes a unified, substantial and universal first stage of the education system, an integrated early childhood *education* that retains its own unique pedagogical identity as well as a clear acknowledgement of the inherent importance of care and full-day opening hours for pre-schools in response to the needs of the great majority of Swedish parents, who are employed or studying. Indeed, Sweden has one of the highest levels of employment for women with a child under 6 years among OECD member states; its employment rate in 2020 was 74 per cent for women with a child under 3 years and 85 per cent for women with a youngest child between 3 and 5 years (including women on parental leave) (OECD Family Database, Chart LMF1.2.C).

As already noted, hardly any children attend pre-schools (or family day care) in their first 12 months, being at home during this time with mothers and fathers who are taking parenting leave, but most enter pre-schools during their second year, and do so without the socio-economic inequalities in attendance documented in split systems. The OECD's Family Database shows that children under 3 years from lower socio-economic backgrounds (i.e., from lower-income families and whose mothers have not had tertiary-level education) are more likely than other children to attend ECEC services in Sweden's integrated system, while the reverse is the case for France, Ireland and the UK, all with split systems (OECD Family Database, Chart PF 3.2.B and C).

This equality of access in Sweden owes much to the changes that followed the transfer of responsibility for ECEC services to education, in 1996. In particular, the introduction of a universal entitlement to such services from 12 months of age, irrespective of parental employment status, and of the *maxtaxa* or maximum fee, increased access to pre-school (as well as to free-time services for school-age children, also transferred to education and subject to the *maxtaxa*). This improvement, along with other positive effects, was documented in an evaluation conducted by the Swedish National Agency for Education, *Ten years after the preschool reform* (Skolverket, 2008). The evaluation showed that an already high take-up of places in early childhood services increased, and, importantly, that the effect of background factors (for example where families lived, parents' employment status, whether parents were born in or outside Sweden) was reduced; in other words, there was greater social inclusion. Another consequence was improved family finances, especially for lone-parent and lower-income families, as parental fees were reduced. The reform had little effect on parental employment, already at a high level and, presumably, because entitlement was extended to children with non-employed parents; employed parents were already entitled to a place. The evaluation also found that pre-school teachers responded favourably to the introduction of a curriculum. Although they believed it merely articulated current practice, many welcomed it for improving the status of the pre-school and supporting its pedagogical work.

More broadly, the expansion of good local services and the move towards the integration of the early childhood system that has taken place since the 1970s have been accompanied by the emergence of new ideas about what constitutes a good childhood, good parenthood and good pedagogy.

> During the 1990s, early childhood education and care services became the first choice for most working and studying parents, even though some still preferred family day care. Enrolling children from age one in full-day pre-schools has become generally acceptable. What was once viewed as either a privilege of the wealthy for a few hours a day [i.e., kindergarten], or an institution for needy children and single mothers [i.e., day care centres], has become, after 70 years of political vision and policy-making, an unquestionable right of children and families. Furthermore, parents now expect a holistic pedagogy that includes health care, nurturing and education for their pre-schoolers. In addition, acceptance of full-day pre-schooling and schooling has complemented the idea of lifelong learning and the understanding of education as encompassing far more than imparting basic skills such as reading, writing and mathematics. (Lenz Taguchi and Munkhammar, 2003: 27)

As this assessment by two Swedish researchers suggests, the emergence of integrated and universally available early childhood services has changed public attitudes towards children's upbringing and the place of pre-schools in that process. There has been a shift away from viewing ECEC services as either an advantage for a better-off minority or a necessary evil for an unfortunate few and towards the pre-school achieving its current standing as a public good widely seen to benefit all children and to be the right of all children and families.

Further confirmation of this shift comes from OECD data on the use of 'informal childcare arrangements during a typical week', which shows that just 0.6 per cent of children under 3 years in Sweden use such arrangements, typically care by grandparents or other relatives, compared with 18 per cent in France, 22 per cent in Ireland and 37 per cent in the UK. This suggests that Swedish parents who are employed or studying neither have to, nor choose to, turn to such informal arrangements when pre-schools are readily available, but perhaps, too, that relatives in Sweden do not feel under pressure to offer their services. One further consequence should be mentioned. As Lenz Taguchi and Munkhammar (2003: 27) note, the emergence of integrated early childhood services in Sweden has been accompanied by new public expectations of what pre-schools are about: 'a holistic pedagogy that includes health care, nurturing and education', together with a broad understanding of education. Structural integration appears to have been matched by conceptual integration.

The transformation of Sweden's early childhood system into an integrated and universal whole has enabled the realisation of Alva Myrdal's ambition, to 'remove the stigma of poverty from child crèches. … Child care should be provided for everyone, and children from all social classes should have the same opportunities for development' (Martin Korpi, 2016: 16); her goal of totally free provision has yet to be fully achieved, however. The transformation has confirmed ECEC services as a fundamental part of the welfare state and of lifelong learning and as a public benefit for all children (Munkhammar and Wikgren, 2010). How can we explain this? What causes may lie behind this transformation?

It seems clear what triggered change in the early childhood system: 'The overwhelming need for women in the work force in the 1970s was the main impetus for the expansion of early childhood services in Sweden' (Lenz Taguchi and Munkhammar, 2003: 28). In this respect, Sweden is not alone; a pressing need for women in the labour force often acts as an impetus for expansion of such services. What marks out Sweden is the direction and form this expansion subsequently took: not just more of the same services but transformation to an integrated and universal system, including services and parenting leave, in which labour-market and gender-equality goals have been matched with children's right to education. What might account for Sweden's distinctive response?

In Chapter 4, we identified welfare regimes and timing as underlying factors in the Anglosphere's split childcare-dominant model, along with the major role it accords private provision and marketisation. These factors also play their part with Sweden and its integrated model, but to very different effect. Alongside the Anglosphere's liberal welfare regime, Esping-Andersen has identified other types of regime, including one that has been called the 'Nordic' or 'social democratic' welfare regime, whose features include universalism, generous benefit levels, extensive services and a high share of social expenditure in the gross national product.

> The social democratic regime is distinct also for its active and, in a sense, explicit effort to de-commodify welfare, to minimize or altogether abolish market dependency. … What, then, is uniquely social democratic is, firstly, the fusion of *universalism* with *generosity* and, secondly, its *comprehensive* socialization of risks. (Esping-Andersen, 1999: 78, 79; emphasis added)

Recently, as we have noted above, that model has been buffeted by the headwinds of neoliberalism, blowing from the Anglosphere, and filling the sails of some willing Nordic sympathisers: the pressure to increase private provision of pre-schools and schools and to marketise these services in Sweden is just one example, tax cuts and growing income inequality another. Yet the Nordic model has resisted being blown to pieces. Significantly, the Swedish early childhood system, as we have seen, started to build its universal and integrated model in the 1970s, before neoliberalism began its global rise to power in the 1980s, and when social democracy was still a power in the land.

The building work benefitted from other strong foundations. The precursive work of past thinkers and activists such as Alva Myrdal, advocating early childhood services provided publicly as a way of 'liberating' both women and children, was an important starting point: 'Sweden's integration of early childhood education and schooling, in terms of the context, the rationales and the process itself, can be seen as the fruit of continuous policy-making dating back as far as the 1930s' (Lenz Taguchi and Munkhammar, 2003: 28).

This policy making, and its context of public discussion, was to culminate in the 'decade of commissions', which provided open and inclusive spaces for the society to investigate, think about and deliberate on what type of early childhood system to build. These commissions can be viewed as expressions of a strong and long-standing national culture of democracy; the country is 2022's top overall scorer for 'democracy quality' on the Sustainable Governance Indicators (https://www.sgi-network. org/2022/Sweden/Quality_of_Democracy). A culture of democracy not only pervaded decision-making processes, but continues to influence the early childhood education to which those decisions gave rise. Thus, for example, the first paragraphs of today's Swedish pre-school curriculum set out clearly that democracy is a fundamental value of the pre-school:

> The preschool is part of the school system and rests on the basis of democracy. ... Education should also convey and establish respect for human rights and the fundamental democratic values on which Swedish society is based. ... Education should be undertaken in democratic forms and lay the foundation for a growing interest and responsibility among children for active participation in civic life and for sustainable development – not only economic, but also social and environmental. (Skolverket, 2018: 5)

But none of these influences could have shaped the Swedish early childhood system without the impetus provided by converging economic and political forces. From the 1960s, the needs of the labour market and the sustained demand for gender equality from a strong women's movement and a new generation of politicians, especially in the governing Social Democratic party, combined to drive the evolution of an early childhood system concerned equally with children and parents.

In this particular political, social and historical context, it was possible for a vision of integrated, universal and public services, and integration between parenting leave and these services, to gain sufficient traction to become established policy and produce a transformation of the Swedish early childhood system in which education played a central role, without neglecting the needs of employed parents and a commitment to gender equality. Put another way, in the late 1960s strong drivers, in particular the need for more workers, made it imperative that something was done in Sweden. As we shall see in the next chapter, a similar situation arose in England in the late 1990s. But whereas England responded by opting for more of the same, doubling down on a fragmented and privatised system, Sweden in the late 1960s had the capacity, the desire and the political bandwidth to stop and think, to consider possibilities, and then to decide to change course: the country acted in time and took time to ensure that what was done was done well.

Notes

1   'Dès l'origine, les fondateurs de la salle d'asile et les administrateurs de l'Instruction publique lui attribuent une double mission: l'assistance et l'éducation.'

2   Some *écoles maternelles* are separate institutions, with a head and three or four levels (years); others are integrated in the same building with *écoles élémentaires*, with one head for both and nine levels. Rarely, in rural zones, some schools have only one or two classes, which include children from 3 to 12 years; generally, villages have either one *école maternelle* or one *école élémentaire*, attended by children from several villages.

3   The main exception in the Anglosphere is Aotearoa New Zealand, which has an extensive network of free-standing kindergartens, not attached to or incorporated into primary schools; they are discussed in Chapter 7. England and Scotland also have some separate 'nursery schools', but their numbers are small and their sustainability uncertain in the face of funding cuts. These kindergartens or nursery schools are only available for two years, rather than the three years of the *écoles maternelles*.

4   Because of the well-paid parenting leave, very few children under 12 months attend ECEC services, so attendance for 1- and 2-year-olds is probably nearly 70 per cent.

5   The free-time pedagogue (*fritidspedagog*) is a graduate professional who works in schools, with a particular focus on free-time services.

6   Sweden's Social Democratic party, a long-established left-of-centre party, should not be confused with the Sweden Democrats, a more recent nationalist and right-wing populist political party.

7   'Tillgodose en ständigt växande efterfrågan på barntillsyn, förväntningar om jämställdhet, barns medborgerliga fostran ... under pedagogisk ledning.'

8   Sweden's parental leave system is very flexible. Leave can be used until a child is 12 years old (though only 96 days can be used after the child is 4 years old). Leave can be taken full-time, part-time, quarter-time or one-eighth time, with the length of leave extended accordingly (for example one day of full-time leave becomes two days of part-time leave or four days of quarter-time leave). It can be taken in one continuous period or in several blocks of time. The system is also very inclusive. In the case of sole custody, the parent with custody receives all of the parental leave days (though in most cases of parents living apart they have joint custody and thus share the right to leave). Same-sex parents have the same rights as other parents and the parental leave is gender-neutral in its construction.

9   For a description and critique of growing inequality in Sweden and the Swedish school voucher system see Pelling (2019, 2022).

6
Trying for transformative change: England

No countries in the Anglosphere, and few beyond, have gone as far as Sweden in achieving transformation of their early childhood systems, both early childhood services and parenting leave. However, attempts have been made elsewhere to, at least partially, reform systems, and in this chapter and the next we examine two cases of Anglosphere countries that have begun to tackle some of the problems in the Anglosphere model that we described in Chapter 3. In Chapter 7, we look at Aotearoa New Zealand, the Anglosphere country that can claim to have come closest to (but still not achieved) transformative change, with bold changes, including to its workforce, curriculum and ways of conceptualising early childhood services. England is the subject of this chapter. Although its reforms have lagged far behind Aotearoa New Zealand's, it merits inclusion (but only just) as a case of attempted transformative change for being the one Anglosphere country to widely introduce an innovative type of integrated early childhood provision, a necessary but often overlooked part of the transformative process. Sadly, this provision, the Children's Centre, has never achieved its full potential, and in recent years has been neglected and allowed to wither. Moreover, while both of these Anglosphere countries show some movement towards more integrated services, neither has managed to address marketisation and privatisation, rampant in both cases, or to develop strong parenting-leave policies that mesh with entitlement to services.

For both countries, we begin with some historical context covering the period leading up to the start of the reform process. This context introduces their systems, and the inherited defects in these systems, as well as some precursors to change and other strengths that could assist a process of transformation. We then consider the history of reform: what was attempted (and what was not) and what was the process followed, leading up to the present day and an assessment of how far each country has got in transforming its early childhood system, or, to put it another way, how far beyond the 'Anglosphere model' each country has managed to get. Each of these two chapters ends with an analysis of the conditions and forces that have favoured change and those that have hindered it.

Historical context

England is the most populous of the four nations that constitute the United Kingdom, with a population of 56.5 million. That population today is ethnically diverse; in 2021, 34.2 per cent of all children born in England and Wales had one or both parents born outside the UK (Office of National Statistics, 2022b). Early childhood, if it is defined as the period before primary schooling starts, is short; though compulsory schooling starts at age 5, most children actually enter the first class of primary school when only 4 years old.

The evolution of early childhood services in England followed a split pattern found in other countries, of 'day care' and 'education' provision. The first day nursery opened in 1850, but nurseries spread slowly and thinly; the National Society of Day Nurseries founded in 1906 represented only some 30 services. The two world wars brought temporary expansions to this form of provision, in response to wartime demand for women's employment: 174 nurseries existed in 1919 and 1,559 in 1944. However, for working mothers with no access to nurseries and no relatives available to care for their young children, other types of 'day care' were available. 'Minders' would look after young children for a small sum of money, and these childminders (the current term in England for family day carers) merged into the institution of the 'dame school'. Long in existence, dame schools increased rapidly in number during the first half of the nineteenth century, mainly taking 2- to 7-year-olds and providing some instruction in reading and writing:

> They served as public nurseries for very young children, being places of security as well (sometimes) as schools; they kept the children of the poor off the streets in towns, and out of the roads and fields in the country. Some dame schools were said to be fairly efficient and to undertake some teaching. But the teachers were often 'elderly or invalid women, who were frequently ignorant … and the business was a source of profit to persons who could earn a living in no other way'. (J. Tizard et al., 1976: 51)

During the second half of the nineteenth century, the demand for dame schools and possibly childminders diminished as fewer mothers were employed and alternative school-based provision spread. Meanwhile, the first real nursery school in the UK had been opened in 1816 by Robert Owen (1771–1858) at his New Lanark mill village in Scotland (now a UNESCO World Heritage site). But the expansion of education for young children in the nineteenth century was to owe far more to another figure, Samuel Wilderspin (1792–1856), who toured the country in the 1820s and 1830s advocating early education and stimulating the opening of infant schools. With the spread of state-aided primary schools from the mid-century, the proportion of pupils who were under 5 years increased, and continued to do so after the introduction of compulsory education from 5 years. Between 1870 and 1900, the proportion of 3- and 4-year-olds who attended primary school grew from 24 per cent to 43 per cent. But numbers then fell back rapidly, to 13 per cent by 1930, partly because of competing claims for education resources and partly because of increasing objections to the principle of schooling for this young age group.

Unfortunately, such school-based infant education was usually drear, starting with Wilderspin, whose 'most noteworthy achievement was to invent the tiered gallery … on which classes of 60 to 100 young children sat in serried rows, on benches, the teacher standing in front of the class, demonstrating, lecturing, hectoring, questioning and teaching by rote'. Overall, the picture of infant education in schools, especially before 1914, is bleak: 'the informality, gaiety and spontaneity of the early Owenite schools was replaced by the infant "system" – rigid, humourless and dreary' (J. Tizard et al., 1976: 54, 56).

There were some bright spots. Nursery education as a distinctive provision was introduced into England. The first Froebelian kindergarten was set up by two German women in London in 1851, with numbers growing after 1870. However, the existence of so much primary school-based infant education, and its powerful backers, militated against England developing a strong kindergarten movement and many actual kindergartens. The National Froebel Union, founded in 1888, focused on training teachers who could influence and introduce kindergarten methods into the public school system. Another notable event in the history of nursery education was the opening in 1911 by sisters Rachel and Margaret McMillan of their nursery school in Deptford (London), providing for the physical, educational and social needs of children from 2 to 8 or 9 years old. But despite this example, and the recommendation of the 1933 Hadow Report that nursery schools be provided, by 1938 just 118 existed.

Provision for young children, in the form of day nurseries, increased rapidly during the Second World War, when women were needed in the labour force, but reversed after 1945, the government sternly insisting that

> under normal peacetime conditions, the right policy to pursue would be positively to discourage mothers of children under two from going out to work ... and to regard day nurseries and day guardians [childminders] as supplements to meet the special needs (where these exist and cannot be met within the hours, age, range and organisation of nursery schools and nursery classes) of children whose mothers are constrained by individual circumstances to go out to work or whose home conditions are in themselves unsatisfactory from the health point of view, or whose mothers are incapable for some good reason of undertaking the full care of their children. (Ministry of Health (UK), 1945)

Public day nurseries, if not closed, as many were, became confined to targeted use by children of single employed mothers or those referred by welfare agencies: a residual service *par excellence*. There was a pervasive indifference, even hostility, to doing anything else to support maternal employment. Even statutory maternity leave was not introduced until the mid-1970s, the UK lagging behind the rest of Europe in this respect. From the start, it consisted of a very long but poorly paid period of leave: 29 weeks after birth, only six weeks of which was paid at a high level, both far longer but lower paid than elsewhere in Europe. (Assiduous readers of the previous chapter will recall that by 1976 Sweden had already moved on from maternity to parental leave, propelled by an active political debate led by the Prime Minister about gender equality, including men's role in the family.)

The 1945 government circular quoted above spoke of making 'provision for children between two and five by way of nursery classes [in primary schools] and nursery schools'. But such provision made only slow progress as other areas of education were prioritised; a commitment in 1973 by the then education minister, Margaret Thatcher, to provide part-time early education for all 3- and 4-year-olds was never realised. The main growth in school provision for young children came from a return of the old policy of admitting children to primary school before compulsory school age; by 1973, the majority of under-5s in school were in such reception classes (J. Tizard et al., 1976). One response to the low priority given to public early education provision was the playgroup movement.

First introduced in Aotearoa New Zealand, playgroups were taken up in England (and some other European countries) in the 1960s, offering part-time places and usually run by parent or other community groups.

Until the mid-1990s, therefore, successive post-war governments had given low priority to early childhood policy, whether services or parenting leave. This neglect showed in the state early childhood services were in by then. Early childhood provision in England was split, between school-based (and teacher-led) services and 'day care' services, the former being the responsibility of the Ministry of Education, the latter the Ministry of Health, with maternity leave, when belatedly introduced, coming under yet another ministry. The amount of school-based provision depended to a considerable extent on local politics and policies, with some (mostly left-wing-controlled) local authorities developing part-time nursery education for 3- and 4-year-olds in nursery classes provided within primary schools; everywhere, more and more 4-year-olds were taken into reception classes. This school-based provision was rounded off by a relatively small number of maintained nursery schools (separate schools provided by local authorities specifically for the education of 2- to 4-year-olds, though most children attending were 3 and over),[1] plus a number of private nursery schools.

Day care services (the term used in legislation up to the 1990s) were similarly fragmented. 'Childminders' were the main formal provision for children whose parents were employed, though for a long time they received little public or research attention. For many years the main providers of day nurseries were local authorities, offering a limited and welfare-oriented service for children deemed to be 'in need' or whose single parent was studying or at work. Private day nurseries were few and far between, at least until the late 1980s.[2] Playgroups provided for many children, but mostly offered only part-time hours and were run on a shoestring, relying heavily on unpaid work and fund-raising by parents and other volunteers.

The split in early childhood services – between schools and day care – also ran through the workforce, which was divided between graduate teachers and classroom assistants (both relatively well paid) in nursery and primary schools, and a diverse group of 'day care workers' in nurseries, playgroups and childminding, with poor qualifications and low wages. The one thing they had in common was that the vast majority, over 95 per cent, were women. Overall, public support for early childhood services, such as it was, depended on local authorities, with support varying widely from place to place, while workforce development figured not at all.

Professor Jack Tizard, the founder and first director of the Thomas Coram Research Unit at the University of London's Institute of Education, summed up the bleak situation thus:

> Today's [early childhood education and care] services are not simply inadequate in quantity; they are also fragmented and unresponsive to changing needs. … The present hotch-potch of pre-school provision (day nurseries, factory nurseries [today we would say 'workplace nurseries'], nursery schools, nursery classes, reception classes, playgroups, minders), and the distribution of children among them, reflect a mixture of historical accident – the needs (of parents especially) for particular hours of care, the local availability of services and the criteria of admission. The needs of the child rarely figure. Each type of service has its own set of hours, not normally adjusted to the needs of parents and child. … [S]ocial segregation occurs when services are neither locally based nor multi-purpose. (J. Tizard et al., 1976: 215)

Tizard was writing in the mid-1970s, but the same could have been written 20 years later.

Jack Tizard is significant. Not only did he offer a prescient analysis of the faults of the English early childhood system (with the exception of parenting leave, about which he had little to say). He also proposed a bold and innovative solution: to replace the existing haphazard and dysfunctional 'hotch-potch of pre-school provision' with a new type of provision, integrated and comprehensive, serving all families within its local catchment area, which he termed the 'Children's Centre'. He went further, managing in partnership with public and private organisations to set up two prototype Children's Centres in London in the mid-1970s. We will return later in the chapter to discuss these prototypes and the subsequent (though very belated) interest of government in this potentially transformative provision; suffice it to say here that these demonstration projects attracted no interest from government at the time or for many years subsequently.

The first signs of change in the system appeared in the late 1980s, not from any policy initiative but because employment among women with young children began to rise rapidly, in particular better-educated women choosing to return to their jobs after maternity leave (Brannen and Moss, 1998). Previously, employment among women with pre-school-age children had been low, overwhelmingly part-time and heavily reliant on informal childcare arrangements (family and friends), but now a new generation of mothers were emerging who needed more hours of care for their children and more formal arrangements. In the absence of public services, the result was an explosive growth in private 'childcare' provision. In England, the number of places with childminders doubled between 1989 and 1997 (from 186,500 to 365,000); this rate of increase, however, was outpaced by private day nurseries, where places nearly quadrupled over the same period (from 46,500 to 173,500) (Department of Health (England), 1997). In less than a decade a large market in private and mainly for-profit 'childcare' had arisen.

Following in the slipstream of these grass-roots changes, the first signs of policy change appeared during the post-Thatcher Conservative government led by Prime Minister John Major (in office 1990–7). Some financial assistance with the childcare costs of low-income families was introduced in 1994, a tentative and limited scheme of demand-side subsidy (i.e., payments were given to the parents using the services rather than to the suppliers of the services). In the same year, the government announced a renewed push for nursery education, with funding to go to any provider that could meet certain standards, not just schools but also playgroups, private nurseries and childminders. Again, a demand-side (and neoliberal) funding strategy was favoured, through the use of vouchers for parents, and this was introduced, on a trial basis, by four local authorities in 1996. Rather than challenge the emergent private market, these initial measures sought to introduce market-building solutions into public policy. The die was cast.

Then came the general election in 1997, a landslide victory for a 'New Labour' government, and overnight early childhood became a policy priority.

Attempting transformation: the New Labour government (1997–2010)

After more than 50 years of post-war policy neglect, from 1997 England's early childhood system became the subject of sustained central government attention; a National Childcare Strategy was launched in 1998 (Department for Education and Employment (England), 1998) and updated in 2004 (HM Treasury, 2004), covering entitlements to early education and increased 'childcare' provision for under- and over-5-year-olds. Two rationales for action were at play here. First was the turn to a positive government attitude towards employed mothers, in part as a response to social changes already underway and in part to support a more productive and competitive economy. Whereas previous governments had been hostile to women with young children working or had assumed a position of official indifference, treating it as a purely personal matter, the Labour government welcomed and supported this employment, through such measures as increasing 'childcare' provision and making this provision more accessible.

The second rationale was a new-found belief in early childhood interventions as an effective 'human technology' for improving educational performance and mitigating a raft of social problems, including child poverty, which had tripled between 1979 and 1996. The Labour government's high expectations concerning early childhood services were expressed in a 2002 'Interdepartmental Childcare Review' document:

> The availability of good quality, affordable childcare is key to achieving some important Government objectives. Childcare can improve educational outcomes for children. Childcare enables parents, particularly mothers, to go out to work, or increase their hours in work, thereby lifting their families out of poverty. It also plays a key role in extending choice for women by enhancing their ability to compete in the labour market on more equal terms ....
>
> Childcare can also play an important role in meeting other top level objectives, for example in improving health, boosting productivity, improving public services, closing the gender pay gap and reducing crime. The targets to achieve 70 per cent employment amongst lone parents by 2010 and to eradicate child poverty by 2020 are those that are most obviously related. Childcare is essential for those objectives to be met. (Department for Education and Skills (England) et al., 2002: 5)

In a few years, government in England had gone from indifference to early childhood services to a strong belief in their almost magical powers for transforming society.

The priority that the incoming Labour government gave to early childhood led to substantial reform, with six main strands.

First, there was a movement to *greater integration* of services. Government responsibility for all early childhood services, previously split between education and health ministries, was settled on one department – education. Similarly, responsibility for regulating all early childhood services was located into one agency, Ofsted, the powerful national schools inspectorate that under the Labour government acquired responsibility not only for schools and early childhood services but also for a whole raft of other children's services (including adoption, fostering and social work) and initial teacher training (today Ofsted's official name is the Office for Standards in Education, Children's Services and Skills). In due course, an early years curriculum, the Early Years Foundation Stage (EYFS), was adopted, covering all services for children under 5 years; the official description of the EYFS statutory framework is 'The standards that school and childcare providers must meet for the learning, development and care of children from birth to 5' (Department for Education (England), 2024). This is today accompanied by a national system of assessment: the reception baseline assessment (RBA) and the EYFS Profile involve assessing children's attainment at the beginning and end of their first (reception-class) year in primary school, when they are aged 4 and 5 years (Department for Education (England), 2023b; Standards and Testing Agency (England), 2023).

Second, an *entitlement to early education* was introduced. Developing the previous Conservative government's belated interest, the Labour administration introduced a universal entitlement to free early education, first for 4-year-olds, then for 3-year-olds, initially for 12.5 hours a week over 38 weeks (475 hours a year), then increased to 15 hours a week (570 hours a year); the increase was announced in 2010 by the Labour government and implemented by the following Conservative-led Coalition government. In 2009, a scheme to extend free nursery education to the poorest 2-year-olds was announced, but not implemented before the Labour government lost power.

The earlier Conservative experiment with vouchers was abandoned, replaced when the Labour government came to power by supply-side funding (a Nursery Education Grant) paid direct to providers. But the Conservatives' market approach was not entirely dropped. The Labour government opened the new early education entitlement to all providers who met certain standards, so as well as school-based provision in nursery classes and nursery schools, early education could now be offered by day nurseries, playgroups and childminders, all competing in a market.

Third, *access to 'childcare'* for employed parents was increased, the government seeking to make 'affordable' and 'high quality' 'childcare' more available. This goal was set out in the National Childcare Strategy, whose targets included two million new childcare places (for both children under and of school age) by 2006, with 1.8 million achieved by 2004. The main means of achieving this goal remained a market of mainly private providers, led by private for-profit day nurseries, but with the government intervening actively in the market. The 2006 Childcare Act placed new duties on local authorities, including securing sufficient childcare by conducting 'childcare sufficiency assessments' and managing the local childcare market; at the same time, the legislation discouraged public provision of 'childcare' services, reducing local authorities to being providers of last resort should private providers prove unavailable (though as we shall see, local authorities were given a more proactive role in the provision of Children's Centres).

The government also sought to bolster the market by the introduction of an extensive system of demand subsidy, the Childcare Tax Credit (1999), a payment to parents through the tax system made available to a substantial number of low- to middle-income families using childcare services. The aim was to support a market approach by increasing parents' financial capacity to buy private services. A final element in the 'childcare' drive was a funding programme – the Neighbourhood Nurseries Initiative – to make 'high quality, convenient and affordable childcare available for working parents' (UK Parliament, 2010) in the 20 per cent most disadvantaged areas, providing some 45,000 new places mainly through private and community-based providers and with the intention that, once established with government support, these nurseries would become self-supporting.

Fourth, *improving qualification levels* in the 'childcare' workforce. In its 2005 consultation paper on a Children's Workforce Strategy (part of its wide-ranging and integrated 'Every Child Matters' approach to children's services, discussed further below), the government spoke of 'our plans to create and support a world-class workforce which is increasingly competent and confident to make a difference to the lives of those they support' (HM Government (England), 2005: 1), an ambition that included the early childhood workforce. To improve leadership in non-school settings, the government aimed to have a graduate leading all Children's Centres (discussed below) by 2010 and all (mainly private) full-time childcare settings by 2015. With this goal in mind and as part of its Children's Workforce Strategy, in 2006 it introduced a new graduate qualification, the Early Years Professional.[3] It also invested money in improving the qualifications of the remainder of the workforce, in particular seeking to increase the numbers qualified at level 3, an upper secondary level, seen as the mainstay of childcare services.

Fifth, *parenting leave* was developed in a number of ways; this was a policy field that previous Conservative governments had not only ignored but actively opposed, for example blocking the adoption of a European Economic Community proposal made in 1984 for a Europe-wide directive to set minimum standards for parental leave. In 1999, the Labour government adopted European Union directive on parental leave that other member states had agreed in 1996 (at that time, the UK had an opt-out from such European social policies), which gave each parent 13 weeks of unpaid leave, though only (unlike in any other country) to be taken in short periods of four weeks per year. This was followed in 2003 by the introduction of two weeks of paternity leave, paid at the same low flat rate as most of maternity leave. Policy attention, however, was lavished mainly on existing maternity leave, the duration of which was extended from nine to 12 months; the period of payment was extended from 18 to 39 weeks, albeit at a low flat rate for all but six weeks (for a fuller discussion of the development of leave policy in the UK, see Moss and O'Brien, 2019).

Sixth, a *new programme, Sure Start, and a new type of provision, Children's Centres*, were introduced. Sure Start was announced in 1998, to be a targeted intervention programme for children under 4 years and their families in areas with high levels of poverty. Sixty 'trailblazer' Sure Start Local Programmes (SSLPs) were named in 1999, and funding was allocated for 250 more SSLPs. Further funding brought the total number of SSLPs to 524 by 2002. Each SSLP was required to provide specified core services: outreach services and home visiting; support for families and parents; good-quality play, learning and childcare; health care and advice about health and development; and support for children with special needs. But each local programme was also free to provide additional services (for a full history of Sure Start, see Eisenstadt, 2011). Jane Lewis, in her study of Sure Start and Children's Centres, describes the former as

> an early intervention programme, intended to bring together a range of services, including family support, health services and support for special needs as well as childcare and education, in disadvantaged areas. The aim was to 'invest' in early childhood[,] ... to improve children's health and their social, emotional and cognitive development, and to strengthen families and communities in disadvantaged areas. ... The policy problem was identified by British policy-makers mainly in terms of family functioning and child poverty among the socially excluded, and the thinking behind the creation of Sure Start focused on finding a more integrated approach to tackling social exclusion among young children and families. (Lewis, 2011: 71–2)

But these targeted Sure Start Local Programmes were not to last. The 2002 Interdepartmental Childcare Review recommended the creation of Children's Centres (CCs) as an effective way of providing good-quality, integrated childcare and early years education as well as a range of other services for children and their families. The main difference between SSLPs and CCs was 'the departure from the notion of a fixed catchment [area] allowing only families living within a small geographical area to use the services, and the absolute requirement of increasing childcare provision for working parents' (Eisenstadt, 2011: 74). Lewis develops the last point, arguing that the transition from SSLPs to CCs marked 'a substantial change in policy, which was nevertheless presented by politicians as continuity. ... [A] focus on support for children and their parents gave way to an emphasis on children's cognitive development ... and parents' employment' (Lewis, 2011: 82). (However, as we show later, by 2010, when the Children's Centre programme was complete, only a minority of Children's Centres, even in disadvantaged areas, offered 'childcare'.)

In 2003, it was announced that SSLPs were to be replaced by Sure Start Children's Centres. The first 32 Children's Centres were opened that year. At this point, we want to turn our focus onto this new type of provision, which earlier we suggested had the most transformative potential of any of New Labour's policy measures. But first we need to go back a bit in time, because, as we have already seen, Children's Centres were not, in fact, new.

Children's Centres: precursors and mass adoption

We mentioned above that in the 1970s Professor Jack Tizard had set up two prototype Children's Centres in London. These projects were intended to demonstrate a new type of provision, integrated and comprehensive, that he envisaged as providing an alternative to the existing fragmented and inadequate 'hotch-potch of pre-school provision'; they would represent a transformation of the early childhood scene in England. It is important to revisit these demonstration projects, and the original vision Tizard had for Children's Centres, to provide a reference point for what happened 30 years later.

Tizard's proposal was 'simple but breathtakingly audacious' (B. Tizard, 2003: 13). Faced in the early 1970s by England's fragmented and dysfunctional system of early childhood services, he came to a clear conclusion: what was needed was total transformation, in the form of a new type of provision that was integrated, multi-purpose, universal, local and free. His argument was that, 'For a society which provides free education, including free higher education, and a free child health service, a free pre-school service is a logical corollary' (J. Tizard et al., 1976: 214). As this comment suggests, he was envisaging this new type of provision as an addition to the existing collection of universal basic services for children and young people already provided by the welfare state.

This new type of provision, the Children's Centre, should be 'the overall responsibility of one authority at national and local level …[,] embrace children from birth onwards and cover education and care'. It should be universal in coverage, each Centre serving a small local catchment area: 'The service must therefore be available to all families [with young children], and not selective in its intake, and must be based on demand, not need.' It must also offer a wide range of services. Some of these would be standard to all Centres; in addition to 'education and care throughout the day and year' (J. Tizard et al., 1976: 214), including for children under 3 years ('the need for provision for this group needs to be accepted'), child health services were essential. But other services would be responsive to the particular needs and demands of local communities, offering as much flexibility as possible in the range of services provided.

> A centre for day-care and education might also offer a range of other services to young families living locally, even perhaps to the local community as a whole. For example a welfare clinic; a toy and book library; clothes-washing facilities[4] …; a meeting place for local groups; a food cooperative. (J. Tizard et al., 1976: 216)

What Tizard was advocating here was a uniform type of provision – the Children's Centre – but with scope for considerable diversity in what each multi-purpose Centre offered.

Two other features of the Children's Centre as advocated by Tizard should be mentioned. First, a reform of the early years workforce was needed, since greater integration

> will require a more rational system of staffing, with a rethink in particular of the existing dichotomy between nursery nurses [the name then used for workers in day nurseries] and teachers … [which] impedes the setting up of a genuinely integrated service in which all needs are met by one group of staff in a multi-purpose neighbourhood centre. (J. Tizard et al., 1976: 218, 219)

Second, there should be substantial parent involvement, which

> does not mean simply helping mothers with difficulties, or holding mothers' classes. It should mean enlisting the active participation of parents in the day-to-day life of the nursery, learning from as well as teaching them, working together. ... Given encouragement, an increasing number [of parents] will probably wish to be involved in the discussion and shaping of aims and methods – and the issue of parent power will become more pressing in the future. (J. Tizard et al., 1976: 218, 226)

While affirming that 'parental involvement in nursery centres is very necessary', Tizard conceded that 'how best to achieve it is not at all clear'.

The two demonstration projects in London that Tizard helped establish in the 1970s continued after Tizard's premature death in 1979, and a few other examples followed (the world-famous Pen Green Centre for Children and Families in the town of Corby opened in 1983). But, as already noted, Children's Centres attracted no interest from government at the time or for decades after. It was not until 2002 that the Labour government adopted the concept, or their take on it, and started a rapid expansion programme. Children's Centres subsequently developed in three phases: the first focused on the 20 per cent most disadvantaged areas in England; the second extended Children's Centres to the 30 per cent most disadvantaged areas, and added some in other areas; and the third achieved full coverage in the remaining 70 per cent of the country.

By 2010, when the Labour government lost power, there were 3,620 Children's Centres (Department for Education (England), 2019), the government having achieved its target of one in every community in England. Children's Centres often built on services developed earlier by the Labour government, including Sure Start Local Programmes and Neighbourhood Nurseries, and on some pre-existing nursery schools. While many were created on existing sites, including nursery and primary schools, many others were in dedicated new buildings, with an estimated capital spend of one billion pounds (Bouchal and Norris, 2014: 4).

Local authorities, marginalised in the provision of 'childcare' services, were given a leading role in the provision of Children's Centres. The central government department with overall responsibility for early childhood services, the Department for Education, renamed the Department for Children, Schools and Families in 2007, delegated to local authorities responsibility for planning and managing the Children's Centre programme in their area. This was later put on a statutory basis by the 2006 Childcare Act, which created legal duties for local authorities to establish and run Children's Centres. Local authorities were responsible for delivering their share of the Children's Centres target as agreed with national government – and they did so. A review of the whole programme concluded:

> The commitment to deliver such a large programme – consisting in part of delivering a capital building programme – on a relatively short timescale was very ambitious, and although it did prove challenging for many local authorities, it was delivered by the deadline. (Bouchal and Norris, 2014: 11)

Although having become a universal service by 2010, in the qualified sense that Children's Centres were to be found in all communities and were available to all families, they were not comprehensive in the services they offered. What was on offer differed in different areas. All Children's Centres had to provide what was known as the 'core offer':

- information and advice to parents on a range of subjects, including looking after babies and young children, and on the availability of local services such as childcare;
- drop-in sessions and activities for parents, carers and children;
- outreach and family support services, including a visit to all families within two months of a child's birth;
- child and family health services, including access to specialist services for those who needed them;
- links with Jobcentre Plus [the government's employment agency] for training and employment advice; and
- support for local childminders and a childminding network.

Children's Centres serving the 30 per cent most deprived communities had in addition to offer integrated early education and childcare places for a minimum of five days a week, 10 hours a day, 48 weeks a year. Children's Centres outside these areas did not need to include such services unless there was unmet local demand, though all were expected to have some activities for children on site. Overall, therefore, the role of the Children's Centres was to provide early education and childcare, but only where the existing market was not able to meet demand; in practice, for most of the country, the focus was on the Children's Centre as an information and support service (Lewis, 2011).

What this meant can be seen in the results of a government-funded Childcare and Early Years' Providers Survey conducted in 2010 (Brind et al., 2011: Table 3.9). In the last year of the Labour government, 85 per cent or more of Children's Centres were providing a wide variety of parent and family support services, including:

- family support outreach and/or home visiting services;
- employment advice links to employment services;
- support for lone and teenage parents and parents with disabled children;
- literacy or numeracy programmes for parents/carers with basic skills needs;
- support for families with drug- or alcohol-related or mental health problems or a member in prison;
- support for particular minority ethnic groups; and
- relationship support.

However, only a quarter provided full-time or sessional childcare, the proportion having declined since the previous year; Children's Centres in the 30 per cent most deprived areas were more likely than those elsewhere to offer on-site full-time childcare (37 per cent compared with 13 per cent elsewhere) and sessional care (28 per cent compared with 22 per cent).

Before we leave Children's Centres and the Labour government, it is important to note that these Centres became part of a much wider policy for children and children's services. This policy was commonly referred to as 'Every Child Matters' (ECM), after the title of a government Green Paper in 2003 (HM Treasury, 2003) produced in response to the report of an inquiry into the death of a young child, Victoria Climbié, killed by the relatives she lived with but failed by a succession of public health, welfare and education bodies. ECM placed a new emphasis on a holistic and integrated approach to working with all children, of both pre-school and school age; this approach included the adoption of a common set of outcomes to cover all services for children and the development of new integrated services, including Children's Centres and Extended Schools (which all schools were to become, providing at least a 'core offer' of services for children and families).[5] Both were presented as combining universal services, which every child could use, and more targeted services for those with additional needs, and as delivering a 'new vision of a universal network of integrated children's services at the local level' (Lewis, 2011: 79).

Processes of change

The Labour government's Sure Start programme, which with Children's Centres was the most innovative result of the new policy interest in early childhood services, originated in a 1998 report from a senior Treasury official, Norman Glass. The report was prepared as part of that government's first Comprehensive Spending Review (CSR), intended to introduce a longer-term perspective to government spending and policy by setting three-year targets for public expenditure. While this initial CSR focused on individual departments, it included three thematic cross-departmental policy reviews, on drugs, youth crime, and services for children under 8 years. It was the last, led by Norman Glass, that recommended and led to Sure Start; the recommendations were based on some key findings that included the particular damage caused by poverty in the early years, the smaller share of public expenditure going to children under 4 years than to those at school, the lack of an overall strategy for services for young children, wide variations in the quantity and quality of early years services across the country, and the potential for the right kind of services to narrow the gap between poor children and the rest (Eisenstadt, 2012).

By contrast, the other parts of government early childhood policy did not benefit from such a process of policy review. There was no comparable report, or any other review process, or indeed any research, that provided a comprehensive and critical analysis of the existing early childhood system, its strengths and weaknesses, or the options available for its future development. For example, although the Labour government inherited a large private for-profit sector of day nurseries and a market in childcare services, there was no discussion, and certainly no evaluation, of privatisation and marketisation before the extension of both became an established part of policy, or, indeed, after this extension. Nor, to take another example, was there any review of parenting leave policy or of the relationship between parenting leave and early childhood services.

If the Labour government was not proactive in taking a critical look at the existing system and possible future directions, it also failed to react to an outside review conducted by the OECD. The *Starting Strong* project was a cross-national thematic review of early childhood education and care policy launched in 1998 by the OECD's Education Committee, and concluded in 2006 with the publication of the second of the project's two detailed and substantial reports. The review covered 20 of the OECD's member states, the countries included having volunteered to participate and to contribute to the costs; most of these countries were in Europe, but they also included Australia, Canada, Korea, Mexico and the United States. Each participating country was reviewed by a multinational team that visited services and met a wide range of stakeholders before preparing a country report, which identified strengths and weaknesses in the country's system and offered proposals for improvement.

Twelve countries took part in the first part of the review, including the United Kingdom, which received an OECD review team in December 1999; its members were drawn from Belgium, Norway, the US and the OECD itself. A report on this initial stage of *Starting Strong* was published in 2001 (OECD, 2001), containing a detailed analysis of early childhood policy in these countries and concluding with a chapter called 'Policy lessons from the Thematic Review', which included eight 'key elements of policy that are likely to promote equitable access to high quality ECEC':

1. a systematic and integrated approach to ECEC policy, including a clear vision, a coordinated policy framework and a lead department in government;
2. a strong and equal partnership with the education system, supporting a lifelong learning approach, smooth transitions and recognising ECEC as an important part of the education system;
3. a universal approach to access, with particular attention to children in need of special support, highlighting the need for more attention to be paid to access for children under 3 years;
4. substantial public investment in services and infrastructure, essential to support a sustainable system of quality, accessible services;
5. a participatory approach to quality improvement and assurance, that engages children, parents and staff;
6. appropriate training and working conditions for ECEC staff, and strategies to recruit and retain a qualified and diverse, mixed-gender workforce;
7. systematic attention to data collection and monitoring, covering the status of young children, ECEC provision and the early childhood workforce;
8. a stable framework and long-term agenda for research and evaluation, with sustained investment to support research on key policy areas.

A further eight countries were reviewed in the second stage of the project, leading to the second *Starting Strong* report, published in 2006. This organised its further findings around the first report's eight 'key elements'. It also included an annex containing extensive and systematic information on the early childhood system in all 20 countries that had participated in the review, and proposed a further 'ten policy areas for consideration by governments and the major ECEC stakeholders':

1. to attend to the social context of early childhood development;
2. to place well-being, early development and learning at the core of ECEC work, while respecting the child's agency and natural learning strategies;
3. to create the governance structures necessary for system accountability and quality assurance;
4. to develop with the stakeholders broad guidelines and curricular standards for all ECEC services;
5. to base public funding estimates for ECEC on achieving quality pedagogical goals;
6. to reduce child poverty and exclusion through upstream fiscal, social and labour policies, and to increase resources within universal programmes for children with diverse learning rights;
7. to encourage family and community involvement in early childhood services;
8. to improve the working conditions and professional education of ECEC staff;
9. to provide freedom, funding and support to early childhood services;
10. to aspire to ECEC systems that support broad learning, participation and democracy.

We have described this comparative study by OECD at some length for a number of reasons. First, the whole exercise was an important example of how the comparative study of early childhood systems can be undertaken in a way that goes deeply into the distinctive identities of different countries, while at the same time drawing out common themes and lessons. The second reason is the 'breadth and the wisdom of the conclusions he [John Bennett, the leader of the review] drew from the many countries that the *Starting Strong* review teams visited' (Moss, 2018: 28); indeed, the whole exercise benefitted from the exceptional leadership of John Bennett, an international expert on early childhood education and care. Third, it was an opportunity, in the words of Joe Tobin, from Chapter 5, 'to push back against [national] provincialism by challenging taken-for-granted assumptions [and] expanding the menu of the possible' (J. Tobin, 2022: 298).

Starting Strong, therefore, offered a unique opportunity for critical analysis and public deliberation about the present system and possibilities for transformation, both in the national report for the United Kingdom (OECD, 2000) and in the two overall project reports. Sadly, the opportunity was wasted by the UK government (unlike, as we shall see in Chapter 7, that of Aotearoa New Zealand). The UK government convened a one-day conference to discuss the national report for the UK, but did nothing further to make use of this rich source of information and provocation to reflection.

If there was little attempt to research, and critically review, the existing system and consider alternatives, or to work with comparative studies to challenge assumptions and stimulate fresh thinking, the Labour government did put considerable funding into some other kinds of research. Notably, it funded two large-scale and longitudinal studies: the Effective Provision of Pre-School Education (EPPE) and the National Evaluation of Sure Start (NESS). The former, the EPPE study, described itself as

> the first major European longitudinal study of a national sample of young children's development between the ages of 3 and 7 years. To investigate the effects of pre-school education, the EPPE team collected a wide range of information on 3,000 children. The study also looks at background characteristics related to parents, the child's home environment and the pre-school settings children attended. Settings (141) were drawn from a range of providers (local authority day nurseries, integrated centres, playgroups, private day nurseries, nursery schools and nursery classes). A sample of 'home' children (who had no or minimal pre-school experience) were recruited to the study at entry to school for comparison with the pre-school group. In addition to investigating the effects of pre-school provision, EPPE explored the characteristics of effective practice (and the pedagogy which underpins it) through twelve intensive case studies of settings where children had positive outcomes. (Sylva et al., 2004: 1)

What EPPE did, therefore, was to look at certain effects of the existing system, and possible causation for these effects, but the information and conclusions so generated were not used as evidence for any critical review of the existing system. Yet what EPPE found did in fact raise major questions about aspects of that system. For example, the researchers concluded that there was a positive relationship between the qualifications of staff and ratings of quality. Children made more progress in pre-school centres where staff had higher qualifications, particularly if the manager was highly qualified. *Having trained teachers working with children in pre-school settings (for a substantial proportion of time, and most importantly as the curriculum leader) had the greatest impact on quality*, and was linked specifically with better outcomes in pre-reading and social development at age 5. ...

Integrated centres that fully combine education with care and have a high proportion of trained teachers, along with nursery schools, tend to promote better intellectual outcomes for children. Similarly, fully integrated settings and nursery classes tend to promote better social development even after taking account of children's backgrounds and prior social behaviour.

Good quality pre-school education can be found in all kinds of settings[;] however[,] the EPPE data indicates that *integrated centres and nursery school provision have the highest scores on pre-school quality*, while playgroups, private day nurseries and local authority day nurseries centers [*sic*] have lower scores. The integrated centres in the EPPE sample were all registered as nursery schools but had extended their provision to include flexible hours for childcare along with substantial health and family support services. ...

Disadvantaged children do better in settings with a mixture of children from different social backgrounds ... than in settings catering mostly for children from disadvantaged families. This has implications for the siting of centres in areas of social disadvantage. (Sylva et al., 2004: 4; emphasis added)

In other words, on the particular measures chosen by EPPE, 'integrated centres' and school-based services, especially nursery schools, and a particular type of worker, namely qualified teachers, performed better. School-based services and teachers were and are, as we have seen, on one side of the early childhood divide in England, and in the minority among early childhood services and workers. Furthermore, integrated centres and nursery schools have fallen into decline since 2010. The results, indeed, appear to throw into question increasing reliance on 'childcare' services, especially day nurseries with their lower-qualified staff and their admission bias towards children from more advantaged backgrounds, the antithesis of 'settings with a mixture of children from different social backgrounds'. Despite this, EPPE has led to no reconsideration or reform of the overall system.

The National Evaluation of Sure Start (NESS) sought to evaluate

> the impact of SSLPs on child and family functioning over time [by] follow[ing] up over 5000 7-year-olds and their families in 150 SSLP areas who were initially studied when the children were 9 months, 3 and 5 years old. The 7-year-old study followed up a randomly selected subset of the children and families studied at younger ages.
>
> The comparison group of non-SSLP children and their families, against which the NESS sample was compared, was selected from the entire Millennium Cohort Study (MCS) cohort. Their selection was based upon identifying and selecting children living in areas with similar characteristics to SSLP areas, but which did not offer SSLP services. This enabled comparisons amongst children and families from similar areas in order to detect possible effects of SSLPs on children and families. (National Evaluation of Sure Start Team, 2012: [3])

The point we would make here is that NESS was conducted as an evaluation, using methods intended to gauge the effectiveness of an intervention. We will develop this point further in the next and final section.

We have argued that the approach taken by the 1997–2010 Labour government to England's early childhood system, having put it in the policy spotlight, lacked any process of critical analysis and public deliberation about that system. But a further feature of the process of policy development was its centralisation: early childhood policies in England emerged from Whitehall, the seat of England's central government in London, through a blizzard of policy missives. This whole way of proceeding was symptomatic of the highly centralised English state, a centuries-old phenomenon that was even more pronounced from the 1980s when Margaret Thatcher's Conservative government hobbled and hollowed out potential centres of opposition to that state, notably trade unions and local authorities. Thus, while local authorities did gain a strategic role in the development of Children's Centres, their place in mainstream early childhood services was increasingly marginalised. As already noted, the 2006 Childcare Act gave them the role of managing the 'childcare market', but made it clear that their role in providing actual services was to be minimal. Their previous role in regulating 'childcare' services was transferred to Ofsted, the central government's agency. All the time, their role in schools continued to diminish. From the 1980s, schools had assumed ever more responsibility for their own management; the first academy schools emerged in the early 2000s, to be followed by mass academisation under post-2010 governments. In effect, this was the privatisation of schools and the transfer of public responsibility to central government. ('Academy' schools are funded directly by central government, with an agreement between the school and the Secretary of State, or chief minister, in the education department.)

Strong and confident local authorities, with an acknowledged and substantive role in providing and planning, as well as supporting, services, might have created important opportunities to experiment with innovative solutions to the deep-seated problems of the English system. Weak and marginalised authorities were unlikely to do so, being in no position to propose or trial alternatives. The result, as we shall argue in the next section, was that increasing the policy priority for early childhood led not to transformation but to more of the same, and to a growing sense that there is no alternative.

Lastly, not only did this highly centralised project not have to contend with strong institutions, such as local authorities, that might have offered alternative views about how a newly prioritised early childhood system could develop. It also met with no sustained alternative positions being advocated by alliances of organisations and expert individuals. Individual voices might be heard responding to this or that policy, but no massed voices speaking in unison merged and emerged.

Giving up on transformation: coalition and Conservative governments (2010–)

In 2010, the Labour government gave way to a Conservative-led coalition government, which was succeeded from 2015 by Conservative-only governments. There have been some further policy developments: the universal early education entitlement for 3- and 4-year-olds has been extended from 12.5 to 15 hours per week, and the proportion of 2-year-olds eligible for free early education has been increased from 20 to 40 per cent; 3- and 4-year-olds are now offered 30 hours of free provision per week (for 38 weeks a year), but only if their parents are employed and meet certain other conditions; the offer itself is presented as 'childcare' and not 'early education' (i.e., these extended hours of free attendance are no longer a universal child entitlement to education but a childcare benefit targeted at certain parents). A universal demand subsidy, 'Tax-Free Childcare', has been added to the existing, more targeted subsidy, offering up to £2,000 a year per child to help with the costs of childcare; a new graduate professional, the 'Early Years Teacher', has replaced the Labour government's 'Early Years Professional', but still without parity of status or conditions with school teachers and with no requirements on providers to employ such workers. At the same time, the Labour government's modest aspiration that a graduate would lead all full-time childcare settings by 2015 has been ditched. Most recently, as outlined in Chapter 3, the Conservative government announced in March 2023 that it would be extending the 30 hours per week of 'free childcare' for employed parents to children from 9 months of age, further emphasising a turn away from a universal right of education for children to a targeted subsidy to support some parents.

While some of these measures represent incremental additions to policies first introduced by the Labour government, in other respects post-2010 governments have undermined what some might consider the Labour government's flagship policies. 'Every Child Matters', the attempt to build a comprehensive and more integrated approach to all services for children and young people, was airbrushed out of existence after the 2010 election. With it went the ambitiously titled Department for Children, Schools and Families, which reverted to its former, narrower label of the Department for Education; this change in name was followed by the ditching of any active support for developing the new types of provision so central to 'Every Child Matters', that is, Extended Schools and Children's Centres. Though not abolished, they have fallen victim to sustained government austerity and neglect, which has seen savage cuts to central government funding of local authorities, who have had to seek large savings in all services which they are not statutorily obliged to provide, including Children's Centres. The impact has been compounded by national guidance on the 'core purpose' of Children's Centres that came out in 2013, which marked

> a significant shift towards targeting families in greatest need and focusing on parenting skills, child development and school readiness, and child and family health and life chances. The requirement to provide full daycare and qualified teachers in the most disadvantaged areas was dropped. Children's centres were expected to signpost families to services, particularly to private and voluntary day care providers. (G. Smith et al., 2018: 7)

A report published in April 2018 (G. Smith et al., 2018) describes some of the consequences of spending cuts and the turn away from a more universal to a more targeted approach. They are summarised in a press release:

> As many as 1,000 Sure Start [Children's] centres across the country have closed since 2009 – twice as many as the government has reported ....
>
> By [the programme's] peak in August 2009, there were 3,632 centres, with over half (54%) in the 30% most disadvantaged areas. However, in recent years, its status as a key national programme has diminished, accompanied by substantial budget cuts, the suspension of Ofsted inspections and increasingly uneven local provision. ...
>
> By 2017, sixteen [local] authorities who had closed more than half of their centres accounted for 55% of the total number of closures. But in areas with fewer closures there's been a reduction of services and staff, leading to fewer open access services such as Stay and Play and more parents having to rely on public transport to find a centre offering what they need. ...
>
> According to the report, 'services are now "hollowed out" – much more thinly spread, often no longer "in pram-pushing distance". The focus of centres has changed to referred families with high need, and provision has diversified as national direction has weakened, leading to a variety of strategies to survive in an environment of declining resources and loss of strategic direction.' (Sutton Trust, 2018)

By 2021, the tally of closed Centres had risen further, the number of full Children's Centres in each local authority area having fallen by more than a third, on average, (Lepper, 2022).

Behind these figures and the narrowed service offer are more than spending cuts and government guidance. There is also a coolness, if not downright antipathy, on the part of Conservative governments to provision closely associated with the preceding Labour government, provision such as Extended Schools and Children's Centres, with their combination of universal and targeted services. In this changed political climate, these innovative forms of provision are out of official favour, and 'Family Hubs' are in; the government announced in 2022 a modest funding programme for these services. 'Family Hubs' are described as 'centres of advice for parents on how to care for their child, keep them safe and healthy and provide services including parenting and breastfeeding support. … [They will] improv[e] access to a wide range of integrated support services for families with children aged 0–19' (Gaunt, 2022). Apart from losing the Children's Centre's focus on pre-school children and families, the Hub model has no provision for early childhood education and care, offering instead a limited menu of advice and support. The Hub is far removed from Tizard's ambitious vision of the Children's Centre as a new universal basic service.

What was achieved

The English story since 1997 is one of stalled integration. The Labour administration moved on the 'low-hanging fruits' of integration: policy making and administration, regulation and curriculum. But it did not attempt to integrate any of the more difficult elements: access, funding, workforce or type of provision. Marketisation and privatisation went unquestioned, indeed were encouraged. Nor was any significant progress made on integrating parenting leave with early childhood services. No further progress has been made since 2010, under Conservative governments; instead, there has been regression, with the ditching of 'Every Child Matters', the decline of Children's Centres and an increasing emphasis on the divisive language of 'childcare' with its exclusive focus on 'working parents' (see Chapter 3, p. 63); any earlier impetus to integration is not only stalled but now dead in the water.

The recent history of the early childhood workforce provides a glaring example of failed integration. The Labour government made some progress in improving the level of qualification among the childcare part of the workforce, but left much still to do and the teacher/childcare worker split untouched. The government's 2010 Providers Survey (Brind et al., 2011) shows the position at the end of Labour's period in office. In school-based early childhood services, two-fifths of staff had a level 6 qualification or higher, reflecting the graduate teacher part of the workforce, while a similar proportion had level 3 or below, reflecting their assistant co-workers (Table 6.4). But in the childcare sector, the profile was very different, despite a substantial increase in qualification levels since 1997. Less than 10 per cent (8 per cent in full-time childcare, 7 per cent in sessional childcare (Table 6.3a), and 3 per cent of childminders (Table 6.3b)) had a level 6 qualification or higher; around half had a level 3 (58 per cent, 57 per cent and 47 per cent respectively) (Tables 6.3a, 6.3b), and most of the remainder had a level 2 or 1 qualification or none at all (16 per cent, 24 per cent and 36 per cent respectively (Tables 6.3a, 6.3b)). The newly introduced graduate worker, the Early Years Professional, was appearing in the workforce by this time, but was still a small part of it – just 4 per cent of workers in full-time childcare and 2 per cent of those in sessional childcare (Table 6.25) – and lacked parity of status and conditions with school teachers. Overall, just under a quarter of heads of full-time childcare services had a level 6 or higher qualification (i.e., were graduates) (Table 6.13a), only 9 per cent of supervisors (Table 6.14a) and just 2 per cent of other childcare workers (Table 6.15a) – a long way from the Labour government's aspiration for graduate-led services.

In sum, despite improvements, the ECEC workforce – in 2010 in particular the predominant childcare part of it – remained at a relatively low level of qualification. Pay, too, remained poor, at least among the great majority of workers not employed in schools. In 2010, workers in school-based services earned on average around £14.50–14.60 an hour, with teachers (at around £20 an hour) earning roughly twice as much as assistants (£10–11 an hour) (Table 5.19). But among childcare workers, the average pay was around £8 an hour, more for heads of services (£9.60 per hour in playgroups, £10.80 in full-day childcare), and substantially less for non-supervisory staff working directly with children (£6.70 and £6.60 respectively) (Table 5.17a). These can be compared with the national minimum wage of £5.93 an hour in 2010, the London Living Wage (intended to provide for 'a minimally acceptable quality of life' in London) of £7.85 an hour, and the average national hourly wage of £14.65 (Brind et al., 2011: 102). Nor do earnings take any account of other benefits, not least pensions. The workforce in schools are generally members of a public sector final salary pension scheme, including a substantial contribution from employers. Staff working in childcare services are unlikely to have access to a similar scheme, and are too low-paid to be able to make adequate contributions to a private pension scheme.

Since 2010, there has been no improvement in qualifications or pay, and even some evidence that qualifications in 'childcare' services have gone backwards. The average wage in the sector was £7.42 an hour in 2018, compared to £11.37 an hour across the female workforce, and in 2019 45 per cent of childcare workers earned so little that they were claiming means-tested state benefits or tax credits. In the private, voluntary and independent sector, the proportion of staff with a level 3 qualification fell from 83 per cent in 2014/15 to 52 per cent in 2018/19

(Nuffield Foundation, 2021: 4). Plans for a graduate-led childcare sector by 2015 have been shelved.

So why include England as a case of trying for transformative change? Because the example of the Children's Centre gives a tantalising glimpse of what transformative change might look like. The Children's Centre as envisaged by Jack Tizard, back in the 1970s, was a transformative type of provision, a universal, integrated and multi-purpose service with early childhood education at its core, that offered a way out of the fragmented, incoherent and dysfunctional services that constituted, and still constitute, England's split system. And as Tizard conceptualised the Children's Centre, it also addressed other divisions, providing integrated access (all children and families in its catchment area entitled to attend), integrated funding (free attendance at a provision directly financed from taxation) and an integrated workforce (rethinking the teacher/childcare worker dichotomy).

Tizard and some other pioneers demonstrated that the Children's Centre was a feasible model of provision, and the Labour government showed the feasibility of deploying Children's Centres widely and at pace. Opening over 3,500 Centres in just seven years was a phenomenal achievement, demonstrating that public services can be extended rapidly if there is sufficient political will; by achieving this, the Labour government undermined one argument for privatised services, that only they can be expanded at pace. They also proved an immediate hit with families; a 2017 report, 'Implementing Sure Start Children's Centres', acknowledged that

> Children's centres also helped generate and sustain popular support for early years' provision, as evidenced by widespread public concern about closures of children's centres after 2010. Children's centres are popular with parents and have achieved high take-up of services. (Bouchal and Norris, 2014: 5)

But, in the end, the transformative concept did not translate into transformative change to the early childhood system. Tizard had seen Children's Centres as a new and universal provision, to replace the existing hotch-potch of pre-school provision, in much the same way that, as we described in the previous chapter, Sweden saw the 'pre-school' as the future shape of their early childhood services, replacing the existing split between nurseries and kindergartens. But the Labour government, by contrast, saw Sure Start and Children's Centres mainly as interventions, a new technology or treatment for reducing social problems; in effect, they supplemented, rather than replaced, the existing hotch-potch, adding to the fragmentation and incoherence. Many Centres, indeed, did not provide even the most basic of early childhood services, education and care. And as an intervention, Children's Centres were subjected to evaluation from an early stage, to determine if they worked, rather than being given the time and sustained support that developing a new type of provision really called for.

Yet at their best, the Labour government's Children's Centres, like Tizard's prototypes 30 years earlier, showed what might be achieved, what transformative change could look like. For instance, in their book *Children, Families and Communities: Creating and sustaining integrated services,* Pat Broadhead, Chrissy Meleady and Marco Delgado (2008) describe the work of a Children's Centre operating in a materially deprived and very diverse area of an English city, and responding to the diverse needs of that community. The Centre provided early childhood education and care, and out-of-school leisure and care services for older children. But it also provided a multitude of other services, in response to the needs of its local community, including: assistance with translation and interpretation; adult education; dance and other workshops; access to legal, health, housing and other services; counselling, advocacy and advice; home care and other domiciliary support workers; respite care for seriously ill parents; support for various other groups, including terminally ill children and their parents, and adult survivors of child sexual abuse, domestic violence and female genital mutilation; and a range of intergenerational activities. It was a genuinely inclusive, multi-purpose community-based service, a true manifestation of Tizard's original vision.

The Labour government failed to transform the Anglosphere model of the early childhood system in England, and the reality is that they never meant to. Instead, they worked to improve the model they inherited, not to replace it. They wanted to increase and support maternal employment, so they encouraged the market in private childcare providers. They wanted to provide further support to working parents, so they built up the existing mainstay of parenting leave policy, an extended maternity leave. They wanted early education to improve later educational performance, so they increased access to existing providers, along with tighter control of the education they provided. They believed early intervention could solve social problems, so they added Sure Start and Children's Centres to the service mix to deliver this intervention.

The result was a series of piecemeal measures that added up to more of the same, with Sure Start and Children's Centres as the one innovation, and then in a muted form. Rather than systemic reform, Labour opted for working with the existing system. Tizard used the term 'hotch-potch' to describe the system in 1970s, which the Cambridge online dictionary defines as a 'confused mixture of different things'. This describes the situation in the 1970s, the 1990s, and still today.

Drivers for and obstacles to transformation

In 1997, the Labour government came to power with a landslide majority. They also came to power with a clear commitment to make early childhood policy a priority. The need for change was driven by the government's belief that the early childhood system had a critical role to play in achieving a number of its key policy objectives, including increasing women's employment, and tackling child poverty and a number of other social problems. There was an awareness, too, that the system itself needed overhauling and that it was not fit for purpose.

So why, given these potential drivers, was the change that followed not transformational? Why, 25 years later, can the summary of a report on early childhood services in England conclude:

> Despite significant investment, there is no national coherent vision for early childhood education and care. Over the past twenty-five years, public policy has sought to address different objectives: improving child outcomes, increasing mothers' labour market participation, and addressing disadvantage. The system accordingly is confused and fragmented. It comprises a diverse patchwork of different services and complex funding arrangements. …
>
> A whole-system review of early childhood services is needed, one which articulates a clarity of purpose and which meets the needs of both young children and their families and makes a difference to disadvantaged children in particular. Given the weight of evidence highlighting the complexities and inefficiencies of current programmes, the time is right for a wholesale evaluation of the purpose and provision of early education and care. (Nuffield Foundation, 2021: 3, 5)

One obstacle to transformational change was the perceived need for quick results. The Labour government wanted more places quickly, especially in 'childcare'. Stopping to review the system they inherited with a view to major reform would have impeded this rapid expansion, which seemed most readily achieved by creating more of the same and by a reliance on the private sector. Review and reflection were limited to the one genuinely new part of their policy, the Sure Start intervention programme, which was to lead to the Children's Centre programme.

At the same time, the government did not face a strong and united campaign calling for transformational change, and articulating what that might mean. Over years of policy neglect, the fragmented system had produced fragmented interest groups, representing different types of provision and different constituencies; there were many voices calling for many different things, but not one concerted call for either a 'whole-system review' or for transformation leading to an integrated public system of early childhood services and synergy between these services and parenting leave. This remains true to the present day.

The Labour government, too, was comfortable with many of the features of the system it inherited, or at least not sufficiently discomfited by them to take on the heavy lifting required to tackle them. Having reconciled itself with – some would say signed up to – the neoliberal sentiments of the preceding Conservative governments, it was ready to accept, and indeed work with, the marketisation and privatisation of early childhood services, and not willing to assess, question or contest their presence. Its aim was to increase private provision and improve the market, through more funding for the parents who used the market and through governing the market and private providers more effectively, via a strong system of centralised regulation.

It readily adopted the 'childcare' discourse, and accepted the childcare-dominant split between school-based and childcare services. It eschewed any attempt to move towards education-based integration, as in Sweden, in favour of a modicum of alignment between fragmented services through consolidation of policy making, curriculum and inspection; it continued to prioritise a need for more 'childcare for working parents' and the need for separate 'childcare services' to deliver it. In the same way, it settled for incremental improvements for 'childcare' workers, rather than radical reform leading to a new integrated graduate workforce across all early years provision; instead of realising the rather grandiosely worded ambition to 'create and support a world-class workforce', it left the low-cost employment model in place. And rather than reform parenting leave on a more gender-equal basis, it settled for enhancing the existing maternalist policy: unlike in Sweden, maternity leave, not parental leave, was the priority, reflecting a party politics in which gender equality, addressing the positions of both women and men, was not a priority. In this respect, Tony Blair was no Olof Palme.

Last but not least, the Labour administration showed little interest in other countries. The exception was the United States, whose research purporting to demonstrate the effectiveness of early intervention programmes influenced the Glass review and the subsequent Sure Start programme. The Labour government's belief in the magical thinking derided by Ed Zigler and described in Chapter 4 manifested itself in its high hopes for what 'childcare' could achieve and for 'Sure Start, which was seen as something of a "magic bullet" that would, in the long term, help to reduce youth crime, teenage pregnancy, family breakdown and poverty' (Lewis, 2011: 73).

While drawn to the technical and economistic approach to early years emanating from the United States – what has been called 'the story of quality and high returns' (Moss, 2014) – the Labour government showed little interest in the experience of other European countries, for example Sweden and its process of creating an integrated early childhood system. Hence, Children's Centres were implemented in a way that was closer to the US Head Start than to the Swedish pre-school. Nor did they engage with the experience of Aotearoa New Zealand, which, as we shall see in the next chapter, was undertaking reforms that could have given them much pause for thought about the possibilities for change in the Anglosphere model.

Notes

1   A report for the government in England published in 2019 states: 'There are currently 392 MNS [maintained nursery schools], although this number has declined from around 600 in 1988' (Paull and Popov, 2019: 9). In 2021, there were more than eight times as many children in nursery classes in primary schools as in nursery schools (Department for Education (England), 2021: 1).

2   In a study conducted by one of the authors in the early 1980s, only 33 private nurseries were identified in the Greater London area that took children under 12 months of age (Brannen and Moss, 1991); today they are over two thousand.

3   In the 2005 consultation paper, the government had discussed other new graduate professionals that might lead an upgrading of the ECEC workforce, namely 'Early Years Teachers' (specialising in work with 0–5-year-olds) and 'Pedagogues', both being professions found in other countries. These options disappeared in the policy documents that followed, replaced by the 'Early Years Professional', a concept unique to England.

4   In 1970, 35 per cent of UK households did not have a washing machine (http://www.statista. com/statistics/289017/washing-machine-ownership-in-the-uk/; accessed 13 October 2023).

5   Extended Schools were to be open from 8 am to 6 pm, and provide access to a range of services, including a 'core offer' consisting of: 'wrap-around' childcare (i.e., before and after the core school day); a 'varied menu of activities', for example homework clubs, study support, and music, dance, drama, and arts and crafts; parenting support (information sessions, parenting programmes); 'swift and easy referral to a wide range of specialist support services'; and wider community access to information and communications technology (ICT), sports and arts facilities (Department for Education and Skills (England), 2005). The government achieved its target of converting all schools in England (over 24,000) to Extended Schools within seven years. For further discussion of the concept and its implementation, see Martin, 2016.

7
Trying for transformative change: Aotearoa New Zealand

We described the English story after 1997 as one of stalled integration; the low-hanging fruits of government responsibility, curriculum and regulation were quickly picked, leaving the hard-to-reach ones untouched, apart from a partial and subsequently rejected attempt to introduce a new type of provision. Aotearoa New Zealand's experience is also of partial transformation, but the process has gone significantly further and, equally important, has not stalled. As a result, Aotearoa New Zealand has gone a long way in the transformation of its ECEC system, or at least of its services, though not of parenting leave. It has achieved not only integrated government responsibility and regulation, but a bicultural curriculum for all children from birth to 5 years that incorporates principles of empowerment and of education in a broad sense; it has worked on innovative methods of assessment and made substantial progress towards a graduate early childhood education (ECE) teaching workforce and pay parity with school teachers.

Transformative change has also occurred in other ways. Alongside the changes mentioned above, and as a separate development, *kōhanga reo* (Māori immersion language nests) developed out of a Māori protest movement that emerged in the early 1970s as part of a broader Māori renaissance whose successes included the Māori language becoming an official language of Aotearoa New Zealand in 1987. *Kōhanga reo* were first established five years earlier and are recognised in this chapter, though its focus is on what are termed in Aotearoa New Zealand 'teacher-led services', mainstream ECE settings.

We begin this chapter with some historical context about the period leading up to the integration of childcare services within an education administration in 1986, the first transformative policy move. We then consider the subsequent record and processes of reform, with the advances and setbacks that have taken place under different political regimes, leading up to the current day, with an assessment of how far Aotearoa New Zealand has got in transforming its early childhood system. We end by analysing the conditions and forces that have favoured change and those that have hindered it.

Historical context

Aotearoa New Zealand is a small island country located in the southern Pacific Ocean. Eastern Polynesian migrants were its first human visitors, arriving in canoe groups around 800 years ago, and the first settlers and indigenous people were Māori. In 2021, the estimated population was 5.1 million, and ethnically diverse. There is a growing population of Māori (17 per cent), and the highest number of Pasifika (Pacific Peoples) in the world.

Compulsory schooling starts at 6 years. Aotearoa New Zealand's early childhood education (ECE) system covers the period from birth to school entry. It has been called a 'paradigm of diversity' (A.B. Smith and May, 2006: 95) because of the variety of types of ECE service and their responsiveness to historical context and community aspirations. Within ECE provision, 'Issues of biculturalism between Māori and Pakeha [New Zealanders primarily of European descent] are now combined with the realities of multicultural diversity'.

The idea of institutions for the care and education of young children emerged in the nineteenth century in Europe, and began to be developed in Aotearoa New Zealand towards the end of that century. The first kindergartens were philanthropic, established around the 1870s and 1880s in the main cities, and by the early twentieth century they were 'a small but established part of the New Zealand educational-charitable scene' (May and Bethell, 2017: 23). Unlike crèches and nurseries, kindergartens were modelled on ideals of the Froebelian German kindergarten movement. The curriculum was based on Froebelian principles of movement, songs, circle games, 'the gifts' (series of geometric educational playthings) and occupations (handcrafts in such mediums as drawing, paper folding, sewing and stick laying). The kindergarten environment was to have attractive play spaces, both indoors and outdoors, and an outdoor garden. The training of women as teachers was a core philosophy.

Following the Second World War, the government released the Bailey Report (named after chairman Professor Colin Bailey) from the

Consultative Committee on Pre-School Educational Services, setting out a blueprint for early childhood education. Its terms of reference were: 'To consider and report on educational services for children below school age, with special reference to the financing and control of such services and the training of personnel' (Consultative Committee on Pre-School Educational Services, 1947: 3). The Committee proposed expansion of ECE through a pre-school education service and training programme as part of a national school system. It was mainly concerned with part-day kindergartens and playcentres, for which it called for state funding and control. The committee portrayed kindergartens as the most acceptable form of early childhood service, since these catered for children aged 3 to 5 years, and their sessional part-day nature gave 'full weight to the place of the home as the all-important element in the nurture of the child' (Consultative Committee on Pre-School Educational Services, 1947: 11). While the committee recognised a limited need for all-day services for mothers who had to work or whose ill health prevented them from 'undertaking the normal responsibilities of the home', it rejected full-day and school day provision on the grounds of cost and because 'Young children spending the whole day from Monday to Friday in a nursery school are deprived of the vital experiences that only a normal home can provide' (Consultative Committee on Pre-School Educational Services, 1947: 11).

The Bailey Report established government interest in and oversight of kindergartens and the shift from a charitable service to a professional service, and acknowledged playcentres as pre-school services. But its rejection of day nurseries as 'not normal' accentuated the divide between 'care' and 'education', and left childcare outside the frame of education and state interest. Helen May argues that the general aims of the report were realised except for the extent of state ownership: 'This was too radical, too costly and resisted by the kindergartens and playcentres, which had invested much in their work. The pragmatic compromise was a state-voluntary partnership, which became the hallmark of all future early childhood services' (May, 2013: 397). The government took responsibility for paying kindergarten teachers' salaries and setting conditions of service, a situation that continued until, under the harsh neoliberal reforms of the 1990s, kindergartens were removed from the State Sector Act 1997 (Davison, 1998; Davison and Mitchell, 2009).

Kindergartens remained largely sessional, catering for 4-year-olds in five morning sessions and 3-year-olds in three afternoon sessions per week. This situation continued until the early 2000s, when the structure of kindergartens began to change. By 2014, 98 per cent of kindergartens had all-day licences offering school day hours and mixed age sessions for children from 2 years of age (May and Bethell, 2017).

Helen May and Kerry Bethell (2017) tell the story of the establishment of a national body of kindergarten associations in the early twentieth century and of the determination of members to promote the case for free kindergartens, with trained teachers for all children, throughout Aotearoa New Zealand. The ideal of free kindergarten education became enshrined in the government's Kindergarten Regulations 1959, which stated: 'No fee shall be payable in respect of the attendance of a child at a kindergarten.' Though these regulations were revoked by the government in 1990, the principle of free, publicly funded ECE, accessible to all children wherever they live and whatever their circumstances, along with staffing by qualified teachers, has endured, and has been central to the advocacy of the wider community-based ECE sector.

Crèches and nurseries were also first established in Aotearoa New Zealand in the late nineteenth century as philanthropic services for the children of the poor and children on the streets. The first two crèches were linked to Auckland kindergartens, to provide for infants and children up to 2 years old whose mothers had to work. Older children could attend the kindergarten. The attempt to provide both care and education in a crèche–kindergarten arrangement lasted only about 12 years in both cases, coming to an end when 'the educational component found a haven in separate kindergarten-only establishments, with the care component remaining hidden amidst private and informal child-minding and baby-farming arrangements' (May, 2013: 214).

The first separate crèche that lasted a long time was set up as a Catholic charity in 1903 for under-3-year-olds whose mothers 'were forced into unfortunate circumstances that required them to earn a living' (May, 2013: 215). By 1907, the age limit was increased to 5 years to meet parental need for arrangements for older children. The focus was on health and welfare, and the nuns caring for the children were trained as nurses. A second crèche was established as a charity under the Anglican Church in 1906. May gives an account of the development of subsequent crèches, and an emerging idea of childcare as a community service with some support offered by city councils, though not by central government; she also discusses the attitudinal and funding barriers and challenges to setting up and running these services, and the split between care and education, nurseries and kindergartens.

These early creche and nursery successes reflect the split between care and education in relation to young children caused by the educational pedagogy of kindergartens, the growth of kindergartens into a movement that excluded under-3-year-olds, and the vocal position of the kindergarten movement about the responsibilities and role of mothers at home. The ideological rationales underlying this split were reflected in the political realities of funding, and it became clear for kindergartens to survive and grow their alignment had to be with the school-based education sector. (May, 2013: 229)

Whereas kindergartens received support from kindergarten associations, no cohesive body advocated for childcare interests.

In the 1960s, women began to move into the workforce in increasing numbers and childcare provision expanded. The Childcare Centre Regulations 1960 came into effect at this time because of scandals arising from the treatment of children in childcare provision. These Regulations provided minimum standards, focused on health and safety. The Child Welfare Division of the Department of Education was made responsible for childcare, rather than the pre-school section, reflecting the conceptual divide between services providing care and those providing education for young children. The demands of the new regulations were a catalyst for the organisation and inauguration of the New Zealand Association of Childcare Centres in 1963, which 'set about improving the quality of childcare through training and better regulations, and calling for government funding, more care for babies and after-school care' (May, 2019: 55). In 1972, responsibility for these services was transferred to the new Department of Social Welfare, further intensifying the divide between childcare and education services (kindergartens and playcentres).

The playcentre movement began in Aotearoa New Zealand in 1942 during the Second World War, to support mothers whose partners were away from home. Playcentres were sessional provision, at first offering only one or two sessions per week, for children of all ages, from babies to school starting age. They are based on a belief in the family as the most important setting for the care and education of the child, and emphasise that both parents and children are learners. Parents assume all roles, including curriculum implementation, management and administration, and undertake training to be educators of their children. Playcentres have been described by Stover and the New Zealand Playcentre Federation (2003: 1) as a 'uniquely New Zealand way of educating families, [which] has moulded its own identity, its own philosophy and practice through a plaiting together of strands – strands of ideas, practices, personalities, and cultures'.

The historical and philosophical differences in the emergence of these three major service types – free kindergartens, playcentres and childcare – were reflected in differences in how they were conceptualised and valued in society. Kindergartens and playcentres were included in the Education Act, while childcare centres in all forms were regulated by the Childcare Centre Regulations; the former were the responsibility of the Department of Education, the latter of the Department of Social Welfare. There were divisions not only in the oversight and administration of these services, but also in their funding, staff training and pay rates. Kindergartens received the greatest amount of government funding, playcentres the next greatest and childcare centres the least. Levels of training and pay rates were similarly higher for kindergarten teachers.

Kindergartens, playcentres and childcare centres were not the only types of provision to emerge in Aotearoa New Zealand. In 1982, the first *kōhanga reo* (Māori immersion language nest) was established outside of these mainstream services. The *Te Kōhanga Reo* movement originated in the resistance politics of the 1960s and 1970s. The movement was a response to the impact of colonisation, which promoted the belief that indigenous people had a cultural deficit, and to assimilationist policies and practices in education. Hilda Halkyard explained the rationale for setting up a separate system of education:

> Māori people have been the scapegoats of the Pākehā education system too long. Enough is enough. What can we do? We have several options: We can accept IT, spit at IT, join in and change IT or make our own alternatives. ... Te Kōhanga Reo is an alternative. (Halkyard, 1983: 16)

Speaking at the first *Hui Taumata Mātauranga* (Māori Education Summit) in 2001, Mason Durie, a Māori leader, professor and researcher, described it as a '*hui* [gathering] about education, but more important it is a *hui* about Māori futures'. He portrayed *kōhanga reo* as a 'Māori centred pathway' that is largely under Māori direction and has an obvious focus on the goal of increasing access to *te ao Māori* (the Māori world). He explained the emergence and importance of a Māori-centred pathway:

> During the twenty-five years 1975–2000, the focus for Māori shifted from assimilation and state dependency towards greater self sufficiency, a celebration of being Māori, and higher levels of autonomy. The message was *tino rangatiratanga* [absolute

sovereign authority] and positive development; the agenda moved away from domination by others and to Māori control of Māori resources. (Durie, 2001: 2)

Te Kōhanga Reo has been described by Reedy (2003: 65) as 'the most vigorous and innovative educational movement in this country (dare I say in the world)'. But it has a *kaupapa* (philosophy) that is much wider than education or care. *Kōhanga reo* are closely connected with Māori communities and aligned with 'the broader goals of Māori development as much as the goals of the education sector' (Durie, 2001: 2). They provide total immersion in the Māori language, are aimed at the revitalisation of Māori language and culture, and are managed by whānau (extended family).

Arapera Royal Tangaere explains that the *kōhanga reo kaupapa* or philosophy

> centres around *'te mana o te whānau'* (the dignity of the family, including the extended family). *Tino rangatiratanga* (self determination), a fundamental principle of Te Tiriti o Waitangi,[1] is also the foundation of the kōhanga movement. Embodied in Te Korowai are four *pou* (or posts) which are the cornerstones of the kaupapa: total immersion in *te reo Māori*, whānau decision-making, management and responsibility, accountability to all cultural, financial and whānau members and groups, and ensuring the health and well-being of the mokopuna and the whānau. (Mitchell, Royal Tangaere et al., 2006: 28)

Another transformation in early years provision during the post-war years was the establishment of Pacific Islands groups. The first, *Lemali Temaita a Samoa*, was set up by a group of Samoan and Cook Islands mothers in Tokoroa in 1972, with more being established from the mid-1980s. The main impetus for setting up these groups came from Pacific women wanting to ensure that their Pacific languages and traditions were passed on to succeeding Aotearoa New Zealand-born generations; 'The focus of these groups was the maintenance and fostering of Pacific Islands language and cultural values' (Robinson, 2002: 8).

One other early type of provision should be mentioned in this overview. Child minding was privately organised, informal and undertaken in the home until the mid-1970s, when 'family day care schemes' began to be established, later to be called 'home-based ECE'. These schemes employed a paid coordinator who recruited carers, made placements, provided resources, collected parent fees and paid carers, and offered support. The carers themselves were always the lowest-paid of all early childhood workers; their pay was termed a 'reimbursing allowance' so that tax did not need to be paid and carers on a welfare benefit could continue to receive the benefit. There were no formal training requirements, until the 1990s.

The push for transformation (1970s–1986)

Advocating for change

The period in Aotearoa New Zealand from the late 1960s to the 1980s was described by May (2019: 103–4) as a time when

> [t]he language of 'order' and 'adjustment' was overlaid by the language of 'rights' and 'liberation'. … [D]emands arose for early childhood institutions to broaden their functions. Campaigns concerning Māori grievances, women's rights and the status of early childhood teachers and workers introduced a new militancy to the politics of early childhood.

In this environment, women involved in the feminist movement of the 1970s were persistent advocates for reform that would bring childcare services into an education administration, and would start to address funding and other inequalities. A recommendation to transfer childcare from the Department of Social Welfare to the Department of Education was first made in parliament by the 1975 Select Committee on Women's Rights, and a similar recommendation was passed in the same year at the Seminar on Equality and the Education of the Sexes, co-sponsored by the Department of Education and the Committee on Women. Rosslyn Noonan, national coordinator of the 1975 International Women's Year, and subsequently general secretary of the Kindergarten Teachers Association (the trade union for kindergarten teachers), later said in an interview:

> 1975 is the crucial year because it brought together early childhood education and the women's movement which had overlapping issues […] Early childhood education people […] were beginning to analyse their inability to deliver what they saw as incredibly important – equality for all children. (cited in May, 2019: 123)

A broader and more concrete recommendation was passed by the Child Care Syndicate of the Conference on Women and Social and Economic Development held in March 1976 to mark the end of International Women's Year. It sought a working group to look at early childhood education and care in Aotearoa New Zealand, the bringing of childcare into the range of funded services, and consultation of organisations, including women's organisations. Geraldine McDonald tells the story of the 'snail-like' progress made in following up this recommendation by a State Services Commission working group,[2] comprising one female and three male government officials; only the woman had 'any prior knowledge of the problems involved ... and more than a peripheral experience of the services' (G. McDonald, 1981: 164). A draft report was widely criticised by early childhood organisations, which dropped separatist divides to take their concerns in a united delegation to the Minister of State Services.

The report was withdrawn and a reconstituted working group was established, with a new chair and including Geraldine McDonald (a researcher and staunch advocate for equitable treatment of early childhood education). It is thanks to her 'guardianship' that the working group's main recommendations were radical. The State Services Commission Report on Early Childhood Care and Education, published in 1980, proposed that:

- administrative responsibility for the three early childhood services (playcentres, kindergartens and childcare) lie with the Department of Education, which would have responsibility for the inspection and recognition of services, and advisory, funding and training functions.
- planning for the needs of areas be 'according to the needs for children and parents, rather than for a particular type of service' (State Services Commission, 1980: 94).
- there be 'equitable' funding for childcare and that 'this be based not on the welfare principle, but on the principle of a contribution to a [legally] recognised service' (State Services Commission, 1980: 95).
- the government eventually subsidise up to 50 per cent of the cost to parents with children in day care. (State Services Commission, 1980: 93–6)

The report also contained a vision for comprehensive planning of services that went beyond 'providing single function centres on an individual basis' (State Services Commission, 1980: 15). Similarly to Jack Tizard's concept of integrated children's centres, discussed in Chapter 6, the report envisaged services as potentially multi-functional and responsive to the needs of local communities. The report also challenged deficit thinking by teachers and providers that hindered some families from taking part in services; instead, parents were conceptualised as 'capable of contributing to the care and education of their children and if they do not, then the fault may lie with the service rather than the women [*sic*]' (State Services Commission, 1980: 11). The report argued that if an aim was that parents should contribute to the care and education of their children, there would need to be 'more flexible patterns of work for both men and women in paid employment, opportunities for part-time work, and leave from paid employment for the care of children' (State Services Commission, 1980: 11). Encapsulated here is a view that transformative change needs to occur, not only in early childhood policy and practices, but far beyond.

The report provided a rationale for breaking the artificial division between care and education services and integrating them within a single education department, in the best interests of the child.

> Whatever is provided for young children is in one sense care, and in another sense education. The two things in relation to the young child cannot be easily distinguished. One cannot provide care for young children without their learning ideas, habits and attitudes; nor can one educate them without at the same time providing them with care. (State Services Commission, 1980: 3–4)

Furthermore, the report argued that 'care and education cannot be divided between separate departments without creating anomalies' (State Services Commission, 1980: 32).

Advocacy with a united voice played a major role in identifying the precise nature of reform that was required. Of 54 submissions to the report by early childhood organisations, educators and researchers, all but two (the Private Childcare Federation and Barnardo's) supported the transfer of childcare to education. This advocacy was to prove persistent over time, not losing sight of these goals and refusing to accept unsatisfactory political responses. Before the publication of the United Nations Convention on the Rights of the Child in 1989, but during a decade when a children's rights focus was being broadened and clarified following the International Year of the Child in 1979 (A.B. Smith, 2016), the vision and argument about the 'best interests of the child' captured imaginations and minds.

Nevertheless, in their responses to the published report, 'Some of the earlier unity dissipated, and groups started to reflect on the impact on their own organisations' (May, 2019: 148). The government used this lack of agreement to justify putting the report aside. But advocates for change increased. In 1982 the Early Childhood Workers Union (ECWU) was established, an industrial trade union for childcare workers that added a strong voice to public debates about equitable pay and conditions for this group, as well as about broader concerns. Childcare issues were further supported by the wider union movement, including the Federation of Labour (FOL), the Combined State Unions (CSU), and the Public Service Association (PSA). The FOL and the PSA both adopted policy on childcare in line with the recommendations of the State Services Commission report.

Transformation gets underway

This combined advocacy influenced the opposition Labour party to adopt the recommendations of the State Services Commission report as its policy. Its manifesto was framed in terms of employment and childcare policies that would enable women to enjoy full and equal participation. In 1984, when the Labour party was elected to government, it announced that childcare would transfer from the Department of Social Welfare to the Department of Education. A forum in parliament, convened by the Minister of Education in 1985, and attended by MPs, academics and representatives of early childhood organisations, confirmed that childcare would be administered by education, and childcare and kindergarten teachers would have common training (Meade, 1990). The transfer happened in 1986.

The one exception to this transfer was *kōhanga reo*, which remained with the Department of Māori Affairs. At the time, transformation for Māori was occurring through *Te Kōhanga Reo*. Writing in 1997, as a teacher working in a childcare centre and a voluntary member of her *kōhanga reo*, Arapera Royal Tangaere (1997: 43) described her perception of *kōhanga reo* as

> a holistic approach to address the survival of our language and the social, economic, and educational problems experienced by Maori people.
>
> To me kohanga reo was more than a language nest. It was more than a childcare centre. Today it has become a social, economic, health, educational, spiritual, political, and cultural renaissance for Maori.

She argued that, given its vision, *kōhanga reo* should remain under the administrative guidance of the Ministry of Māori Affairs.

Shifts in early childhood services were not only departmental. They were also occurring in the language used in official policy documents: the terms 'childcare', 'day care' and 'pre-school' were replaced with the term 'education and care'. This shift reflected the transformative vision of the campaigners in the 1970s and 1980s, that childcare centres are an educational and social service for children and their families and that care and education are inseparable, and their rejection of the prevailing discourse that childcare is 'a last ditch welfare service to substitute for inadequate or incapable parents'. Their arguments foregrounded the need and right of young children to experience educational programmes of 'high quality'. For this reason, they advocated equitable funding for all early childhood services. Divisions between service types, in forms of training and pay of workers, were also of concern.

The transfer of childcare services to education in 1986 was to be a momentous turning point. It placed Aotearoa New Zealand as a world leader in dissolving the artificial divides that had separated care and education. It also highlighted the further integration needed to address the splits that existed within the workforce between teachers and carers, and inequities in their training, pay and working conditions. In this transformative move, ECE was brought from the shadows to the centre of government and public attention.

Transformation takes two steps forward, one step back (1986–2019)

This section looks at developments and reversals in transformative reform in early childhood education, the term increasingly adopted in Aotearoa New Zealand from 1986 to the 'Early Learning Action Plan 2019–2029'. The main focus here is on what are termed in Aotearoa New Zealand 'teacher-led centre-based ECE services', i.e., 'education and care centres' (the name today for what were childcare centres) and kindergartens. The integration of childcare into the Department of Education in 1986 was significant in promising an education focus for all children in early childhood services. But other policies, related to staffing, funding and provision, were needed to achieve the goal of offering all children access to a good education that also supported their families. In particular, the inequitable working conditions of staff (including low pay), and their varied qualifications, needed addressing, as the campaigners of the previous decades had advocated.

Global trends in policy thinking, the policies of the elected political parties in different periods, and the understandings and influence of successive ministers of education were all significant factors in ECE policy reforms. These reforms were struggled for against a backdrop of the new right or neoliberal economic theory that was becoming dominant internationally; in Aotearoa New Zealand it was applied systematically, first under the fourth government of the traditionally social democratic Labour party (1984–90), and then more harshly under the centre-right National government (1990–9), in what Jane Kelsey (1997) called 'the New Zealand experiment'. Kelsey describes the fundamentals of the country's 'structural adjustment programme' as market liberalisation and free trade, limited government, a narrow monetarist policy, a deregulated labour market, and fiscal restraint. State services were privatised, extreme reductions in benefit levels were made in the 1991 government budget, taxation was reduced for high earners and increased for low earners. As part of the deregulation of the labour market, the 1991 Employment Contracts Act (New Zealand Government, 1991) actively favoured individual over collective bargaining and removed good-faith bargaining provisions and union representatives' right of workplace access. Kelsey writes of the impact:

> What were once basic priorities – collective responsibility, redistribution of resources and power, social stability, democratic participation, and the belief that human beings were entitled to live and work in security and dignity – seemed to have been left far behind. Poverty, division and alienation had become permanent features of New Zealand's social landscape. (Kelsey, 1999)

This was the unpromising context for the initial years of the transformation of ECE.

Policy transformations but market mechanisms (1986–1990)

The Labour government that came into power in 1984 after nine years in opposition 'was persuaded that there was a crisis in early childhood, and that an increased investment would bring benefits to children, women, families, communities and the nation. Early childhood education moved to centre stage on the government's agenda' (May, 2019: 204). Both the Minister of Education, Russell Marshall, and the Prime Minister, David Lange, were outspoken supporters of early childhood education, which Helen May considers 'the result of 20 years of lobbying by some, and a decade of strategic planning' (May, 2019: 205). Having transferred government responsibility for all early childhood services (except the *kōhanga reo*) to education, in 1988 the Labour government introduced a new integrated professional qualification, a three-year early childhood teacher education programme in Colleges of Education, exactly comparable in length and status to primary teacher education programmes. This replaced the previous divided system, in which there had been a two-year training for kindergarten teachers and a limited one-year training for some childcare workers. New teacher education programmes were required to 'be inclusive of care and education, cover programmes for the care of babies, and have more emphasis on education studies and the cultural and family context of children's lives' (May, 2019: 207).

During the period 1988 to 1990, when there was immense pressure to make cuts in government spending, sell off state assets and reduce the role of the state, new policy was being developed for schools and ECE. The ECE policy was formulated in two stages: first in the form of a working group report, *Education to be More* (Early Childhood Care and Education Working Group, 1988), and later in the formal government policy document, *Before Five* (Lange, 1989).

Education to be More described the role of early childhood education as addressing the interests of the child, of caregivers, and of cultural survival and transmission. Its stated aims were to address issues related to the status of early childhood education (including variations in quality, remuneration and training), equity of access, Māori determination and control over the development of *ngā kōhanga reo*, the status of women, and funding inequities and levels. Subsequently, *Before Five* adopted a framework that largely followed the proposed administrative structure outlined in *Education to be More*, and confirmed that 'At all levels of education, the early childhood sector will have equal status with the other education sectors' (Lange, 1989, 2). It promised funding levels that would promote good-quality care and education, the aim being for ECE to be funded on an equitable basis with the school sector. Substantial government funding was needed to realise this, but such increased funding was contrary to new right economic theories that government spending and the role of the state should be reduced. Politicians and government officials were polarised. The Treasury even wrote a cabinet paper arguing for minimal funding increases for non-kindergarten services and a funding decrease for kindergartens for reasons of equity (Meade, 1990)!

In this context, and seeking the support of the public and of sympathetic politicians, the ECE trade unions, the Kindergarten Teachers Association (KTA) for kindergarten teachers and the ECWU for childcare workers, organised the 'Campaign for Quality Early Childhood Education', aimed at improving quality and funding for the ECE sector. The unions invited participation from other ECE organisations and women's groups, launched a petition calling for increased funding, and arranged for campaigners to present the petition to their local MPs, with the result that 42 MPs were required to read the petition out in parliament. A rally outside parliament resulted in a meeting between politicians and the ECE campaigners. A day of action brought the campaign to public attention in Aotearoa New Zealand's biggest city, Auckland.

These actions coincided with intense lobbying inside parliament by the women's caucus. Anne Meade, who was on secondment to the Prime Minister's advisory group, wrote, 'I believe that the players inside Parliament Buildings would not have achieved worthwhile funding against those supported by "captains of industry" without the political activity of the Campaign for Quality Early Childhood Education' (Meade, 1990: 109). Prime Minister David Lange spoke in July 1990 at the announcement of a huge funding increase of NZ$43m, or 125 per cent, in the early childhood education budget; referring to his struggles with cabinet colleagues and government officials who were proponents of new right economic theories, he said that gaining this increased ECE funding was 'like snatching raw meat out of the jaws of a rottweiler'.

While public funding of ECE had risen substantially, the government's neoliberal orientation was apparent in the way the funding was dispensed to support market approaches. The method adopted, termed 'bulk funding', was a competitive mechanism based on per capita amounts and involved cash being allocated to institutions or individuals to enable them to act autonomously in a market environment, rather than direct government funding of staffing and infrastructure (Wylie, 1998). In other words, the government supported a *quantum* of education rather than *processes* of education. Moreover, under the *Before Five* policy, funding was largely the same for all services regardless of intake (children) or of cost drivers. Government saw itself as a purchaser of education rather than as a provider: as the Ministry of Education (New Zealand) (1995) put it, 'Under current policies the government buys educational hours of a particular quality from early childhood centres and overall is neutral in terms of service type.'

The impacts of bulk funding compared with direct funding of staffing and other costs were evidenced in the kindergarten sector. From 1948 until 1997, kindergarten teachers and associations formed the only early childhood group legislated to be part of the state sector; kindergartens were 'the flagship of government support for New Zealand early childhood education' (Wylie, 1993: 3). Before bulk funding was introduced, government funding for kindergartens included direct payment of teacher salaries, an administration grant, an operating grant, funding for professional support, a special needs grant, and an administrative grant to the kindergartens' representative body. This funding mechanism and the state involvement in negotiating kindergarten teachers' salaries and conditions ensured a level of government responsibility for meeting costs and for how funding was spent. Once they were bulk-funded, however, and removed from state sector bargaining arrangements, kindergartens were effectively privatised; their funding levels stagnated and kindergarten associations were left with the costly and complex business of negotiating employment conditions. Studies during these years showed negative impacts on teachers' pay and conditions, and that group sizes were increased, kindergarten maintenance was deferred, and costs previously met by government were loaded onto communities. Low-income communities were particularly disadvantaged (Mitchell, 1996; Wylie, 1993).

In the absence of linkages to the costs of individual services, and because there was no transparent formula specifying what the funding was intended to cover, under bulk funding the level of funding for individual services was easily eroded and there was leeway for management to use funding as it wished, including for private gain. Provision was not planned; instead any provider could establish a service and receive public funding as long as they met rather minimal regulatory requirements. These market arrangements effectively opened the door to a private for-profit sector keen to capitalise on business opportunities. Prime Minister David Lange, who had supported the transfer of childcare to education and the ECE funding increases, made it clear that nevertheless the government was politically committed to privatisation and marketisation.

> The Government does not want to become the owner of a squad of private child-care centres. What those people do well they ought to do, in contract with the Government and subject to the safeguards that are essential for children. (Lange, 1988: 8229, cited in Gallagher, 2022: 49)

Gallagher has termed the approach 'state-led marketization'.

At this time, outside of government structures, the two unions in the ECE sector, the Kindergarten Teachers Association and the Early Childhood

Workers Union, continued to be powerful advocates of transformation. In order to offer a strong, united ECE teacher voice, they amalgamated in 1990 to form *Te Rau o te Aroha o te Kōhanga ki Aotearoa*: the Combined Early Childhood Union of Aotearoa. Underlying the amalgamation was a goal, debated within the membership and by the national executives of each union over a period of five years, of working collectively to influence ECE policy and fight for equitable employment conditions. Later, in 1993, the new union further amalgamated with the primary teachers and support staff union to form *NZEI Te Riu Roa*, the New Zealand Educational Institute, to better resist the extreme attacks on unionism and workers' rights experienced during these times. Like the Campaign for Quality Early Childhood Education, the amalgamated union continued to organise campaigns and working groups during the 1990s and 2000s; these not only focused on improving teachers' pay and employment conditions, but also brought other ECE organisations together with them to identify and advocate additional transformative ECE policy directions.

A minimal state approach (1990–9)

Gains made under the *Before Five* reforms were eroded substantively by a centre-right coalition government led by the National party (1990–9), especially in its first years, which adopted a 'minimal state' approach (Royal Commission on Social Policy, 1988: 128). In 1991, there were major reviews of every aspect of ECE, including funding; these were followed by reductions to funding levels for centres with children under 2 years and by diminished accountability requirements. Policy emphasis was placed on individual parental and service responsibility for standards and provision, and a competitive market framework was introduced into advisory support services and teacher education provision (Mitchell, 2005). The previous Labour government had introduced a policy that the benchmark minimum qualification in ECE would be the three-year integrated Diploma of Teaching (ECE) offered at Colleges of Education. The aim had been that by the year 2000 all staff, starting with the 'person responsible' in an ECE centre, would either be in training for or hold the Diploma. A 1991 budget decision relaxed the agreed timeframe, and 'mish mash, chop change' policies concerning training and qualifications (May, 1996: 5) created huge problems in moving towards a better-qualified workforce.

The intention was clearly for ECE services to operate as much as possible like businesses in a competitive market. Scandals emerged during this time when private owners running 'childcare' services as businesses made huge personal gains through spending government bulk funding on property upgrades. Staff and children did not receive any benefit. As already noted, the 1991 Employment Contracts Act removed requirements for employers and employees to bargain 'in good faith' (for an explanation of this term, see Employment New Zealand, 2023), scrapped trade unions' right of entry to the workplace, and actively promoted individual workplace, as distinct from collective bargaining, arrangements. At that time a national award covered the majority of workers in the 'childcare' sector and was negotiated between the union and employers. When the term of the award expired, profit-making employers refused to take part in the collective bargaining process for its renewal. Consequently, any hope of a national unified pay scale disintegrated, as employers pursued individual site employment agreements.

There was a steady rise in the proportion of 'education and care centres' run as 'private services' during this period, which has continued: 48 per cent in 1992 (Mitchell, 2002), 55 per cent in 2002, 64 per cent in 2012, and 74 per cent in 2021 (Ministry of Education (New Zealand), 2021c). In other words, between 1992 and 2021, the proportion of 'education and care centres' run as private for-profit businesses grew from just under half to nearly three-quarters, leaving 'community-based services' in the minority.

Underfunding and bulk funding were used as mechanisms in the systematic drive by the centre-right government coalition to fully privatise early childhood education. Their effect was especially apparent in kindergartens; almost immediately on taking office, the National party government removed the legal impediment to kindergartens charging fees, and halted the staffing scheme aimed at improving kindergarten staff:child ratios. In March 1992, the public funding of kindergartens was fundamentally changed, with the introduction of bulk funding. Before this date, as we have seen, kindergarten funding had been calculated according to particular costs and allocated to be spent on those costs; teachers' salaries, the biggest cost component, were paid directly by the government's central payroll system, and there were also grants for other costs. But once they were bulk-funded, the government virtually froze kindergarten funding. Finally, in 1997, kindergarten associations and teachers were removed from the State Sector Act, in legislation passed 'under urgency', meaning without advance notice and without debate. In the kindergarten case, a select committee process to enable public submissions was bypassed. Negotiation of the kindergarten teachers' national employment award was devolved to individual kindergarten associations, and the national collective employment contract for all teachers splintered into 18 separate awards as kindergarten associations negotiated separately (Mitchell, 2019). Once 'the flagship for Government support' (Wylie, 1992: 2), kindergartens were effectively privatised.

Yet three significant developments at this time served to continue the transformation agenda for early childhood education. The first was the development and publication of the national ECE curriculum, *Te Whāriki* (Ministry of Education (New Zealand), 1996), covering all services for children under 6 years. Helen May described the government rationale for developing a national curriculum framework for ECE, at the same time as the national schools' curriculum, as 'part of an international trend to strengthen connections between the economic success of the nation and education' (May, 2019: 244). Yet running counter to these trends, and resisting any possibility of 'schoolification' and downward push from the schools' curriculum, *Te Whāriki* was developed as a bicultural curriculum catering for all children from birth to school starting age.

The story of its development has been told in many publications (Carr and May, 1992, 1993; Lee et al., 2013; May, 2009; Nuttall, 2003). *Te Whāriki* has endured to the present day, with a revision in 2017 (Ministry of Education (New Zealand), 2017a) that retained its original aspiration statement, principles and strands. The commitment to the Te Tiriti o Waitangi partnership of Māori and Pākehā and the development of the curriculum as a bicultural document fitting for Aotearoa New Zealand was made possible by the collaboration with *Te Kōhanga Reo* National Trust (TKRNT). Tilly and Tamati Reedy from TKRNT worked in partnership with Margaret Carr and Helen May from the University of Waikato to construct the curriculum framework. The development process included working groups, with ECE sector representatives, and consultation on a draft curriculum, which was published in 1993. The partnership and the high level of expertise of the curriculum writers, and the careful, deep and extensive consultation, ensured the final document was soundly based and enjoyed the trust of ECE sector organisations.

This curriculum is quite different from traditional developmental curriculum approaches.

The title 'Te Whāriki', suggested by Tamati Reedy, was a central metaphor. The early childhood curriculum was envisaged as a whāriki, translated as a woven mat for all to stand on. The principles, strands and goals provided the framework, which allowed for different programme perspectives to be woven into the fabric. There were many possible 'patterns', depending on the age and interests of the children, the cultural, structural or philosophical context of the particular service, and the interests of parents and staff. This was a curriculum that provided signposts for individuals and centres to develop their own curriculum weaving through a process of talk, reflection, planning, evaluation and assessment. (May, 2019: 245)

Ideas about outcomes and how these should be assessed reflect wider ideas about what learning is valued and the nature of knowledge. Following publication of *Te Whāriki*, and outside of government policy at this time, Margaret Carr (2001) and others developed a unique narrative approach to assessment; it used 'learning stories', a strength-based assessment approach that documents the weaving together of knowledge and skills with dispositions and attitudes that support 'learning how to learn' and 'life-long learning'. A learning story is

> a documented account of a child's learning event, structured around five key behaviours: taking an interest, being involved, persisting with difficulty, expressing a point of view or feeling, and taking responsibility (or taking another point of view). ... A Teaching Story, on the other hand, is about evaluating practice. (Carr, May et al., 2000: 7, 8)

Assessments 'can be formative of democratic communities of learning and teaching' (Carr, Cowie et al., 2001: 29) in a number of ways:

- Assessments can construct and highlight valued outcomes for living in a democracy.
- Assessments can assist participants in the community to develop trajectories of learning.
- Assessments can provide opportunities for children to self-assess.
- Assessments can provide spaces for families and community to contribute to the curriculum.

Margaret Carr contrasts this formative model of assessment and associated outcomes, which is consistent with the sociocultural framing of *Te Whariki*, with a traditional model of assessment whose outcomes of interest are a 'list of fragmented skills and items of knowledge that describe competence, often with a reference to school entry' (Mitchell and Carr, 2014: 14, Table 1). In the formative model, the 'children dictate stories and take photographs, the *families* contribute comments, the *practitioners* add stories, and revisit the collection with the child or children, enabling re-telling, re-cognizing, and the collaborative construction of trajectories of learning'. 'Learning stories' adopts an ecological and participative viewpoint about learners and learning, and is a democratic practice emphasising '[i]nterpreted observations and dialogue', and '[c]ommunication with four audiences: children, families, other staff and self (the practitioner writing the story, perhaps for or with the children)'.

By contrast, in the latter, more traditional approach, assessments are made by practitioners, emphasising 'objective observation'. The psychometric and behavioural viewpoint tends to construe learning as an individual acquisition, and enables surveillance by external agencies and planning for 'filling the gaps in skill or knowledge'. This decontextualised perspective distorts results, and is of limited value in understanding children's learning and potential. Gee writes:

> To fairly and truly judge what a person can do, you need to know how the talent (skill, knowledge) you are assessing is situated in – placed within – the lived social practices of the person as well as his or her interpretations of those practices. ... [M]any a standardized test can be perfectly 'scientific' and useless at the same time; in a worst case scenario, it can be disastrous. (Gee, 2007: 364)

Under a later government, professional development and narrative assessment resources compatible with the sociocultural framing of the curriculum were to be developed (Ministry of Education (New Zealand), 2005).

The second action to forward the transformative agenda during this period was the groundwork laid by the unions to achieve parity of pay between ECE and school teachers. The full story of the union campaign for pay parity has been told in other publications (Mitchell, 2019; Mitchell and Wells, 1997). The story starts during the 1990s, when equal pay for ECEC teachers was hard to achieve in a deregulated labour market and without legislated and enforceable backing. Pay rates were well below those of teachers in the schools sector. In 1999, experienced registered teachers with a degree on the best union negotiated collective agreements in the childcare sector (Consenting Parties Early Childhood Teachers' Collective Employment Contract) and kindergarten sector (Kindergarten Teachers' Collective Employment Contract) earned 52% and 46%, respectively, below comparable teaching positions in the school sector (Mitchell, 2005). Many early childhood teachers in the childcare sector earned considerably less than this. (Mitchell, 2019: 111)

As noted above, the union for early childhood and kindergarten teachers amalgamated with the primary teachers and school support staff union in 1994 to become NZEI Te Riu Roa. The consolidation within a larger union and with primary school teaching colleagues offered a strong foundation for advocating pay parity. Primary teachers were seeking parity of pay with secondary teachers, and in turn the union supported teachers in ECE in their advocacy and in a job comparison. The slogans 'A teacher is a teacher is a teacher' and 'Shoe size shouldn't shape salaries' were used in both campaigns. The union planned a very deliberate campaign, which first lobbied for increased government funding for ECE, since this was a precursor for improving pay.

Unlike pay equity claims, which compare the pay of a female occupational group with the pay of a predominantly male occupational group that is similar in skills, qualifications and experience, the case for pay parity for ECE teachers used internal comparisons with the largely female primary teacher workforce. A job evaluation to compare the skills, experience and qualifications of kindergarten teachers with those of primary teachers was commissioned by the kindergarten employers and the trade union and undertaken by a researcher, Janice Burns, who had considerable expertise in the design and implementation of job measurement methodologies. A key finding was that:

> The roles of kindergarten teachers and basic scale / senior primary teachers are similar in size, and there is an area of considerable overlap. There appears to be no justification for the difference in salary at any time of the three levels of the pay scales, either in terms of qualifications required or the size of the job being undertaken. (J. Burns, 1999: 5)

Teachers brought the case for pay parity to their kindergarten families, local media and local politicians. However, it was not until a Labour government was elected that pay parity for kindergarten teachers was achieved – albeit on the groundwork laid down in the 1990s – and it is only now being realised for the whole ECE teaching sector. Looking back, it is clear that pay parity had required several conditions:

> an understanding of the policy context; a thorough analysis of the legitimacy of the case for pay equity for early childhood teachers; a persuasive collective campaign that captured the imaginations and hearts of the public – the public did support ideas because these were articulated well; strategic thinking – timing action around

key political events when there was greater effect; government politicians who supported the claim; and intervention by the state to enact pay parity. Persistence was crucial. (Mitchell, 2019: 111–12)

The third action contributing to transformation, and again laying the groundwork for later developments, was the report of a working group set up to examine the challenges and hardships experienced by ECE services in the 1990s and the policies and political actions that would help the sector move forward. The working group was the Early Childhood Education Project, and their report, co-written by Linda Mitchell and Clare Wells and published in 1996, was *Future Directions: Early childhood education in New Zealand*. NZEI Te Riu Roa, the teachers' union, initiated this work by inviting representatives from national community-based ECE organisations to work in partnership 'on a major project on the future directions of early childhood education' (Early Childhood Education Project, 1996: 2). The seven largest ECE organisations in the sector participated; the working group was chaired by Geraldine McDonald, a respected researcher with high credibility in the ECE sector and whom we have already met as a strong advocate, back in the 1980s, of the integration of childcare within education. The group called for submissions and built widespread support for its work, including its recommendations: each participating organisation used its established networks to invite the wider ECE community to participate and contribute their views. Five government agencies and the Ministry of Education were asked to outline how they contributed to quality in ECE, and they all responded.

The terms of reference, crafted by the working group, included an overall aim of providing 'a rigorous and coherent review of the current situation of ECE in Aotearoa New Zealand and the access of children to it', and a specific aim to 'develop proposals on the structures and funding required to ensure quality education for young children' (Early Childhood Education Project, 1996: 4). The work of various government agencies, their relationships with ECE providers and their contribution to quality ECE for young children were also examined. The final report proposed three main policy goals.

1. The long-term goal for ECE services to be universally funded on a basis equitable with the schools sector, with both sectors funded in the same way. [Schools had resisted bulk funding of teachers' salaries when it was proposed in the 'Tomorrow's Schools' report (Ministry of Education (New Zealand), 1988; school teachers continued to be paid by the government through the teachers'

payroll, with a teachers' collective agreement negotiated between the two teachers' unions (NZEI Te Riu Roa for primary teachers and PPTA for secondary teachers) and the Secretary for Education];

2. The development of policy at national, regional and local levels to be undertaken as a partnership between the government, providers, practitioners and parents/caregivers;

3. The development by government of a strategic plan for early childhood education, to include how society can offer holistic support for families/whānau raising young children.

Recommendations under each goal were highly detailed.

The launch of the final report of the working group was held at the Beehive – the seat of government. Leaders of the main political parties and their education spokespersons responded, including the then leader of the Opposition, Helen Clark, who was to become Prime Minister in 1999. She praised the report for its credibility, its broad base, and the very extensive consultation undertaken with the sector. This marked the beginning of a sustained campaign to keep the report and proposals in front of the public and politicians, a campaign that was organised nationally by NZEI Te Riu Roa and delivered locally in idiosyncratic ways. Analysis by Clare Wells (1999) of the specific goals and recommendations and subsequent policy development showed that by 1999 the influence of the report was spreading to the Labour party's policy proposals.

A child rights approach (1999–2008)

A new Labour government was elected in 1999, in coalition with the left-wing Alliance party. The transformation momentum picked up again under this government, which made far-reaching changes to the ECE system; they have been discussed in many publications (e.g., May, 2019; Mitchell, 2015, 2019). These changes were influenced by several factors. One was an emerging understanding of ECE as a public good and a child's right. These ideas were circulating in international academic circles (e.g., Moss and Petrie, 1997), and were promoted in publications and debated intensely in Aotearoa New Zealand forums. *Te Whariki*, the ECE curriculum, reflected a view of the child as a citizen and active contributor to society. Professor Anne Smith, the inaugural Director of the Children's Issues Centre established in the University of Otago in 1995, influenced thinking through the breadth of her public speaking and publishing on children's rights, and made the links between research on children's issues and government policy.

Other notable speakers contributed to debate in Aotearoa New Zealand. In her keynote address to the Combined Early Childhood Union of Aotearoa's millennium teachers' conference, Gunilla Dahlberg from Sweden argued:

> Early childhood institutions ... need to be open to *all* families with young children. Access should not be constrained either by cost or by admission criteria, for example the employment status of parents. To be so, early childhood institutions should be largely or wholly publicly resourced and available as *a right to all local children*, as such being not only forums, but also community institutions. (Dahlberg, 2000a: 8; emphasis original)

Rosslyn Noonan, speaking at the New Zealand Council for Educational Research (NZCER) research conference in 2001, as Chief Commissioner at the Human Rights Commission, entitled her speech 'Early childhood education: A child's right?' She set out a vision in which, as a right, every child should be able to access quality and appropriate ECE services, arguing that achieving this requires universal and fully funded services (Noonan, 2001: 67).

There was much debate during this time about the role of the state (e.g., Child Poverty Action Group, 2003; Mitchell, 2002). The OECD's *Starting Strong I* and *II* reports (OECD, 2001, 2006; see also Chapter 6), with their specific policy recommendations and evidence about the value and importance of quality ECE, were also influential. These were known to academics, and made available and used by participants in the collaborative advocacy forums established at different times, including the *Future Directions* working group and the later *Quality Public ECE Project*. The policy decisions of the new Labour government were consistent with this changing discourse about children and their place in society, assisted by a Minister of Education, Trevor Mallard, who had had close connections with the ECE sector for many years and championed the aims and strategies set out in the *Future Directions* report, including the visions for a qualified teaching workforce, universal funding and pay parity for teachers. His policy advisor during his first years in office was Clare Wells, co-writer of the *Future Directions* report, and previously a trade union leader and kindergarten teacher.

Last but not least, as already suggested, the groundwork for the transformation agenda's regaining momentum had already been laid by the *Future Directions* working group and report and the solid base of support it had garnered from the ECE sector and politicians. Advocates and organisations had subsequently kept its ideals alive.

Almost immediately, in March 2000, the new government introduced legislation to return kindergartens to the state sector, and so resume responsibility for teachers' employment conditions. In making the announcement, Trevor Mallard said:

> The previous Government saw early childhood education as a business. We see it as an integral part of the education system and we want to help as many children as possible have access to quality early childhood education.
>
> Teachers are the key to that quality. By taking responsibility for the terms under which they are employed, the Government is taking leadership for setting benchmarks for standards. (New Zealand Government, 2000)

Acting on the recommendations of the *Future Directions* report, the government set up a representative group to work in a consultative way with the ECE sector to develop a 10-year Strategic Plan for ECE. This plan, *Pathways to the Future: Ngā Huarahi Arataki* (Ministry of Education (New Zealand), 2002), led to far-reaching changes to the ECE system, with its clear focus on three major goals: to improve the quality of ECE, to increase participation in quality ECE, and to promote collaborative relationships between ECE and schools, and with families and with health and social services. The government's vision was 'for all children to participate in early childhood education no matter their circumstances' (Ministry of Education (New Zealand), 2002: 1).

The Strategic Plan linked the three main goals with strategies to achieve them. Over the period 2002–9, a raft of new policy initiatives were put into place:

- *Targets were set for regulated staff* in teacher-led services (i.e., education and care centres and kindergartens) to be qualified and registered ECE teachers: all persons responsible for centres by 2005; 50 per cent of other staff by 2007, 80 per cent by 2010 and 100 per cent by 2012, with some leeway between 2010 and 2012 for a small percentage to be studying for the approved qualification. Similar to the registration process for school teachers, registration for ECE teachers involved a two-year period of professional supervision. The targets were supported by a wide range of initiatives, most notably higher funding for services with more registered teachers.

- *Support was introduced to enhance practising teachers' professional capabilities* and to generate a culture of enquiry within ECE services as communities of learners. The Ministry of Education published a series of assessment resources (Carr, Lee et al., 2004–9; Ministry of Education (New Zealand), 2009), an ICT strategy (Ministry of Education (New Zealand), 2005) and a self-review resource (Ministry of Education (New Zealand), 2006). These resources were consistent with the sociocultural framing of *Te Whāriki*, and also featured exemplars of practice from all the diverse ECE service types, with government funding for professional development related to these exemplars. ECE services that had innovative approaches to teaching and learning could apply in a competitive process to be designated as Centres of Innovation (COIs); COIs were funded to work over a three-year period with research associates to research these innovative practices and disseminate findings (Meade, 2005, 2007, 2009, 2011).
- *A new funding system*, established in 2005, supported, and differentiated between, ECE services on the basis of their costs. Five funding bands introduced in 2005 were linked to the proportion of staff who were qualified and registered early childhood teachers. In recognition of their extra costs, an equity funding system provided additional funding: for ECE services in low-income communities; for services for children with special needs or from non-English-speaking backgrounds; for ECE services teaching in a language and culture other than English; and for services in isolated communities. This constituted a significant shift from the bulk-funding model, which had differentiated between costs only on the basis of the number of children that attended, their ages and the hours they spent in the service; the new system started to recognise, through funding, some of the structural conditions that have been linked in research to good-quality early childhood education, such as the qualifications, pay and conditions of teachers and other workers, high staff:child ratios, and small groups of children.
- *Pay parity* for kindergarten and school teachers was negotiated in 2002, which placed an implicit responsibility on the government to meet the rises in pay rates by increasing kindergarten funding levels.
- *Twenty hours free ECE* for 3- and 4-year-olds in teacher-led services was launched on 1 July 2007, following some political struggle both over the development of the policy proposal and in its initial reception by private providers. The Ministry of Education and Treasury officials

initially costed and promoted a highly targeted funding model that was based on the service being neither universal nor free, but the Minister of Education required officials to go back, working closely with Linda Mitchell and Raewyn Ramage (members of the Funding Taskforce Group), 'to report on the "cost of providing totally free ECE by the year 2012" and develop scenarios for the amount of free entitlement that could be provided' (May, 2019: 288). The '20 hours free ECE' policy was intended 'to send a strong signal of the importance of ECE and the public benefits that accrue from ECE participation' (Cabinet Policy Committee, 2004: 9). However, ECE services needed to opt in to the scheme, which did not guarantee a place; in other words, it was not an entitlement but depended on parents being able to find a place in a service that had opted in. Moreover, providers could seek optional charges and voluntary donations from parents.

- The funding levels for 20 hours' free ECE were set at the average cost of providing ECE at the regulated quality level, and the initial response from the sector 'ranged from full support to adamant opposition, with many undecided' (Bushouse, 2008: 43). A main concern was whether the funding levels would cover costs. The Early Childhood Council (ECC), representing many private providers, was most vociferous in its condemnation of the policy, 'calling 20 Hours Free "dangerous" and [it] called on the government to allow top up fees. The Minister shot back with a statement to commercial childcare chains that they could not expect to deliver a return to shareholders funded by the government ECE programmes' (Bushouse, 2008: 45).

- A small gesture was made towards the idea of *integrated ECE services*, with a Parent Support and Development Programme providing funding for a three-year pilot in eight ECE centres in 2006, extended to 16 in 2007. ECE centres were free to design their own programmes.

In combination, these policies encouraged more accessible provision and democratic participation and practice. A longitudinal evaluation of the strategic plan carried out with the same ECE services over 2004, 2006 and 2009 (L. Mitchell, Meagher-Lundberg, Mara et al., 2011; L. Mitchell, 2011) showed that difficulties in affording the cost of ECE experienced by low-income families in 2004 and 2006 were largely dispelled by 2009. According to parents, the '20 hours free ECE' policy had contributed to parental decisions to participate in ECE and encouraged more regular and sustained attendance by 3- and 4-year-olds.

During the Labour government's implementation of the strategic plan, Aotearoa New Zealand made substantial progress towards achieving the teacher qualification target; by 2009, 64 per cent of teachers in 'education and care centres' and kindergartens were qualified and registered, up from 37 per cent in 2002. The employment of qualified teachers and take-up of professional resources and development were linked positively to ratings of process quality and indicators of 'good' assessment, planning, evaluation and self-review processes. These included an opening up of the curriculum to parents and whānau (extended family) through invitations to be involved in assessment and planning. The story of the kindergarten's transformation, and the positive impact on families, can be found in Jeanette Clarkin-Phillips's doctoral study (2016) of one of the pilot centres in the Professional Support and Development Programme.

Interventionist approach (2008–2017)

The Labour government lost the 2008 election. The National party regained office and held it until 2017. A contrasting policy agenda marked a shift 'from a child rights to an interventionist approach' (L. Mitchell, 2015), as discourses of children as 'priority' replaced a focus on citizenship, and a turn occurred away from universal to targeted approaches aimed at encouraging ECE participation by a minority. This was a time of heated debates, particularly over universal versus targeted funding, and the value of and need for qualified teachers in ECE. Researchers in ECE were influential in bringing research-based evidence to politicians, the ECE constituency and the public.

Professor Anne Smith was a member of the Early Childhood Education Taskforce, established by the new government in 2010 to develop a ECE funding model that moved away from cost drivers, reduced the level of universal funding, and targeted funding towards priority children. Her concerns about the Taskforce's focus on economic development rather than children's rights and well-being, and the proposed turn away from universalism to a targeted funding model, provoked her to write an independent dissenting report. In addition, she asked the Canadian economist Gordon Cleveland to examine the consequences of the funding model, and his analysis offered her valuable justification. As it turned out, the new funding model was never finalised (May, 2019: 313).

The Prime Minister, John Key, also expressed his view that having a high proportion of qualified ECE teaching staff was a matter of personal belief'. In response, two academics at the University of Waikato wrote:

> We find it startling that questions are being raised about whether educators in early childhood centres should be qualified, when we now know so much more about the significance for life-long learning of the early years and about the complexity of the care and education task. The Prime Minister has said that 'it is a matter of personal belief as to whether a high proportion of all centre staff should be trained teachers'. This is not so. It is a matter of an informed and evidence-based educational decision. These questions would never be raised about the adults who teach 5- and 6- (or older) year-olds in school. … We had hoped that 100 per cent qualified teachers for *all* children in early childhood … would contribute to the government's aim of equitable and quality outcomes for children from all backgrounds. (Carr and Mitchell, 2010: 1).

When the Minister of Education, Ann Tolley, claimed there was no evidence that centres with 100 per cent qualified teachers were better than those with a lower percentage, the New Zealand Childcare Association (now Te Rito Maioha Early Childhood New Zealand) initiated a research project to provide evidence on the subject. A key finding was that, compared with children in centres with 50–79 per cent qualified teachers, children in centres with 100 per cent qualified teachers had:

- more interactions with qualified teachers;
- more conversations with these teachers;
- more episodes of sustained shared thinking;
- more teacher mediation of their concept development; and
- slightly higher scores on indicators to do with independence and concentration.

(Meade et al., 2012: xii)

The main shifts and losses in this period of National party government were:

- The almost immediate removal from its website by the Ministry of Education of all reference to the previous government's Strategic Plan and the dropping of the word 'free' from the previous '20 hours free ECE' policy.

- The cutting of funding for professional development and COIs.
- The extension from 2010 to 2012 of the timeframe for reaching targets of 80 per cent qualified and registered ECE teachers in centres, with the 100 per cent target dropped altogether. Funding of the top two funding bands for teacher-led services employing more than 80 per cent regulated staff was cut, putting the onus on management to find extra funding or else employ less qualified staff.
- A new emphasis placed on targeted policies to support the participation of children deemed to be 'priority' and who were not attending ECE, namely Māori, Pasifika and children from low socio-economic homes. Six initiatives were trialled in communities where a high proportion of children had not attended ECE before starting school. These included: increased support for parent playgroups; the Engaging Priority Families Initiative whereby brokers worked with families to encourage ECE participation; and Targeted Assistance for Participation (TAP) grants for helping establish new services and child spaces in those communities where they were needed. An evaluation commissioned by the Ministry of Education found support from parents and providers for integrated ECE:

> [Services funded with a TAP grant] were most responsive when they were connected to the local community through offering an integrated service with early childhood education alongside other family services, or where they held a hub of connections with community agencies and organisations. All but one TAP service provider interviewed did these things and this is what made them successful with priority families. (L. Mitchell, Meagher-Lundberg, Davison et al., 2016: 100)

- The removal of the only funding differentials between community-based and privately owned ECE services. Equity funding became available to the private sector and private centres became eligible for TAP grants, which enabled private owners to use taxpayers' money to fund capital works, which might later be sold for a profit.

In these ways, Labour's policies were undermined and private for-profit ECE was further incentivised through substantial government funding and weak accountability requirements. Such provision continued to grow, increasingly bringing into ECE the world of foreign investors and shareholders. As an example, in late 2014, a publicly listed company, Evolve Education Group, bought two large ECE companies, LollipopsEducare, with 30 education and care centres, and Porse, an accredited home-based provider and trainer. It also bought an additional 55 education and care centres and an ECE Management organisation and stated its intention to expand. The Evolve Education Group prospectus foregrounded the money-making potential of ECE, treating ECE as a business opportunity, as a commodity to be sold to parent consumers as they participated in the workforce. The first duty of Evolve as a listed company was to make money for owners or shareholders, and profitability was a key criterion for selecting and acquiring Evolve's ECE centres. The whole approach of Evolve Education Group was at odds with the aims of a public system of education. As we shall see below, the company soon moved on to pastures new.

Renewed movement (2017–)

The election of the Labour-led government in 2017 brought a renewed interest in the ECE workforce, including commitment to teacher qualifications and pay parity, and new interest in public provision of ECE services. The government opted for developing another Strategic Plan, called the *Early Learning Action Plan*. The new Minister of Education, Chris Hipkins, announced in its terms of reference an agenda of 'investing in and backing our world-class, public education system for all students. This involves turning the tide away from a privatised, profit-focused education system.' It promised to 'ensure that community-based early childhood education services have well-maintained facilities and are able to expand to meet growing demand' (Hipkins, 2017).

The development of the Strategic Plan was led by a ministerial advisory group, chaired by Professor Carmen Dalli from the Victoria University of Wellington. Members of the Early Childhood Advisory Committee (comprising representatives of national ECE organisations) and of the ECE Research Policy Forum (notable academics, and officials from the Ministry of Education and from the Education Review Office, the government agency that evaluates and reports on the education and care of all children in ECE services and schools) were the Reference Group. This more democratic model of policy development, involving input from those involved in the grass roots of teaching, managing and researching ECE, contrasted with the less consultative approach of the preceding National government when it appointed its Taskforce.

However, Ministry of Education officials had a strong role in the Reference Group's work, and controlled what was reported to government ministers. For instance, Helen May and Linda Mitchell, both members of the Reference Group, prepared a paper (May and Mitchell, 2018) that detailed explicit, concrete and workable ways to implement the Minister's intention to 'turn the tide' in ECE away from private profit-focused provision and from a market approach to provision. Despite much debate, the final report, written by Ministry officials, made no mention of the issue or of policy solutions. However, a mechanism to move from a market approach to a planned approach to provision of ECE services did make it into the final report, proposing a new and radical initiative.

The *Early learning action plan 2019–2029* was published in 2019 (Ministry of Education (New Zealand), 2019). The economic and future-oriented focus of the National government's Taskforce report was replaced with a primary concern for learning and well-being at the time of attendance at ECE services. In the Foreword, Minister of Education Chris Hipkins wrote: 'High quality early learning services benefit children, families and whānau. They support parents and help children in their early years to enjoy a good life, learn and thrive' (Ministry of Education (New Zealand), 2019: 5). Recommendations for policy were detailed under five 10-year objectives: learners with their whānau at the centre, barrier-free access, quality teaching and leadership, future learning and work, and a world-class public education system. We present below some of the key recommendations, which were the focus of policy action and contribute to a continuing transformative agenda, along with comments on their implementation.

- *Incentivise for 100 per cent and regulate for 80 per cent qualified teachers* in teacher-led ECE, leading to regulation for 100 per cent. As at March 2023, the Ministry of Education was still planning consultation about regulatory change.
- *Implement a mechanism that improves the level and consistency of teachers' salaries* across the ECE sector. Higher rates of funding, called 'parity funding rates', have been available from 1 January 2023 for education and care centres whose management chooses to adopt at least the same salary levels as the first six steps of the kindergarten teachers' pay scale. Since many managers did not make this choice, this partial pay parity was not guaranteed for all teachers in education and care centres. Furthermore, the government funding levels have been insufficient to cover the costs

of kindergarten teachers' pay rates and decision-making processes have been fraught with problems, as explained by Te Rito Maioha Early Childhood New Zealand (Wolfe, 2023):

> Centres without the scale or profit margins to absorb the extra costs are being forced to make untenable choices. Less than 40% of eligible services have been able to afford to opt-in to the new pay parity rates. Many of our members have told us that even though they can barely afford it, they felt compelled to opt in to pay parity, both morally and to compete for staff against larger corporate centres. To do so, they're going into debt, cutting staff to minimum ratios and increasing whānau fees. In other words – the choices are lower quality ECE for children, more expensive fees for parents and whānau, or no access to ECE at all, ultimately setting up future generations to fail.

- *Introduce a managed network approach* to ensure high-quality, diverse and sustainable ECE provision. This is at odds with a market approach, where there is no requirement for planning and ECE providers alone are responsible for determining where a new ECE service is located. Amendments have been made to government legislation: the Education and Training Act (2020) requires anyone who wants to operate a new licensed early childhood service to apply for network management approval from the Minister of Education before applying for licensing. The applicant now has to demonstrate that 1) there is a need for a new service of the type and location being offered and 2) the applicant is suitable (fit and proper), capable to provide a service, and has sufficient finances.

The Action Plan contains some contested recommendations. One that began to be implemented almost immediately was 'Co-construct a range of valid, reliable, culturally and linguistically appropriate tools to support formative assessment and teaching practice.' Scholars from the Early Years Research Centre at the University of Waikato had argued in their submission (Early Years Research Centre, 2019) that such an action should be set within the framework of *Te Whāriki*, and implementation should only be considered after improvements had been made to reach targets for qualified teachers, adult:child ratios, and other supports. However, the recommendation was one of the first to be implemented. Academics from two other universities were contracted to develop 'practice and progress tools' in the area of social-emotional learning, and further tools are being developed in literacy and mathematics.

The 'Draft practice and progress tools (Kōwhiti Whakapae), social-emotional learning' were trialled during 2022. A critical review (Mitchell et al., 2022) by 13 researchers and teachers raised concerns 'that the tools represent a significant departure from current assessment approaches [e.g., 'learning stories'] and have potential to impact on early childhood curriculum and shape the direction of ECE assessment in Aotearoa New Zealand'; they concluded that the tools were incompatible with *Te Whāriki*. The review team discussed their concerns and the problematic features with Ministry officials, who later said that major changes had been made. A senior Ministry official commented, 'We have significantly iterated the tools [that were] critiqued and they look very different now. We have been working with our sector reference group and they are very happy with the changes (as is the user testing group)' (J. Ewens, personal communication, 3 May 2023). A revised version of the tools and framework was published in October 2023 (Ministry of Education (New Zealand), 2023c).

Another contested consequence of the Action Plan concerns terminology. The Action Plan replaces the terms 'early childhood education' or 'early childhood education and care' with 'early learning', and children are renamed 'learners'. These terms now appear in the Ministry of Education official websites and information. Scholars from the University of Waikato Early Years Research Centre (Early Years Research Centre, 2019: 6) have argued that ECE is 'not just about early learning, it is education in its broadest sense' and is 'grounded in discourses of democracy, equitable opportunities for all children to care, education and development'.

Other recommendations of the 2019 Action Plan have a longer timeframe and lack specific aims. These recommendations include: improving staff:child ratios and gaining advice about group size and environments; facilitating wrap-around health and social services to support children and their whānau to engage in early learning; and reviewing equity and targeted funding (a review is underway).

What was achieved

Over decades of political change, Aotearoa New Zealand has confronted many problematic issues in ECE systems that are features of the Anglosphere model. There are a number of dimensions along which

Aotearoa New Zealand has transformed its early childhood system, and which cumulatively have taken the country further along the transformative path than other Anglosphere countries – and brought it nearest to a nearly completely transformed system like Sweden's.

First, Aotearoa New Zealand has moved away from its pre-1986 childcare–education divide in policy making and administration to an integrated system, in which all ECE services are commonly administered and regulated by the Ministry of Education. The Ministry of Education describes itself as the government's lead advisor on Aotearoa New Zealand's education system, developing policy and undertaking research, evaluation and monitoring. Integration within an education ministry provided a foundation for further integration with respect to curriculum, the workforce and funding. The movement towards integration is also reflected in changes in the language used. What were formerly termed 'daycare' and 'childcare' centres, emphasising their 'care' function, are now 'education and care' centres, emphasising that education and care are intertwined; there has been strong support for a discourse of 'early childhood education' rather than 'childcare', although this discourse is now somewhat contested.

Second, Aotearoa New Zealand's curriculum, *Te Whāriki*, offers an image of all young children as 'competent and confident learners and communicators, healthy in mind, body and spirit, secure in their sense of belonging and in the knowledge that they make a valued contribution to society' (Ministry of Education (New Zealand), 2017b: 2). Its four principles foreground empowerment, attending to the wider family and community, reciprocal relationships and holistic development. Outcomes include learning dispositions and working theories that contribute to lifelong learning. The approach taken differs from curriculum models that emphasise acquisition of discrete and decontextualised skills. This is an integrated curriculum, used by a wide diversity of ECE services that includes kindergartens, playcentres, education and care centres, home-based services and certificated playgroups. In this respect, it plays 'an important unifying role by providing principles for curriculum development, strands that describe valued learning, goals relating to the provision of a supportive learning environment, and learning outcomes' (Ministry of Education (New Zealand), 2017b: 8). The curriculum for *kōhanga reo* is a document in its own right (Ministry of Education (New Zealand), 2017b). Both curriculums have the same framework of principles and strands.

Third, the curriculum approach is supported by government policies intended to build and sustain a qualified and professionally supported early childhood workforce. Indeed, Aotearoa New Zealand has gone a long way towards ensuring a qualified ECE workforce of graduate professionals, in teacher-led centres and as coordinators of home-based services; in 2021, 70 per cent of these staff held an ECE graduate teaching qualification that leads to registration with the Teaching Council of New Zealand. (Staff at playcentres and home-based educators are not included in this definition, while data on *kaiako* (teachers) at *kōhanga reo* is not provided to the Ministry.) However, while all kindergartens and some education and care centres employ 100 per cent qualified teaching staff, some education and care centres employ only the regulated minimum of 50 per cent; the target of 100 per cent qualified staff in all centres is still to be reached. Despite these variations between centres, Aotearoa New Zealand today has the highest level of graduate and specialised early years teachers in its early childhood education workforce of any country.

Fourth, parity of kindergarten teachers' pay with the pay of primary teachers has been achieved, though only limited progress has been made towards pay parity for teachers in education and care centres. A remuneration survey of staff in education and care centres, kindergartens and home-based services, carried out between August and October 2020 (Ministry of Education (New Zealand), 2021b: 3), found wide differences in rates of pay; the average annual salary for a qualified teacher at an education and care service was NZ$55,964, compared to NZ$72,880 for a similarly qualified teacher at a kindergarten. The new 'parity funding' rates, effective from January 2023, have not covered costs and the bulk-funding mechanism has disadvantaged individual services, including many that are community-based and in low socio-economic communities. Offering 'incentives' for raising teacher pay and conditions is not enough to ensure pay parity for all early childhood teachers, since teachers rely on employers 'opting in' to paying parity rates. A bold transformational step, in line with a view of ECE as a public service, would be for the government to accept ECE teachers as public servants, make the Secretary of Education a party to a national collective agreement on pay parity rates, and pay teachers' salaries through a centralised payroll, as is done for school teachers.

Fifth, funding is mainly delivered as supply-side funding and is becoming increasingly responsive to the actual costs of services. The original bulk-funding formula, based on a global calculation of the number and ages of children and their hours of attendance, has been modified to take into account some of the costs of employing and paying qualified teachers, with the intention of acting as an incentive to improve levels of both qualified teachers and their pay. Additional equity funding takes into account the nature and economic resources of the community that a centre or kindergarten serves. As bulk funding has increased, and become increasingly related to actual costs, the funding system has become more integrated under an educational administration, although another form of funding is still in use, namely the Work and Income Childcare Subsidy, a targeted subsidy to reduce parental fees for certain groups. However, as argued above, bulk funding of teacher salaries is a problematic mechanism, since the amount available to be spent on teachers' pay and conditions does not reflect actual costs, competes with other spending purposes, and is at the discretion of employers.

Aotearoa New Zealand has achieved much since transformation began in the 1980s, but there remain some unresolved issues. Take, for instance, access. The total proportion of all children aged 0–4 years old who attended a licensed early learning service during the 2020 ECE Census week was 60.7 per cent (down from 63.9 per cent in 2019). This included 91.5 per cent of 4-year-olds and 86.2 per cent of 3-year-olds, down from 94.2 per cent and 89.8 per cent respectively in 2019, which was probably due to the impact of Covid (Ministry of Education (New Zealand), 2021a). Overall, therefore, access to and participation in ECE are high for 3- and 4-year-olds, and Aotearoa New Zealand has gone some way to making ECE free for this age group in its '20 hours ECE' policy. But there is as yet no entitlement to a free place in a suitable ECE service, either for all children or just for 3- and 4-year-olds. Free hours of attendance depend on availability and, in some instances, the policy aims have been thwarted by service managers who offer 20 hours' free ECE on condition that families enrol their children for more than 20 hours, with high costs for additional hours.

Transformation has also failed to deal adequately with issues of provision of ECE. There is no fully integrated form of provision similar to Sweden's 'pre-schools' or England's 'Children's Centres'. Moreover, the government does not directly provide any ECE, apart from *Te Kura* (the Correspondence School), and has relied instead on a market approach. This has allowed for-profit providers to establish ECE without any regard for planning, leading to oversupply in some communities and undersupply in others.

The growth of private services has also seen the arrival in Aotearoa New Zealand of international financialised companies, such as Evolve in 2014 (discussed above) and Busy Bees in 2022 (discussed in Chapter 3). Both are publicly listed companies, whose primary aim is to make profits for shareholders. But they are not alone. In February 2022, this advertisement was placed by the Institute of Directors New Zealand for the position of Chair for an 'ECE Rollup', the aim of which was to expand the company through acquisitions, not by the creation of new places, make money, and get out.

> *ECE rollup. Expansion in New Zealand through acquisitions 'and exit'*
>
> We're going to dominate the fragmented early childhood education industry in New Zealand through acquisition growth with commercial debt, equity and vendor finance.
>
> Our goal is to consolidate 100 facilities in the early childhood education sector & exit.
>
> Early childhood education has performed extremely well, with 5000 facilities & 100–150 new facilities being built in New Zealand for the last 5 years.
>
> We have a group of experienced Board of Directors [*sic*] specialising in early childhood education, legal, finance, accounting and mergers & acquisitions.

Acquisitions and exit are the story elsewhere. It was recently announced that Evolve has sold its 105 education and care centres, seeking a better financial return by reinvesting in Australia.

> The company has entered into a conditional agreement to sell its 105 childhood centres, which it owns through local subsidiary, Lollipops Educare Holdings, to an acquisition vehicle managed by Australian private equity firm, Anchorage Capital Partners, for [NZ]$46m – but the final price would be subject to revisions.
>
> 'The rationale for the transaction is largely to accelerate the execution of Evolve's Australian growth strategy by redeploying proceeds to acquire assets in Australia,' the company said in an announcement to the stock exchange. (Radio New Zealand, 2022)

The new network management approach proposed in the latest strategic plan, which will enable government to intervene in the market to shape the development of new services, may mitigate some of the problems arising from allowing a market free-for-all to determine provision. Under the network management approach, too, new forms of provision, such as integrated ECE services, could be envisaged and developed. However, early indications are that the new approach will not 'turn the tide on private provision' and foster a rebound of community-based

ECE services, with their more democratic culture. They have a long tradition of involving families and communities as members of decision-making bodies; community-based kindergartens and education and care centres involve elected parent, staff and community representatives on management committees and boards, while parent/whānau-led services embed family involvement within their total operation and decision-making. This is not the case with private for-profit ECE centres, which are first and foremost accountable to their shareholders; there are no government requirements for families and communities to be represented in formal governing and decision-making bodies.

A final gap in the transformative programme should be noted. Parenting leave entitlements remain weak, the absence of entitlement to an ECE place not being matched by an entitlement to well-paid leave; the two parts of the system lack synergy. Aotearoa New Zealand still has much work to do in this policy area.

Drivers of and obstacles to transformation

This account of the historical context and the advances and reversals from 1986 to 2022 offers some insight into the drivers and obstacles to transformation of the ECE system in Aotearoa New Zealand, and the reason why it has come further than other Anglosphere countries. First and foremost, the country has demonstrated a capacity to think, discuss and create a widely agreed vision of an integrated system of early childhood education, and then to advocate effectively and consistently over time for its realisation through broad and strong alliances; individuals and organisations have shown an ability to work collectively, even where there is disagreement, and to gain public support through personal networks, campaigning and other means. Trade unions (which have shown an ability to cohere and integrate) and community organisations, as well as academics, have played important roles in this collective effort. Advocates have developed and drawn on shared understandings of pedagogy and curriculum, and the reality of lives and working conditions of participating families and ECE teachers, to analyse problematic issues and to envisage, detail and campaign for transformative policies.

Enlightened politicians, with an understanding of ECE and a political will to transform the system, have also played a part as key players in advancing government policy. The history of Aotearoa New Zealand's ECE reform demonstrates the influence of individual prime ministers and education ministers, and of the political beliefs of (some) elected governments. The major transformations were made during the terms of left-leaning Labour governments; it is interesting to note, however, that the transformative process started under a Labour government with a strong neoliberal orientation, susceptible to economistic arguments for early childhood investment, but also open to influence from the strong early childhood lobby referred to above.

The democratic and participatory theme keeps recurring in the Aotearoa New Zealand narrative. A democratic approach to policy development undertaken in genuine consultation with the many stakeholders in ECE occurred in the development of Aotearoa New Zealand's forward-thinking policies, including the creation of the internationally renowned curriculum, *Te Whāriki*, in the 1990s, the development of the 10-year Strategic Plan for Early Childhood Education published in 2002, and, most recently though only partially, the development of the Early Learning Action Plan published in 2019. Wide consultation can enable rich policy solutions that respond to context and are widely understood and supported. On the other hand, the diversity of thinking and backgrounds among stakeholders in the sector means policies are not always agreed upon; for example, issues related to teacher qualifications and to funding granted to for-profit ECE providers have been contested, and these differences of view are still not resolved.

In sum, the policies that have contributed most to transforming the ECE system have been developed through consultative processes and have incorporated a vision, goals and very specific strategies. The 2002 Strategic Plan for ECE offers an example; the vision is outlined in the Minister of Education's Foreword, though it does not go so far as to express a commitment to a public early childhood education as a child's right and a public good. Nor does it include visionary statements about the purpose of education. But there are three clear goals – increasing participation in quality ECE, improving its quality, and promoting collaborative relationships – and the plan details a raft of policy strategies and a timeframe for achieving these. (It has to be admitted, though, that the timeframe was for an extended period, leaving the Plan's implementation vulnerable to the election of a new government that rejected its direction, which has happened in Aotearoa New Zealand more than once.)

One other feature of this democratic theme should be noted. The transformative history of ECE in Aotearoa New Zealand has been significantly influenced by the Māori resistance movement, the emergence of *kōhanga reo*, and aspirations for a bicultural society. An important example of this influence is *Te Whāriki*, the unique early childhood curriculum, with its distinctive conceptual framing and process of development.

Evaluation, research and monitoring have been valuable for formulating and refining robust policy and for identifying both its intended and its unintended consequences (OECD, 2001, 2006). The Ministry of Education has contracted evaluations for its major strategic policies in ECE, and has piloted specific initiatives, before revising them. These evaluations have undoubtedly helped to pinpoint valuable approaches, and helped in the refinement of policies. Research funding grants for the Teaching and Learning Research Initiative and for Centres of Innovation have supported worthwhile research in innovative pedagogy and curriculum, carried out as collaborations between academic and teacher researchers. But it should be noted that, as in England, no evaluation of the twin policy pillars of marketisation and privatisation has been commissioned.

This is relevant, as the main obstacles to transformative reform are undoubtedly marketisation and privatisation, neoliberalism's solutions to every need, including education. Four decades of neoliberalism started with Labour government reforms in the 1980s, and intensified in the 1990s under the succeeding National government. Private for-profit services provide 62 per cent of the total 222,913 licensed places in the whole of the ECE sector (teacher-led and parent/whānau-led), including 69 per cent of licensed places in the teacher-led sector. These places are all in the home-based and education and care sectors, where private services predominate (Ministry of Education (New Zealand), 2023b).

Private providers have obstructed the implementation of the '20 hours free ECE' offer. They have hindered an even and equitable distribution of services. They have also hampered workforce reforms. In particular, the divide that exists between the pay and conditions of teachers in kindergartens and schools and those of teachers in mainly private education and care centres remains an unresolved issue; it is hard to achieve parity for teachers employed in education and care centres, where bargaining arrangements with individual employers are the norm. A shift to state responsibility for the whole ECE teaching workforce, in line with kindergarten teachers, would be a major step forward, enabling pay parity and appropriate working conditions to be achieved for all.

Aotearoa New Zealand still has some way to go before it achieves the transformative goal of a fully integrated public system of early childhood education, which is itself integrated with a strong parenting leave policy, with entitlements in leave and ECE services coordinated to ensure synergy. Still, it has travelled far and shown the possibility of systemic change, rather than relying on tweaking a long-standing but dysfunctional split system; its reformation of the early childhood workforce, for example, is remarkable in its ambition and execution. The country has also suggested some of the conditions and processes that can enable transformation, as well as some of the most significant obstacles. We shall draw on this experience and these lessons as we turn in our final chapter to consider the Anglosphere's model for its early childhood system and how the latter might be transformed.

Postscript to Chapter 7

A new government was elected on 14 October 2023, made up of three right-leaning parties led by the NZ National Party with Act NZ and NZ First as coalition partners; political commentators have argued that the government could be the most right-wing government since the early 1990s (Frost, 2023; Slaughter, 2023). The government's proposed policy changes include:

- The reversal of many years of affirmative action for Māori, the public use of *te reo Māori* (the Māori language) and co-governance, and a review and possible referendum on Te Tiriti o Waitangi; the opening of parliament saw thousands taking part in protests against 'anti-Māori' government policies.
- The dilution of worker rights through a repeal of 'Fair Pay' legislation and the reintroduction of 90-day trial periods for all businesses (workers can be dismissed during the trial without reason). This will disadvantage early childhood teachers in the education and care sector, as their claims for parity with kindergarten and school teachers rest on the 'Fair Pay' legislation and increased government funding; their claims have been further disadvantaged by the recent discovery of a NZ$252m shortfall in the Ministry of Education's funding forecasts under the previous government to cover the cost of pay parity (Ministry of Education (New Zealand), 2023a).
- A shift in education towards individual choice, privatisation and prescriptive curriculum. Primary and intermediate schools will be required to teach one hour a day each of reading, writing and maths, starting in 2024, and the curriculum is to be refocused 'on academic achievement and not ideology, including the removal and replacement of the gender, sexuality, and relationship-based education guidelines' (New Zealand National Party & New

Zealand First, 2023: 8). Partnership, or charter, schools are to be reintroduced, while a promised regulation sector review is likely to include early childhood education and to diminish staffing standards. While other early childhood education policies have not yet been announced, the change in government is likely to see a shift towards demand-side funding.

There is now, more than ever, a need for democratically organised networks and community groups to give voice to and persist in collective efforts to progress ideals for early childhood education as a public good underpinned by Te Tiriti o Waitangi, and for a qualified and well-paid ECE workforce.

Notes

1   A distinct feature of New Zealand with respect to the indigenous population is Te Tiriti o Waitangi, the Treaty of Waitangi, an agreement made in 1840 between representatives of the British Crown and around 500 Māori chiefs. Most Māori signed the Māori version of Te Tiriti o Waitangi, which differed in significant ways from the English version (the Treaty of Waitangi). Te Tiriti o Waitangi was an agreement in which Māori gave the Crown rights to govern and to develop British settlement (Article 1), while the Crown guaranteed Māori tino rangatiratanga, their absolute sovereign authority over their lands, villages and everything that they value (taonga katoa) (Article 2). 'In article 3, the Crown promised to Māori the benefits of royal protection and full citizenship. This text emphasises equality' (Waitangi Tribunal, 2023). In a further, verbal undertaking, the Governor said 'that the several faiths (beliefs) of England, of the Wesleyans, of Rome, and also Māori custom shall alike be protected'. Since the signing of the Treaty there have been 'repeated failures to honour these founding promises' (Human Rights Commission, 2023). Te Tiriti is the basis for a country that includes Māori and English as official languages, a vision of a bicultural society, and a bicultural curriculum in early childhood education.
2   The State Services Commission (now the Public Service Commission) is the central public service department of Aotearoa New Zealand charged with overseeing, managing, and improving the performance of the state sector and its organisations.

8

Transforming early childhood in the Anglosphere

The prevailing [free market] ideology of the last 40 years has blinded the public to alternatives by deliberately confining the boundaries of public debate.

(*The Guardian*, 2022)

This final chapter is about alternatives and possibilities at a time of great and converging crises, about hope, therefore, but also about urgency. We ask how the countries of the Anglosphere might transform their early childhood systems: to what end, and how they might get there. The ideas we offer are not put forward as a blueprint. They are meant, rather, as a provocation to thought and deliberation: they are one transformative possibility. If readers don't like them, because they don't think they would work for their country, or for any other reason, that's fine, but then we would challenge those readers to come up with alternative analyses and ideas, to offer their own transformative possibilities. The urgency, it seems to us, is to escape neoliberalism's TINA ('there is no alternative') – that 'free market' ideology that has for decades 'blinded the public to alternatives by deliberately confining the boundaries of public debate' (*The Guardian*, 2022) – and so to rediscover a world of possibilities and political choices, and with them a renewal of a democratic politics of education more generally, and of early childhood education in particular. We want, in short, to help the public to see alternatives and to blow away the assumptions that have confined the boundaries of public debate.

We start the chapter by recapping our earlier argument that there is an Anglosphere model for early childhood systems, a model that is deeply flawed and dysfunctional, and that has so far proved resistant to transformation, despite increased policy priority for early childhood services and parenting leave. We will contend that now is the time for transformation, because the neoliberal era, which has been so influential in shaping and maintaining the Anglosphere's model, is coming to an end, and because our societies urgently need to be better equipped to respond to this terminal condition and to the other converging crises of our times: a combination, in short, of opportunity and necessity. We will propose our ideas for transformation, our provocation to thought and action, starting with a reconceptualisation of early childhood systems, as public, universal, education-based and integrated. We will emphasise, too – at the risk of repeating ourselves because the point is so important – that the fact that this integrated system is education-based does not mean ignoring care, the needs of working parents or the many other needs and rights of young children and families that go beyond education – indeed, quite the opposite. We propose that this transformed system should not only work with a broad concept of education, but also be imbued with an ethics of care and inclusive values of democracy, equality and cooperation, and adopt a form of provision that can accommodate a range of projects, including the support of employed parents. We will end by considering what the process of transformation might involve, for example how we might set about de-privatising and de-marketising early childhood services.

Throughout the chapter we will refer back to some of the countries we have featured in this book and which offer examples of how things can be different. Please note, though, that these countries are put forward as examples of possibility, to provoke thought, not as policy solutions that can or should be taken off the shelf and imported. These examples are: Sweden and its near-totally integrated and universal public early childhood system, spanning services and parenting leave; Aotearoa New Zealand and its radical reform of the early years workforce and its innovative curriculum; England and its Children's Centres, an attempt (not fully realised) to rethink and reform provision for young children; and Canada and its commitment to use public funding to halt the spread of privatisation.

The case against the Anglosphere model

Before recapping our basic critique of the Anglosphere's early childhood systems, we should make it clear that we are not saying that the Anglosphere model is uniquely problematic. Most early childhood systems suffer from a number of similar problems with similar problematic consequences: the great majority have split services, although school-based or kindergarten services mostly dominate, and a split between these services and parenting leave; most have systems that have developed piecemeal and haphazardly over a long period; and, most important, most now have systems that no-one would propose if they were starting from scratch today; yet these systems, the legacy of historical accident, are rarely the subject of thorough review to determine their suitability for the present day. Only Sweden and a handful of other countries have escaped these deep systemic problems, showing it can be done.

The splits in the system are the foundational problem: splits between school-based and kindergarten services and their workforces on the one hand and 'childcare' services (in group settings or provided by individuals in their homes) and their workforces on the other; and splits between early childhood services and parenting leave policies, which leave these policies failing to mesh. In the Anglosphere, as we have shown, the split has left the 'childcare' sector as the dominant provider of services and (except in Aotearoa New Zealand) 'childcare workers' as the majority in the workforce; elsewhere, schools or kindergartens and their workers are mostly predominant. That dominance of childcare provision gives rise to and is reinforced by endless talk about 'childcare', a 'childcare' discourse, which reflects a deeply embedded and narrow way of thinking about early childhood services, a conceptual split that seems to prevent people and society from imagining something different, thereby 'confining the boundaries of public debate'.

But there is a further systemic problem, which is particularly prevalent in Anglosphere countries. This is an increasing reliance on marketisation and privatisation, with a growing presence of for-profit 'childcare' providers, in other words providers who operate as businesses in a market, selling a commodity to consumers and in competition with each other. These private 'childcare' markets are assuming a new character under the growing influence of corporatisation and financialisation; 'childcare centres' themselves are increasingly the subject of acquisitions and mergers, of wheeling and dealing, in an inexorable search by a rampant capitalism to extract more profit. Coming late to prioritising early childhood, whether services or parenting leave, and relying mainly on the childcare sector, with its low-cost employment model, the Anglosphere has been characterised by low levels of public expenditure, though this is moving up in most countries.

The Anglosphere's model for its early childhood system is, we have contended, extremely problematic. It produces many adverse consequences, documented earlier in this book. They include: fragmentation and discontinuities; inequalities and social divisiveness;

an undesirable and unsustainable approach to the workforce; an over-emphasis on 'childcare' for certain children (i.e., those with employed parents) and an under-emphasis on care for all, indeed on meeting the needs of all children and all parents; privileging the competitiveness of the market over the cooperation of the network; and increasingly turning what should be a public good and common space into a private benefit and tradeable commodity.

This Anglosphere model has a long history and many of its adverse consequences are not new; it is the product, in part, of historical developments and well-established liberal welfare regimes and their associated values and beliefs. But its dysfunctional features and troubling results have been exacerbated by neoliberalism, an ideology and movement that has been especially influential in the Anglosphere since the 1980s. Under the influence of neoliberalism and of its educational wing, the Global Education Reform Movement, early childhood services have been afflicted not only by marketisation and for-profit privatisation, with attendant competition and commodification, but also by increasing standardisation and a restricted economic rationale, and at a deeper level they have been infected and affected by the 'economisation' that is the 'crucial signature of neoliberalism' (Brown, 2016: 3, cited in Chapter 1); human capital, *homo economicus*, commodification and return on investment cast a long shadow.

We dwelt at some length, in Chapter 4, on the way neoliberalism economises everything and everyone (including our images and our rationales), because it is important to understand how this 'prevailing [free market] ideology of the last 40 years has blinded the public to alternatives by deliberately confining the boundaries of public debate'. But neoliberalism has not only confined debate. It has also shaped the way we understand the world, tending to confine the way we think to the economic, and indeed a particular idea of the economic, in which people serve a highly competitive, growth-driven and greedy economy, too often destructive of human and environmental well-being. Transformation calls for breaking free from these neoliberal-imposed boundaries, to seek a wider and richer view of what matters and of what we, as individuals and societies, might want, and now is the time to do that.

Now is the time for transformation

The neoliberal era, that 'prevailing ideology of the last 40 years', is coming to an end. The 2008 financial crisis demonstrated the failure of neoliberalism's belief in self-regulating markets and imposed huge costs on ordinary people and society at large. Neoliberalism's irrelevance to other crises confronting mankind has become glaringly apparent. It offers no credible solutions to the environmental catastrophes surrounding and closing in upon us; indeed, it is complicit in their intensification. Faced with the Covid pandemic, societies looked to public intervention to provide solutions, not to the market and the exercise of individual self-interest. These seismic events point to one conclusion: with the 'collapse of the neoliberal economic model. ... The idea that markets can resolve most social problems, and that government should simply provide the basic institutions to allow this to happen, has run out of political capital' (Hopkin, 2020: 256, 257). The verdict of Nobel prize-winning economist Joseph Stiglitz is even more stark and foreboding: 'If the 2008 financial crisis failed to make us realise that unfettered markets don't work, the climate crisis certainly should: neoliberalism will literally bring an end to our civilisation' (Stiglitz, 2019b). The historian Adam Tooze (2021) picks up the 'end of neoliberalism' theme, arguing that we can see 2020 and the Covid pandemic 'as a comprehensive crisis of the neoliberal era – with regard to its environmental, social, economic and political underpinnings', and that this 'helps us find our historical bearings. ... [T]he coronavirus crisis marks the end of an arc whose origin is to be found in the 70s.'

The neoliberal project has comprehensively failed, and at a great cost. As it enters its terminal crisis, neoliberalism leaves a trail of rubble in its wake: individuals, families, communities and societies have been left diminished and damaged by growing inequality and insecurity, the relentless emphasis on individual choice and competition, the undermining of solidarity and caring relations, the weakening of welfare states and the damaging of democracy, and the worshipping of growth and consumption. The neoliberal legacy is immiseration, alienation and disenchantment. But the crisis of neoliberalism also leaves a dangerous vacuum as the world enters a transitional period similar in some important respects to an earlier period vividly described, over 90 years ago in the 1930s, by the imprisoned Italian Communist leader Antonio Gramsci (1971: 276): 'The crisis consists precisely in the fact that the old is dying and the new cannot be born; in this interregnum a great variety of morbid symptoms appear.' Faced by this perilous moment, more of the same with fingers crossed won't do; we need both analyses of past failures and proposals for fundamental change that can assist the new to be born.

That, we believe, is the task facing our societies today. We can only offer our ideas in the field of early childhood, but we do so with an awareness that these proposals need to engage and entangle with proposals for fundamental change in many other fields, certainly other sectors of education, but also *inter alia* economics and the environment, participatory democracy and restoring the public domain, health and housing. These parts, too, need not only to relate to each other, but to form part of a broader political narrative, which brings us back to Gramsci's view of the process of transformation and the need to enable the new to be born. The German sociologist Jens Beckert brings that diagnosis up to date when he offers his diagnosis of where we are today:

> [Neoliberalism's] promises did not survive the test of the real world. Today, they are largely exhausted. … [But] there are currently no politically strong narratives that would point to alternatives to the neoliberal logic of competition, markets, and coercion in ways that are firmly guided by the principles of social justice and a democratic polity. (Beckert, 2020: 322, 327)

The prize for giving birth to the new is immense and will come from creating interconnecting meta- and micro-narratives. That prize is to move from our present time of morbid symptoms to healthier societies that are more just and equal, more democratic and solidaristic, more caring and sustainable. So now is the right and necessary time to talk about and plan transformation, a process that requires opening up the 'boundaries of public debate' and overturning the dictatorship of 'no alternative'.

Transforming early childhood in the Anglosphere: reconceptualising and reforming

Images

Transformation is, of course, a process; it cannot happen overnight and should not be rushed. In our view, and taking a leaf out of Sweden's and Aotearoa New Zealand's book, an essential first part of the process is critical, reflective and participatory review of and discussion about the early childhood system, that investigates 'how and how well the system currently works and how it should change in order to meet the needs of children and society during the coming decades'. We are quoting here the terms of reference of the Cambridge Primary Review (Hofkins and Northen, 2009: 4), which was a non-governmental review of primary education in England, running between 2007 and 2009, under the leadership of Professor Robin Alexander; the wording is, however, only indicative, not sacrosanct, and may need to be elaborated. The structure, process and exact scope of review are very much open to debate: a four-year government commission, as in Sweden, is just one model, the sequence of working groups in Aotearoa New Zealand another. But it needs to be public, well resourced (including having its own research capacity), and seek views and evidence from a wide range of sources (including children).

An important part of the transformation process, we would argue, and for reasons we discussed in Chapter 4, must be to address the issue of images, in particular of the child, the parent and the early childhood service. The challenge is to construct images for a post-neoliberal world that are no longer predominantly economic and highly reductive, this being part of a wider process of 'de-economization' and of reimagining a better world. This does not mean that the economic no longer has a part to play in thinking about early childhood systems, their rationale and the images that underpin them. It does, but when considering what that part might be, we must avoid what the economic historian and sociologist Karl Polanyi (1886–1964) called 'the economistic fallacy'; that is, 'the attribution to the economy of a privileged analytic and historical status relative to all other spheres of human behavior … [,] a distortion in thought that paralleled the distortion of a society in which the market had become dominant' (Block and Somers, 1984: 48, 63).

Deposing the economic from this privileged position means putting it in its place as just one of many 'spheres of human behavior' and placing it at the service of more important goals, including flourishing lives for all, strong communities and a sustainable existence. This is an ambition explored by Kate Raworth, an economist focused on the social and ecological challenges of the twenty-first century, in her book *Doughnut Economics*:

> For over 70 years economics has been fixated on GDP, or national output, as its primary measure of progress. That fixation has been used to justify extreme inequalities of income and wealth coupled with unprecedented destruction of the living world. *For the twenty-first century a far bigger goal is needed: meeting the human rights of every person within the means of our life-giving planet.* … Today we have economies that need to grow, whether or not they make us thrive: what we need are economies that make us thrive, whether or not they grow. … In the twentieth century, economics lost the desire to articulate its goals: in their absence, the economics nest

got hijacked by the cuckoo goal of GDP growth. It is high time for that cuckoo to fly the nest so that economics can reconnect with the purpose it should be serving. So let's evict that cuckoo and replace it with *a clear goal for twenty-first-century economics, one that ensures prosperity for all within the means of our planet.* (Raworth, 2017: 25, 30, 32; emphasis added)

A useful starting point for thinking about a post-neoliberal image of the child is Loris Malaguzzi, whom we introduced in Chapter 3, one of the greatest educationalists of the twentieth century and a leading figure in the creation and evolution of the world-famous early childhood education in the Italian city of Reggio Emilia. He was very clear about the importance of the image of the child, since he understood that this image was productive in so many ways: pedagogically, culturally, socially, politically. He was also very clear about the importance of being explicit about the choice of image, which should be a democratic political choice made from an array of alternative images: 'A declaration [about the image of the child] is not only a necessary act of clarity and correctness, it is the necessary premise for any pedagogical theory, and any pedagogical project' (Malaguzzi, quoted in Cagliari, Castagnetti et al., 2016: 374).

His declaration, his political choice, shared by the educators in Reggio Emilia, was very clear and very bold:

There are rich children and poor children. We [in Reggio Emilia] say all children are rich, there are no poor children. All children[,] whatever their culture, whatever their lives[,] are rich, better equipped, more talented, stronger and more intelligent than we can suppose. (Malaguzzi, quoted in Cagliari, Castagnetti et al., 2016: 397)

This 'rich' child is born with a hundred languages,[1] and is a protagonist and an active citizen of society; such children are 'not bottles to be filled' but 'active in constructing the self and knowledge through social interactions and inter-dependencies', 'not the ... bearers of needs, but the bearers of rights' (Malaguzzi, quoted in Cagliari, Castagnetti et al., 2016: 266, 377). Such children are, in the words of *Te Whāriki*, Aotearoa New Zealand's innovative early childhood curriculum, 'competent and confident learners and communicators, healthy in mind, body and spirit, secure in their sense of belonging and in the knowledge that they make a valued contribution to society' (Ministry of Education (New Zealand), 2017b, 51). They have great potentiality, whose full extent is unknown and unknowable, going far, far beyond the employment-related capabilities of human capital theory: as the philosopher Baruch Spinoza (1632–77) puts it, '[w]e don't know what a body can do' (Spinoza, 1996: 71). Rather than the child as a *foretold* becoming, this is the child as an *untold* becoming.

The post-neoliberal image of the parent is no longer as a consumer, but as an active citizen with rights, a protagonist, who should be actively involved with their child's education, with the opportunity to be (in Jack Tizard's words) 'active particip[ants] … in the day-to-day life of the nursery. … Given encouragement, an increasing number [of parents] will probably wish to be involved in the discussion and shaping of aims and methods' (J. Tizard et al., 1976: 218, 226).Malaguzzi shared this ambition, arguing, 'Families must be taken from a passive position as pure consumers of a service and brought to an active, direct presence and collaboration' (Malaguzzi, cited in Cagliari, Castagnetti et al., 2016: 113), and went on to make this a reality through the system of 'social management' operated in the schools of Reggio. This, we could say, is an image of the 'rich' parent, recognised as a competent citizen, 'competent because they [parents] have and develop their own experience, points of view, interpretation and ideas, which are articulated in implicit or explicit theories and are the fruit of their experience as both parents and citizens' (Cagliari, Barozzi and Giudici, 2004: 30).

Because children are a constant source of wonder and surprise because they do what is totally unexpected, beyond what the adults around them could have imagined, they demand educators able to recognise, value and respond to this vivid image of the child: in short, an image of the 'rich' child requires an accompanying image of the 'rich' early childhood worker. This is someone able to work with multiple languages, to welcome the unexpected and uncertainty, and to assume the role of researcher; research is understood, in the words of Carlina Rinaldi (2021: 145) from Reggio Emilia, as 'a way of thinking, of approaching life, of negotiating, of documenting'.

Two other images come to mind, also very much at odds with the neoliberal image of the early childhood worker as technician or as businesswoman. First is the early childhood worker as 'democratic professional', comfortable with working collaboratively and non-hierarchically with children and adults; they are supportive of democratic methods of managing the centre in all its aspects, pedagogical as well as administrative; they welcome diversity, of values, of ideas, of understandings: in the words of the Brazilian educator and philosopher Paulo Freire, 'I must respect even positions opposed to my own, positions that I combat earnestly and with passion' (Freire, 2004: 66). The educator as democratic professional may offer her 'reading of the world', but at the same time her role is to 'bring out the fact that there are other "readings of the world", different from the one being offered as the educator's own, and at times antagonistic to it' (Freire, 2004: 96), and therefore that there are political choices to be made.

Second is the early childhood worker as an 'intellectual', someone who is curious about new ideas and what is going on in the world, 'a producer of knowledge connected with the demands of society', and a critical thinker able to introduce 'a critical attitude towards those things that are given to our present experience as if they were timeless, natural, unquestionable: to stand against the maxims of one's time, against the spirit of one's age, against the current of received wisdom' (Rose, 1999: 20). This is someone, too, who can make, and work with, connections between theory and practice. For Carlina Rinaldi, from Reggio Emilia, 'Theory and practice should be in dialogue, two languages expressing our effort to understand the meaning of life' (Rinaldi, 2021: 144).

Finally, we look at the image of the early childhood service. Here, our starting point is an image from an earlier book that one of us co-authored, which proposed that early childhood services should be understood as 'public forums situated in civil society in which children and adults participate together in projects of social, cultural, political and economic significance' (Dahlberg et al., 2013: 73); the original reference, written 25 years ago, omitted 'environmental' projects, though these are clearly relevant and important today. This image foregrounds the public nature of early childhood services, that they are a public good and a public resource as well as a public space and part of the public domain; they might also be termed a 'universal basic service', alongside existing universal basic services such as health, compulsory schooling and libraries. Some have argued that other services should be added to the list, such as public transport and the internet, all available as of right to all citizens in a renewed welfare state (cf. Social Prosperity Network, 2017; Coote and Percy, 2020).

As a universal and basic public service, early childhood services should be considered a public responsibility, requiring public funding, and should be democratically accountable to the public. To be clear, this means that these are publicly provided or community-based services that have entered into an agreement with a public body to act as a provider on behalf of that body. It also means that these services are democratically managed and adopt what Alfredo Hoyuelos describes, in writing about Loris Malaguzzi and the schools of Reggio Emilia, as 'the ideological and ethical concept of a transparent school and transparent education ... [as well as a political idea], which is that what schools do must have public visibility[,] thus "giving back" to the city what the city has invested in them' (Hoyuelos, 2004: 7).

This image, with its reference to 'children and adults [participating] together in projects' of many kinds, defines the early childhood service not only as a public resource, available to all and contributing to the common good, but also as having the capacity and potential for doing many things, in other words, for being 'multi-purpose', responsive to the diverse needs of the citizens of all ages that it serves. To emphasise this enormous potentiality of the early childhood service functioning as a democratic public space and resource, we can add complementary images: the early childhood service as a workshop where an infinity of projects can be hatched and undertaken, and as 'a laboratory for not-yet' contributing to 'recreating society through ongoing experimentation' (d'Agnese, 2018: 154, 157). Once we start working with these images, the possibilities are endless, the sky's the limit.

Education and care

Having said that, we propose that the multi-purpose early childhood service should be, first and foremost, educational, with early childhood education at its centre, and situated within the education system, indeed as the first stage of that system. To be clear, we see no place any longer in a transformed early childhood system for 'childcare' services and therefore no place for the split between school-based or kindergarten services and childcare services. The end of 'childcare' services brings the end of this split; and, with it, the 'childcare' discourse can be pensioned off for good and the term 'early childhood education and care' (or indeed 'early learning and care') can be replaced by 'early childhood education'.

But to reiterate what we have said earlier, so that we leave no doubt or ambiguity, an 'early childhood education' service in an education system does not dismiss or devalue care. It can and should value care as a universal requirement, for all children and all adults, care being understood as an ethic, an ethics of care, which should imbue all relationships. What do we mean by an 'ethics of care'? Joan Tronto, a leading proponent of this concept, describes it as 'a *practice* rather than a set of rules or principles', combining two elements: 'It involves both particular *acts of caring* and a *general "habit of mind"* to care that should inform all aspects of a ... moral life' (Tronto, 1993: 126, 127; emphasis added). Understood in this way, as an ethic, care is about meeting physical needs and undertaking other 'particular acts': care as work. But it is also relational, a way of approaching relationships, a 'habit of mind' that includes several dispositions or qualities: attentiveness (to the needs of others), responsibility, competence and responsiveness. As Andrea Doucet puts it, 'Tronto's approach to care and care labour entangles relationalities, responsiveness, and responsibilities', adding, 'care is more than tasks or units of time. ... [It] cannot be captured on a tally sheet' (Doucet, 2023: 21, 23) – or indeed be commodified and marketed by 'childcare' services.

Furthermore, caring, understood as an ethic, should be widely applied: it is, say Tronto and her co-author Bernice Fisher, a 'species activity that includes everything that we do to maintain, continue, and repair our "world" so that we can live in it as well as possible' (Fisher and Tronto, 1990: 40); so this means care not only of other people, but also of communities, societies and the physical environment. We would add that care as such a relational ethic and as such a universal requirement has a number of implications. It means care is not something needed primarily by the very young (and the very old); rather, care is needed by all ages and should, therefore, permeate all education sectors up to and including universities (and indeed all other public services, from hospitals to prisons, and beyond, into the private sector too). It means that care is not a separate activity, lower in the pecking order than education, a simple physical task to be delegated to 'assistants'; care is a complex relationship closely enmeshed with education, and is everyone's responsibility.

The primacy we attach to education in early childhood services has several justifications. The first is, as already noted, the 'right to education during early childhood ... beginning at birth', an interpretation by the UN Committee on the Rights of the Child (2006: para. 28) of the UN Convention on the Rights of the Child's 'right of the child to education'; the main rationale for early childhood services is no longer that it is a requirement of employment for some parents ('childcare') but as an entitlement for all children ('education'). However – and we cannot repeat this too often so we leave no doubt – the creation of an 'early childhood education' service in an education system does not dismiss or devalue the needs of working parents or the importance of gender equality: early childhood education services as proposed here recognise that most parents today are employed, studying or otherwise engaged in what Ulrich Beck terms 'public work' (Beck, 1998) or else might be labelled 'civic or community engagement'. They therefore have opening hours that, as far as possible, support such activities, as well as working in close synergy with parenting leave to ensure there are no gaps in support:

this is what happens in Sweden, which has a system of early childhood education services, but a system organised to support the many employed parents in that country. Nor, and again we want to be totally clear on this point, does this education service confine itself to education, important as this is, but, as a public space and public resource, offers many other projects, just as, in our view, schools for older children should do.

The second reason for the primacy of education is the importance in a public service for young children of adopting the principles that underpin education services in most high-income countries, in particular that they should be universal in coverage and free to attend, and employ well-qualified staff. 'Childcare' is not associated with any of these principles.

Third, we attach primacy to education because we understand 'education' in a very broad and holistic sense; indeed, we prefer it to the term 'learning' for this reason, agreeing with the Aotearoa New Zealanders quoted in the previous chapter who contest their government's replacement of 'early childhood education' with 'early learning', on the grounds that early childhood education is not just about learning. The UN Convention on the Rights of the Child refers to education as being directed towards the 'development of the child's personality, talents and mental and physical abilities to their fullest potential' (Art. 29.1(a)), to which we might add the child's moral, aesthetic and participatory abilities.

We also see education as being primarily an emancipatory project, contributing to the formation of children and young people 'who can think and act for themselves' and can participate fully in society as democratic citizens. This view of education conveys the image of a human being who builds or creates herself or himself, and in a way that is not preordained, a process of self-development or self-formation, though always in relationship with others. Or, in the words of Loris Malaguzzi, talking about early childhood education in Reggio Emilia, 'it is clear our choices have been in the direction of currents of thinking that define children first and foremost as disposed to and active in constructing the self and knowledge through social interactions and interdependencies' (Malaguzzi, quoted in Cagliari, Castagnetti et al., 2016: 377).

This emancipatory and proactive understanding of education has roots in a far older tradition: the concept of *Bildung*, which emerges in eighteenth-century Germany, but was influenced by an earlier, English philosopher, Anthony Ashley Cooper, 3rd Earl of Shaftesbury (1671–1713), 'who was the first to emphasise the importance of "inner Bildung", our inner formation' (Rowson, 2019: 5), and indeed 'formation' is a direct English translation of the German word. *Bildung* is '[d]ifficult to translate, [but] in essence it refers to the inner development of the individual, a process of fulfillment through education and knowledge, in effect a secular search for perfection, ... an interior process whereby an individual could work on himself, or herself' (Watson, 2010: 53). In *Bildung* are to be found 'elements of education, enculturation and also realisation; the sense of fulfilling one's nature or purpose in response to the challenges of a particular historical and societal context. ... Bildung entails a dynamic world view that values independence of mind and spirit grounded in ecological and social interdependence' (Rowson, 2019: 3).

Bildung is holistic in scope, concerned with all aspects of the individual: 'humans are viewed as bio-psycho-social-spiritual organisms; ... the bio-psycho-social-spiritual process [lies] at the heart of Bildung' (Rowson, 2019: 6, 12). It is a continuous and unending process, a flow that ignores the artificial sectorisation of education systems and makes a nonsense of talk about one sector 'readying' children or young people for the next sector. Viewed from this perspective, *Bildung* is

> the way that the individual matures and takes upon him or herself ever bigger personal responsibility towards family, friends, fellow citizens, society, humanity, our globe, and the global heritage of our species, while enjoying ever bigger personal, moral and existential freedoms. It is the enculturation and life-long learning that forces us to grow and change, it is existential and emotional depth, it is life-long interaction and struggles with new knowledge, culture, art, science, new perspectives, new people, and new truths, and it is being an active citizen in adulthood. Bildung is a constant process that never ends. (Andersen and Björkman, 2017: 5)

This understanding of *Bildung* has much in common with the educational aims of the municipal schools for young children in Reggio Emilia, with their image of a human being as a protagonist who builds or creates herself or himself, and in a way that is not preordained. *Bildung* is

> an active business that entails an educator of ability who increases the individual's possibility of freedom ... One of the Enlightenment project's basic ideas was faith in humans' reasoning ability to free humans socially, politically and culturally. This emancipatory way of thinking came from the idea that all humans have the possibility to actively create knowledge and the courage to think for themselves. (Dahlberg and Lenz Taguchi, quoted in Moss, 2013: 29)

Such a concept of education – broadly conceived, emancipatory in purpose, a continuous process of formation, without predetermined outcomes (or at least, with much that is necessarily uncertain and unknown) – is a long way from the tenets of the Global Education Reform Movement and much of GERM-infected contemporary education policy, with its economistic framing and readying purpose and its focus on achieving certain predetermined, disconnected and narrowly conceived outcomes. Given the widespread influence of this impoverished and impoverishing view of education, we understand the concerns of those who are wary of putting education at the centre of an integrated early childhood system. But far richer views exist and education does not have to be this way, as many have demonstrated in practice. To state the obvious, 'education' (like 'care') is a contestable concept, with no agreed meaning: the view of education adopted is central to any transformative project.

Integration

Starting from images or understandings – first principles, you might say – we make a political choice, arguing for an early childhood system that includes *public* early childhood *education* at its core. But we would add a third defining feature: a transformed system that is *integrated*. That means integrated early childhood services, covering the seven dimensions we introduced in Chapter 3, and which have been so nearly achieved in Sweden, as we described in Chapter 5:

- Policy making and administration: within national, regional and local education departments;
- Regulation: within a single education agency or department, nationally, regionally or locally;
- Curriculum or similar pedagogical guidelines: a single curriculum from birth to at least compulsory school age;
- Access to services: a universal entitlement to access early childhood services from birth (though as most children, in our schema, would be cared for at home by parents taking parenting leave during their first year, access during this period would mainly be to activities where the young child was accompanied by a parent or other carer);
- Funding (including who pays and how payment is made): all early childhood services, as part of the education system, to be funded in the same way as compulsory schooling, that is, directly (services

rather than parents receive funding) from taxation, and to be free to attend for at least the equivalent of compulsory school hours. Parents might contribute to additional hours, but only up to a low maximum ceiling;

- Workforce (including structure, education and pay): to be adequately qualified and paid and based on a graduate[2] early childhood teacher, a specialist in working with children from birth to at least 6 years and having parity of employment conditions with school teachers; all staff required by regulation to work with children and families should have this professional qualification and conditions of employment, though staff with different specialist skills may be employed on a supernumerary basis to provide additional support where needed;

- Type of provision: multi-purpose centres for children from birth to compulsory school age, serving a defined catchment area, delivering education and a variety of other projects for children and adults, including but not limited to support for employed parents. This type of provision might be called a 'Children's Centre' or by some other name; for the remainder of this chapter we will switch from referring to 'early childhood services' to 'early childhood centres'.

What about individuals working in their own homes, namely 'family day carers', 'childminders', 'homebound educators' or similar? We think that they would have a place in a transformed system, but that over time their numbers would diminish, as has happened in Sweden. We say this for two reasons. First, the supply of women wanting to do this work will decline over time, a process already underway, at least in England. A 2022 think tank report, titled (predictably) *Better Childcare*, describes childminders in England as 'a declining profession', and notes that in the 'last 10 years, the number of childminders has halved, and the number of places has fallen by more than a quarter' (MacDonald and Kelly, 2022: 27). (The right-wing think tank that published this report sees increasing childminder numbers as playing an important role in fixing a 'constrained supply of childcare' (p. 6), which has produced a dysfunctional market in which '[c]hildcare in the UK is too expensive, and the options available to parents are too limited' (p. 6); its own perspective on early childhood services is constrained by an unquestioning adoption of a childcare discourse and a neoliberal commitment to markets).

Second, we think parents will increasingly choose to use early childhood centres, especially if they are readily accessible and as they become accustomed to attending them with their children while on parenting leave or otherwise not in employment. For the same reason, we think parents will increasingly choose centres rather than relatives; there is evidence that this has already happened in countries with well-developed early childhood centres. In 2019, according to the OECD Family Database, during a typical week parents made use of informal childcare arrangements for 36.9 per cent of children under 3 years in the UK and 21.6 per cent in Ireland, compared with less than 1 per cent in Sweden (https://www.oecd.org/els/family/database.htm: PF3.3).

Underpinning integration of these seven *structural* dimensions would be what might be termed *conceptual* integration, early childhood centres being conceptualised, as we have already set out, as multi-purpose, education-led public spaces working with an ethics of care. The integration of the early childhood system would be completed by the synchronisation of early childhood centres with parenting leave. This would mean 12 to 15 months of parenting leave, well paid, designed to promote shared use by parents, and viewed as an essential condition for achieving gender equality, work–family balance and a good childhood; this might be achieved either by leave being an individual and non-transferable entitlement, so that if one parent did not use their full entitlement, it would be lost; or by some form of incentive for families where both parents use leave, for example offering additional months of leave (O'Brien and Moss, 2020). As indicated above, early childhood centres would provide a range of activities for parents, other carers and children while parents were on leave, as well as subsequently. Once leave ended, children would be entitled to attend their local early childhood centre without being accompanied by a parent. Parenting leave would be rounded off, as in Sweden, by well-paid leave for parents to care for sick children, which would avoid conflicts of interest between children, parents and centres and further support employed parents.

While we believe that most parents would choose such an arrangement, we recognise there may be some parents who would want or need to take a shorter leave period, resuming employment or studying when their child is below 12 months of age. How this could best be accommodated within the system requires discussion and the examination of options.

Public not private

We have addressed most of the defects we see in today's early childhood systems in the Anglosphere. But one more needs to be discussed: privatisation and marketisation, or, as some have put it, the commodification of early childhood services. We want again to be very clear. We see no place for private businesses (those operated for profit) or for markets in a future public, universal, education-based and integrated system of early childhood centres.

This is not just because of the current failings in how early childhood markets and private businesses work, as discussed in Chapter 3. It is a matter of moral value and political choice; the words of the political philosopher Michael Sandel resonate with us:

> And so in the end the question of markets is really not an economic question. It's a question of how we want to live together. Do we want a society where everything is up for sale? Or are there certain moral and civil goods that markets do not honour and markets cannot buy[?] (Sandel, reported in Wintour, 2012)

To these questions we would answer respectively 'No' and 'Yes'. Markets may have their place in society, as do private businesses. But what that place should be, what 'moral and civil goods' should be excluded from marketisation, is contestable. We would agree with the conclusion of Fred Block and Margaret Somers that

> most of what makes life possible is not actually produced to be sold on the market and will be endangered by being treated as such. These are the necessities of social existence that, along with material sustenance, make it possible for us to be full members of the social world we all inhabit interdependently – above all, education, health care, a sustainable environment, personal and social security, and the right to earn a livelihood. It is when these public goods are turned into commodities and subjected to market principles that social life is threatened fundamentally and major crises ensue. According to Polanyi, these necessities of social life have to be protected from the market by social and political institutions and recognized as rights rather than commodities, or human freedom will be endangered. (Block and Somers, 2014: 8–9).

Consequently, we reject, as a moral and political choice, the whole idea that early childhood education is for sale, a private commodity to be traded in the marketplace, with its image of early childhood centres as private profit-making businesses selling to private consumers; this is quite incommensurate with our images of the child, of the parent and of early childhood services. We do not think parents are consumers, and we do not think that early childhood centres are businesses selling commodities to parents-as-consumers, an image that has no place for the child as we envisage her or him: the 'rich' child, the citizen, the subject of rights entitled to education from birth. While we are clear what early childhood centres are not, we are equally clear what we think they are: public goods, public spaces and public resources, universal and inclusive basic public services available to everyone as of right as part of a strong public domain where 'strangers encounter each other as equal partners in the common life of society, a space for forms of human flourishing which cannot be bought in the market-place' (Marquand, 2004: 27).

Strangers encountering each other as equal partners in the common life of society do so not as consumers in a market but as citizens in a democracy, for, as David Marquand further argues, 'people are consumers only in the market domain; in the public domain, they are citizens' (Marquand, 2004: 135). At the heart of our argument against marketisation and privatisation is the need to restore a strong and democratic public domain, which means diminishing the market domain and restraining (once again) capitalism, which, under the neoliberal hegemony of recent years, has broken free of social restraint and run rampant with such terrible consequences. Of course, in theory a private for-profit business could deliver a non-marketised public service under contract to a public authority. But why even consider this option? It means public funds contributing to private profits; and it means expecting a private business, whose first responsibility is inevitably towards its owner(s) and to making a profit, to work for the common weal, creating a potential conflict of interest.

But there is another reason for thinking twice before attempting to involve the private for-profit sector in a public system. Profit-seeking businesses cannot be expected to adopt the values of cooperation and equality, inclusion and democracy, which we argue for below; that is not what businesses are about, their values being inevitably about competitiveness, efficiency and return on capital, their interests focused on market share and profitability. We want instead to see publicly funded and publicly accountable centres, many directly provided by public bodies, working together cooperatively in local networks, and complemented by a competent system of individuals and organisations providing to centres and to their networks varied forms of support and opportunities for experimentation, innovation and development.

To state this is not to blame or criticise businesses, but to emphasise that they are not public services and cannot aspire to being democratic organisations. With values and interests at odds, participation of the private for-profit sector in a public system is likely to lead to constant friction between the public system and participating businesses, with the very real danger of the latter, by their demands and lobbying, constantly undermining and weakening the former. An example comes from Canada. As we saw in Chapter 3, the federal government has initiated a Canada-wide Early Learning and Child Care (CWELCC) Plan, with the intention of increasing the number of places, improving workforce conditions and reducing fees to parents. There is also an intention of focusing the expansion of services on the public and not-for-profit private sectors. In an article titled 'Give them an inch and they'll take a mile: The story of for-profit child care in Ontario' (Cleveland, 2022), the economist Gordon Cleveland describes the results of implementing the CWELCC Plan in Canada's most populous province, following the provincial government's signing of an agreement with the federal government to gain access to the new federal funding. In this Ontario–Canada Canada-wide Early Learning and Child Care Agreement, the province has 'committed itself to the vision of building a largely not-for-profit system of accessible, affordable, inclusive child care services of high quality with federal money'.

Cleveland describes how the Ontario provincial government wanted for-profit 'child care operators' to opt into the CWELCC system, and so has 'bent over backwards to accommodate' them, conceding much ground on the conditions they must meet in return for public funds. This leads to a situation where fees

> in no way validate the costs and earnings [of for-profit providers] that are covered by the new government revenues. There is effectively no reporting on what these costs and earnings are. There is no way to calculate the amount of surplus taken by operators, or to see how it is used. ... No requirement for reporting on how the public funds they receive are spent until well into 2024. Even then, only a requirement for an annual audit. No need to justify the salaries paid to management. No need to justify the profits they claim each year, which are built into the fees they charge. (Cleveland, 2022)

Cleveland observes that this is 'the way the for-profit operators like it. ... They don't want detailed accountability for the public funds they receive.' He concedes that, from 'an economic point of view, the position of the for-profit operators is quite rational'. However, the operators' demands are 'just not very good for Ontario children, families and for the building of a financially accountable child care system'.

It is important to remember that Canada is the Anglosphere country with the lowest penetration of for-profit providers into the early childhood system. The influence of this sector, therefore, is likely to be far stronger in other countries.

Values

We have already touched on the question of ethics for the transformed system, indicating the important role that could be played across all services by the adoption of an ethics of care. That would not necessarily preclude working with other ethical approaches. We would welcome more discussion of such approaches, as ethics seems to us to be of critical importance to early childhood education (indeed to all education), yet has received far too little attention in policy-making, research and discussion.

We would also argue that the transformed system should be founded on clear values, and not those that pervade contemporary neoliberal-influenced systems, such as competition, individual choice and calculation. We have already indicated two that we find important: cooperation, closely related to solidarity, and gender equality, which we would extend to equality in general. There are two others we consider equally important.

The first is inclusion, that is, ensuring that the early childhood system includes every child and every family, with no eligibility or other conditions that could mean, for example, that some families missed out on parenting leave or were unable to attend early childhood services alongside their fellow citizens.

The second is democracy, where we join a long tradition of viewing democracy and education as closely linked. For example, education has been seen as a means of renewing democracy, a view expressed in the famous words of John Dewey: 'Democracy has to be born anew every generation, and education is its midwife' (Dewey, 1980: 10:139). One way education can contribute to this goal is by supporting the formation of the democratic citizen, able to think critically and to participate fully in society. That task and the more general role of education in democratic rebirth or renewal is particularly urgent today, given the 40 years' erosion of democracy in our societies by a hostile neoliberalism and inimical marketisation, while a vibrant and participatory democracy is one important condition for effective societal responses to the converging crises of our times.

We will not go in great detail into what democracy as a value would mean in early childhood systems. We offer just a few pointers here, and direct those who want to go deeper to a number of publications specifically about democracy in early childhood education (see, for example, Moss, 2009, 2021; Sousa, 2020; Sousa and Moss, 2023). There is a much larger literature about democratic education in compulsory schooling.

We understand democracy as having a number of dimensions. It is about a way of governing at multiple levels (from the classroom right up to national level), and including decision-making (from macro-decisions such as allocating resources and making policies to micro-decisions about everyday life), managing public services (including the democratic or social management of early childhood centres), and service accountability (the idea of democratic accountability as opposed to managerial accounting). Important issues here may include: determining what constitutes the public or common good; the application of multiple methods for 'listening' and otherwise enabling wide participation among children and adults; and the importance of equality as an enabling condition, for in a 'fully democratic society, all people would have broadly equal access to the necessary means to participate meaningfully in decisions about things which affect their lives' (Wright, 2012: [7]).

But we can also understand democracy in other ways – which are not either/or but and … and … and. Democracy can be a way of life and of living together, indeed a relational ethics to complement an ethics of care. This was the way the American philosopher John Dewey thought of democracy, describing it as 'more than a form of government; it is primarily a mode of associated living, of conjoint communicated experience' (Dewey, 1980: 9:93), and as 'a way of life controlled by a working faith … in the capacity of human beings for intelligent judgment and action if proper conditions are furnished' (Dewey, 1939: 2).

The French pedagogue and education reformer Célestin Freinet also saw democracy in relational terms, but understood it as a way of opening up possibilities for change: democracy, he wrote, could be viewed as 'a space for valuing diversity and heterogeneity, as a form of participation and cooperation, and as a means to create innovative reflections and transformative practices in education and society' (Sousa, 2020: 152–3). The Brazilian philosopher Roberto Unger develops this idea of democracy providing opportunities for innovation and transformation when he introduces the concept of 'democratic experimentalism' in public services, whose provision, he argues,

> must be an innovative collective practice, …. [That can no longer be] by the mechanical transmission of innovation from the top. It can only happen through the organisation of a collective experimental

practice from below. ... Democracy is not just one more terrain for the institutional innovation that I advocate. It is the most important terrain. (Unger, 2005: 179, 182)

We are attracted to the ideal of an integrated system of early childhood education as one that encourages and enables experimentation, in pedagogy and in projects undertaken, with a strong element of democratic experimentalism.

We would add one final point about democracy in early childhood, or any education. Rather than democracy being treated as a subject to be taught, it should be approached as a disposition to be acquired and nurtured through doing: it should be a lived experience, what Tom Bentley describes as 'everyday democracy' in 'everyday institutions', which is

> the practice of self-government through the choices, commitments and connections of daily life. Everyday democracy means extending democratic power and responsibility simultaneously to the settings of everyday life. ... *It means that people can actively create the world in which they live*. (Bentley, 2005: 20, 21; emphasis added)

This is democracy as an everyday culture, as a lived experience, as a value, ethics and practice of a democratic community.

We have set out above how we would like to see early childhood systems in the Anglosphere transformed, while emphasising that we do not claim a monopoly of wisdom and good ideas. What we do want to insist on is the urgent need for the Anglosphere countries to think critically about the systems they have, challenge taken-for-granted assumptions, consider alternatives, and expand the menu of the possible. This requires a process of public deliberation, with wide participation informed (and provoked) by a comparative, cross-national approach. The end result should be a clear vision of and convincing rationale for the transformed system that has been chosen, and a clear process and timeline for making the vision a reality.

What about the pedagogy?

We have focused in this chapter, indeed in the whole book, on systems and on the need for systemic transformation. We have had far less to say about pedagogy, what goes on in the educational projects of transformed systems, whether it be content (including curriculum), methods of working, or assessment. With what understandings and in what ways does or should a fully integrated and universal public early childhood system conduct its education?

To this we would reply, 'It depends.' For, where that system is imbued with democratic values, answers to that question should be the product of democratic dialogue and deliberation, deliberation that accepts that there is no one correct answer to the questions posed by education. That is why Loris Malaguzzi argued that

> pedagogy is not totally cultural, and that politics plays the role it has to play, so that our discourse inevitably is also always a political discourse whether we know it or not. It is about working with cultural choices, but it clearly also means working with political choices. (Malaguzzi, cited in Cagliari, Castagnetti et al., 2016: 267)

Our hope is that the transformed system, including the values with which it is inscribed, would be supportive of such political discourse and such choices about pedagogy and related matters of content, and that the system, with its well-educated workforce, cooperative ethos and competent supportive systems, would be conducive to the introduction and implementation of whatever political choices were arrived at. The experience of Aotearoa New Zealand, with its innovative curriculum and methods of assessment, gives some support to such hopes. It is similar in Sweden, where the pedagogical thinking and ways of working in the early childhood education of Reggio Emilia have been inspirational and widely disseminated among the country's pre-schools and well-qualified pre-school workforce:

> Reggio Emilia, a Mecca in northern Italy for thousands of Swedish preschool teachers and commissions, committees and ministers, had developed a preschool pedagogy that had become an important and extensive source of inspiration for the Swedish preschool. ... This contains the fundamental characteristics which are also part of Swedish preschool pedagogy – the child as an active, competent and exploring being, project and theme oriented working approaches, and the democratic perspective on the child's acquisition of knowledge and learning ..., but in a more audacious and sharper form. (Korpi, 2016: 64)

But, important as the influence of Reggio Emilia has been, the Swedish system has enabled pedagogical work informed by other theories and practices; one could say it is a country with a uniform system and diverse pedagogies.

Thinking the unthinkable

There is never a good time for transformative change, disruptive as it is bound to be. Countries like Sweden and Aotearoa New Zealand, which began their transformations decades ago, have done all or some of the heavy lifting that is needed, for example reforming their workforces. The progress both countries have made shows that it can be done, given time, money and sustained political will, including ensuring that members of existing workforces can participate in and benefit from the transformation. England's experience with Children's Centres and Sweden's in replacing nurseries and kindergartens with pre-schools likewise demonstrates how fragmented and dysfunctional services can be redesigned, again given time, money and political will.

Perhaps the most challenging task in the implementation of the transformed system we have proposed is to de-privatise the existing system. This means removing for-profit 'childcare' services from the system and replacing them with new forms of multi-purpose, education-based centres, both public and community-based, and de-marketising, replacing markets in which providers compete for customers and seek to maximise profit rather than to meet needs with networks of collaborating services whose distribution is decided by public bodies in the public interest. Even raising this as a possibility can seem like thinking the unthinkable, but the starting point for transformation must be to think about, and recognise the legitimacy of, alternatives, alternatives we may find functioning examples of in other countries, or imagine as a precursor to experimentation. This means recognising that neoliberalism has 'blinded the public to alternatives by deliberately confining the boundaries of public debate', and that we have all, to a greater or lesser extent, embodied neoliberalism's ideas about, on the one hand, what is normal and self-evident and, on the other, what is 'unrealistic' or 'off the wall'.

Irina Domurath, a Chilean academic, has written about how this process of normalising neoliberal values, assumptions and images has worked in Chile. She describes her country as a 'neoliberal laboratory' following a military coup in September 1973, backed by the United

States, which 'implemented a neoliberal experiment' that made the military regime headed by General Augusto Pinochet a 'forerunner of marketisation and privatisation in Latin America – in healthcare, education, pensions, housing and so on':

> When a state has abrogated responsibility for the wellbeing of its citizens and those citizens have internalised the rationale that everyone is the architect of their own future, the social contract breaks down.
>
> There is no (legitimate) state any more – only an administrative organ. There are no longer citizens. What remain are individuals, wolves among wolves, distrustful of each other, void of feelings of solidarity, void of hope for change. (Domurath, 2022)

Similarly, in relation to early childhood services, the Anglosphere has come to accept the following as normal and self-evident:

- that these important public services should be provided for profit by businesses competing in a market;
- that there are no longer citizens, including young children with a universal right to education, only consumers needing to purchase a commodity of 'childcare';
- that there should be separate 'childcare' services for some children;
- that children should be economised and subjected to 'readyfication', where preparing or readying children for the next stage of education becomes a major pedagogical goal;
- that people working in these services should be treated as cheap labour; and
- that there is no hope of fundamental change.

But there is hope, because alternatives are possible and the world never stays still: what goes up inevitably – eventually – comes down again. Susan George (1999) reminds us: 'In 1945 or 1950, if you had seriously proposed any of the ideas and policies in today's standard neo-liberal toolkit, you would have been laughed off the stage … or sent off to the insane asylum.' So, it is short-sighted and ahistorical to think anything is unthinkable; as Milton Friedman, one of the godfathers of neoliberalism, once famously remarked, it is important to develop and sustain alternatives to be ready for when 'the politically impossible becomes politically inevitable' (Friedman, 1982: ix), acknowledging that the time for change always comes round; as we have already suggested, that time is approaching, as the end of the neoliberal hegemony is nigh.

We need to be ready. Once we dare think the unthinkable, we can begin to imagine and discuss and plan for how the unthinkable might actually happen. How might de-privatisation and de-marketisation be brought about? How might we drop 'childcare' services and ditch the 'childcare discourse'? How might we create parenting leave, indeed leave policies spanning the life-course that promote gender equality and a more satisfying relationship between employment and care responsibilities? How might we move from dysfunctional systems to systems that are fit for a world that aspires to be more just and equal, more democratic and solidaristic?

And it is important to remember that thinking the unthinkable is going on elsewhere too. We can place de-privatisation of early childhood services in a wider context: that of a movement to bring a range of basic services that have been privatised back into the public domain. 'Public Futures' is a research collaboration between the Transnational Institute and the University of Glasgow: its premise is that '[p]rocesses of bringing essential services and infrastructure into public ownership are taking place across the globe'. Its website (https://publicfutures.org/) collects information on examples of such de-privatisation, with over 1,700 examples worldwide to date, though none, so far, in the field of education.

The driver for the de-privatisation of early childhood services and the building of a public system is political will. But the lever for change is public funding. In the case of early childhood services this does not mean using public funds to buy services back into public hands. Rather, it involves public subsidies that now go to private, for-profit providers, and have lured many businesses and their financial backers to enter the market for childcare provision, being used instead to rebuild and support a public system. As a first step, public funding might no longer be available to new for-profit providers, as Canada is attempting to do with its recent federal funding initiative. Then subsequently, over time, public funding might be gradually withdrawn from existing private, for-profit 'childcare' providers, and increasingly transferred to a system of public services – inclusive and democratic, education-led and multi-purpose, publicly provided or community-based – as these are developed. What 'over time' might mean is open to debate, but we suggest a 10-year transition period as a basis for discussion.

What might happen to existing for-profit providers, who would face this gradual withdrawal of public funding over the transition period? De-privatisation does not mean they would be closed down by fiat or taken into public ownership; it means that they would be outside the emerging public system. In these conditions, some might decide to go entirely private, catering as private schools do in England to a privileged, affluent elite; this is the antithesis of an inclusive public system, but not a development that can be prohibited. Others might decide, and be able, to transfer to non-profit status and so become part of the public system, if they were able to meet stringent conditions. Some would go out of business in any case over the transition period, since even in current conditions there is a constant churn of new 'childcare' providers entering the market and existing ones dropping out; for example, in England between 1 April 2021 and 31 March 2022 around 14 per cent of 'childcare providers' left the sector, leading to a net loss of around 4,000 (6 per cent) providers (Ofsted, 2022b: Figures 8 and 5).[3] This would leave some that would decide to pack up and leave the business altogether, assessing their centres to be no longer viable in a changed funding environment.

All these considerations, it should be added, are set against a backdrop of the increasing consolidation of private for-profit provision in the hands of large corporate businesses, with their private equity and other financial backers in search of high returns on investment. Anglosphere countries need to confront this trend and ask: Is this what we really want for our children, families and communities?

With de-privatisation would go de-marketisation, assuming that our societies chose to build collaborative networks of mutually supportive public services and not maintain or introduce competition between private services. Places in early childhood centres would be allocated on the presumption that children and families attended their local service, unless there was a very strong reason for an alternative placement. In other words, the local centre would be the default placement.

An interesting indicator of how this turn away from prioritising parental choice and market competition might work in practice comes from a comparison of the contrasting allocation policies in England and Scotland for compulsory schooling; England, unlike Scotland, prioritises parental choice. In this situation, where approaches to school choice have diverged substantially in the past 35 years,

Around 90 per cent of Scottish children attend the catchment secondary school allocated to them by their local authority, most of them by default, and only a small minority actively apply to an alternative. However in England all families are expected to apply to between three and six schools, with the result that only half of children attend their nearest secondary school. ... While choice is generally seen as a good thing, the Scottish system seems to provide adequate opportunity to offer a preference for most families, and satisfaction is similar if not higher north of the border. At the same time, English families tend to be more stressed, anxious, harassed and regretful than their Scottish counterparts. School choice policies have been more psychologically toxic than their originators might have imagined. (Battacharyah, 2023: 60)

In other words, while most parents want to feel they could exercise some choice if needed, and this should remain a possibility, the great majority would probably opt for a good, local service where that was the default position. To this we might add that choice does not have to be exercised only individually; participation in a school or other service run democratically also enables choice to be exercised, but through collective deliberation and decision-making.

Given the extensive evidence that 'childcare' markets do not work particularly well in their own terms, and often work perversely to the advantage of those with more resources, de-marketisation would not represent the loss of a successful mechanism but the discarding of a rather unsuccessful experiment. Moreover, non-marketised networks of public services would not simply be left to their own devices, to sink or swim as best they can. Competent systems and collaborative networks of services would provide external overview and support, while parents' influence would be felt through their participation in democratic management of services.

On that note we come to the end of our enquiry into the early childhood systems in the Anglosphere. We reach this point with mixed emotions: frustration and some sorrow at how things are today; some understanding mixed with anger at how things have got to where they are and why change is not readily achievable; some excitement when we can see clearly that those things could be made different, especially when that vision is informed by actual examples; and some hope that the times are right and ripe for deep change. On the other hand there is also anxiety that we may be overwhelmed by the converging crises of our times rather than being able to muster the resources and other conditions to bring about that deep change.

Notes

1   Vea Vecchi, an *atelierista* from Reggio Emilia, has explained the theory of the hundred languages of children in the following way:

> In Reggio pedagogy, a choice has been made to extend the term language beyond the verbal and consider *languages* as the different ways used by human beings to express themselves; visual language, mathematical language, scientific language, etc. In a conversation on the relationship between pedagogy and atelier, Claudia Giudici, pedagogista, puts it like this, 'When we speak of languages we refer to the different ways children (human beings) represent, communicate and express their thinking in different media and symbolic systems; languages, therefore, are the many fonts or geneses of knowledge'. *Poetic languages* are forms of expression strongly characterized by expressive or aesthetic aspects such as music, song, dance or photography. (Vecchi, 2010: 9)

2   By 'graduate' we mean having a qualification at ISCED 6, bachelor's or equivalent level, and having parity of qualification with primary school teachers.

3   This period includes the disruption caused by the Covid pandemic. However, the number of 'childcare providers' leaving the sector was higher in each year between 2015–16 and 2019–20 than in 2021–2; most leavers will have been childminders rather than group settings but there is no breakdown of providers leaving by type of provider or the number of places lost in each type of provision (Ofsted, 2022b).

References

Andersen, L.R. and Björkman, T. (2017) *The Nordic Secret: A European story of beauty and freedom*. Stockholm: Fri Tanke.

Archer, N. and Oppenheim, C. (2021) *The Role of Early Childhood Education and Care in Shaping Life Chances: The changing face of early childhood in the UK*. London: Nuffield Foundation. Online. https://www.nuffieldfoundation.org/wp-content/uploads/2021/10/Role-early-childhood-education-care-life-chances-Nuffield-Foundation.pdf (accessed 31 October 2023).

ASX (n.d.) 'Investing in A-REITs'. Online. https://www2.asx.com.au/investors/learn-about-our-investment-solutions/a-reits (accessed 25 October 2023).

Australian Associated Press (2022) 'Australia needs 16,000 new educators to fill shortfall in childcare sector, inquiry told'. *The Guardian*, 31 October. Online. https://www.theguardian.com/australia-news/2022/oct/31/australia-needs-16000-new-educators-to-fill-shortfall-in-child-care-sector-inquiry-told#:~:text=1%20month%20old-Australia%20needs%2016%2C000%20new%20educators%20to,in%20childcare%20sector%2C%20inquiry%20told&text=Australia%20will%20need%20to%20hire,pledged%20billions%20in%20childcare%20subsidies (accessed 25 October 2023).

Australian Children's Education & Care Quality Authority (2018) 'National Quality Standard'. Online. https://www.acecqa.gov.au/nqf/national-quality-standard#:~:text=The%20National%20Quality%20Standard%20(NQS,are%20important%20outcomes%20for%20children (accessed 15 January 2024).

Australian Competition and Consumer Authority (2023) 'Review of childcare policy to better meet the needs of families'. Online. https://www.accc.gov.au/media-release/review-of-childcare-policy-to-better-meet-the-needs-of-families (accessed 13 January 2024).

Australian Productivity Commission (2023) *A Path to Universal Early Childhood Education and Care*. Draft report. Online. https://www.pc.gov.au/inquiries/current/childhood/draft#:~:text=Media%20release-,A%20path%20to%20universal%20early%20childhood%20education%20and%20care,to%20a%20Productivity%20Commission%20report (accessed 13 January 2024).

Ball, S.J. (2003) 'The teacher's soul and the terrors of performativity'. *Journal of Education Policy*, 18 (2), 215–28. https://doi.org/10.1080/0268093022000043065.

Ball, S.J. (2020) 'Preface'. In G. Roberts-Holmes and P. Moss, *Neoliberalism and Early Childhood Education*. Abingdon: Routledge, xv–xviii.

Battacharyah, A. (2023) 'School choice in Scotland and England: Divergent paths and different destinations'. *FORUM*, 65 (1), 55–62. https://doi.org/10.3898/forum.2023.65.1.08.

Beach, J. and Ferns, C. (2015) 'From child care market to child care system'. *Policy Alternatives*, Summer 2015, 53–61.

Beck, U. (1998) *Democracy without Enemies*, trans. M. Ritter. Cambridge: Polity Press.

Becker, G. (2002) 'Human capital'. Paper given at the University of Montevideo. Online. http://www2.um.edu.uy/acid/Family_Economics/Becker%20-%20Family%20%26%20Human%20Capital.pdf (accessed 25 October 2023).

Beckert, J. (2020) 'The exhausted futures of neoliberalism: From promissory legitimacy to social anomy'. *Journal of Cultural Economy*, 13 (3), 318–30. https://doi.org/10.1080/17530350.2019.1574867.

Bengtsson, H. (2022) 'Sweden: Less special than it was'. *Social Europe*, 23 September. Online. https://socialeurope.eu/sweden-less-special-than-it-was (accessed 25 October 2023).

Bentley, T. (2005) *Everyday Democracy: Why we get the politicians we deserve*. London: Demos.

Berger, I., Ashton, E., Lehrer, J. and Piginhi, M. (2022) 'Slowing, desiring, haunting, hospicing, and longing for change: Thinking with snails in Canadian early childhood education and care'. *In Education*, 28 (1b), 6–21. https://doi.org/10.37119/ojs2022.v28i1b.658.

Berger, P. and Luckmann, T. (1966) *The Social Construction of Reality: A treatise in the sociology of knowledge*. Garden City, NY: Doubleday.

Bernheim, D. and Whinston, M. (2008) *Microeconomics*. Boston, MA: McGraw-Hill Irwin.

Biden, J. (2022) 'Remarks of President Joe Biden: State of the Union address as prepared for delivery'. Online. https://www.whitehouse.gov/state-of-the-union-2022/ (accessed 25 October 2023).

Blakeley, G. and Quilter-Pinner, H. (2019) 'Who cares? The financialisation of adult social care'. Institute for Public Policy Research briefing paper, London. Online. https://www.ippr.org/files/2019-09/who-cares-financialisation-in-social-care-2-.pdf (accessed 25 October 2023).

Block, F. and Somers, M. (1984) 'Beyond the economistic fallacy: The holistic social science of Karl Polanyi'. In T. Skocpol (ed.), *Vision and Method in Historical Sociology*. Cambridge: Cambridge University Press, 47–84.

Block, F. and Somers, M. (2014) *The Power of Market Fundamentalism: Karl Polanyi's critique*. Cambridge, MA: Harvard University Press.

Borger, J. (2023) 'Doomsday Clock at record 90 seconds to midnight amid Ukraine crisis'. *The Guardian*, 24 January. Online. https://www.theguardian.com/world/2023/jan/24/doomsday-clock-at-record-90-seconds-to-midnight-amid-ukraine-crisis (accessed 25 October 2023).

Bouchal, P. and Norris, E. (2014) 'Implementing Sure Start children's centres'. Online. https://www.instituteforgovernment.org.uk/sites/default/files/publications/Implementing%20Sure%20Start%20Childrens%20Centres%20-%20final_0.pdf (accessed 7 November 2023).

Bouve, C. (2010) *L'Utopie des crèches françaises au XIXᵉ siècle. Le pari sur l'enfant pauvre*. Berne: Peter Lang.

Brannen, J. and Moss, P. (1991*) Managing Mothers: Dual earner households after maternity leave*. London: Unwin Hyman.

Brannen, J. and Moss, P. (1998) 'The polarisation and intensification of parental employment in Britain: Consequences for children, families and the community'. *Community, Work & Family*, 1 (3), 229–47. https://doi.org/10.1080/13668809808414234.

Brennan, D., Cass, B., Himmelweit, S. and Szebehely, M. (2012) 'The marketisation of care: Rationales and consequences in Nordic and liberal care regimes'. *Journal of European Social Policy*, 22 (4), 377–91. https://doi.org/10.1177/0958928712449772.

Brind, R., Norden, O., McGinigal, S., Garnett, E. and Oseman, D. with La Valle, I. and Jelicic, H. (2011) *Childcare and Early Years Providers Survey 2010*. London: Department for Education. Online. https://assets.publishing.service.gov.uk/government/uploads/system/uploads/attachment_data/file/219458/osr17-2011.pdf (accessed 26 October 2023).

Broadhead, P., Meleady, C. and Delgado, M.A. (2008) *Children, Families and Communities: Creating and sustaining integrated services*. Maidenhead: Open University Press.

Brown, W. (2016) 'Sacrificial citizenship: Neoliberalism, human capital and austerity politics'. *Constellations*, 23 (1), 3–14. https://doi.org/10.1111/1467-8675.12166.

Bryant, L. (2022) 'Three things I'd fix as Australia's (fantasy) minister for early education and childcare'. *The Guardian*, 6 June. Online. https://www.theguardian.com/commentisfree/2022/jun/06/three-things-id-fix-as-australias-fantasy-minister-for-early-education-and-childcare (accessed 26 October 2023).

Burns, J. (1999) *Kindergarten and Primary Teachers: A comparison of their work*. Wellington: New Zealand Educational Institute.

Bushouse, B. (2008) *Early Childhood Education Policy in Aotearoa/New Zealand: The creation of the 20 Hours Free programme*. Wellington: Fulbright New Zealand. Online. https://www.fulbright.org.nz/wp-content/uploads/2011/12/axford2008_bushouse.pdf (accessed 26 October 2023).

Busy Bees (2024) 'Expanding our portfolio'. Busy Bees Nurseries. Online. https://www.busybeeschildcare.co.uk/expanding-our-portfolio (accessed 9 January 2024).

Butler, J. (2022) '"The aspiration of universal childcare": Anne Aly on what drives Labor's ambitious plans'. *The Guardian*, 13 June. Online. https://www.theguardian.com/australia-news/2022/jun/14/the-aspiration-of-universal-childcare-anne-aly-on-what-drives-labors-ambitious-plans (accessed 26 October 2023).

Cabinet Policy Committee (New Zealand) (2004). *Minute of decision. Early childhood funding: proposed new system*. 31 March. Cabinet Office, released under the Official Information Act.

Cagliari, P., Barozzi, A. and Giudici, C. (2004) 'Thoughts, theories and experiences for an educational project with participation'. *Children in Europe*, 6 (March), 28–30.

Cagliari, P., Castagnetti, M., Giudici, C., Rinaldi, C., Vecchi, V. and Moss, P. (eds) (2016) *Loris Malaguzzi and the Schools of Reggio Emilia: A selection of his writings and speeches 1945–1993*. Abingdon: Routledge.

Cameron, K. and Boyles, D. (2022) 'Learning and teaching in a neoliberal era: The tensions of engaging in Froebelian-informed pedagogy while encountering quality standards'. *Global Education Review*, 9 (2), 99–117.

Carr, M. (2001) *Assessment in Early Childhood Settings: Learning stories*. London: Paul Chapman Publishing.

Carr, M., Cowie, B., Gerrity, R., Jones, C., Lee, W. and Pohio, L. (2001) 'Democratic learning and teaching communities in early childhood: Can assessment play a role?' In B. Webber and L. Mitchell (eds), *Early Childhood Education for a Democratic Society*. Wellington: New Zealand Council for Educational Research, 27–36.

Carr, M., Lee, W. and Jones, C., advised and assisted by Walker, R. and Cowie, B. (2004–9) *Kei Tua o te Pae/Assessment for Learning: Early childhood exemplars*, 20 books. Wellington: Learning Media for the Ministry of Education. https://www.education.govt.nz/early-childhood/teaching-and-learning/assessment-for-learning/kei-tua-o-te-pae-2/ (accessed 15 January 2024).

Carr, M. and May, H. (1992) *Te Whāriki, early childhood curriculum guidelines*. Early Childhood Curriculum Project. Hamilton, New Zealand: Waikato University.

Carr, M. and May, H. (1993) *Te Whāriki curriculum papers*. Early Childhood Curriculum Project. Hamilton, New Zealand: Waikato University.

Carr, M., May, H., Podmore, V., Cubey, P., Hatherly, A. and Macartney, B. (2000). *Learning and Teaching Stories: Action research on evaluation in early childhood education*. Wellington: New Zealand Council for Educational Research.

Carr, M. and Mitchell, L. (2010) 'Young thrive with skilled teachers'. *NZ Herald*, 24 June. Online. https://www.nzherald.co.nz/nz/education/young-thrive-with-skilled-teachers/6AIFRWTYAR5YTSTHHSHVCWJ5WI/?c_id=466&objectid=10654148 (accessed 16 January 2024).

Chambers, J., Clare, J. and Aly, Anne (2023) 'Productivity Commission inquiry to consider universal early education system'. Media release, 9 February. Online. https://ministers.treasury.gov.au/ministers/jim-chalmers-2022/media-releases/productivity-commission-inquiry-consider-universal-early (accessed 3 November 2023).

Child Poverty Action Group (2003) *Our Children: The priority for policy* (2nd edn). Online. https://www.cpag.org.nz/publications-clone-1701161639419/our-children-priority-for-policy-cpag-2003?rq=our%20children%3A%20the%20priority%20for%20policy (accessed 13 January 2024).

Childcare Research and Resource Unit (2022) 'What now for child care?' Online. https://childcarecanada.org/resources/issue-files/what-now-child-care (accessed 27 October 2023).

Chomsky, N. and Waterstone, M. (2021*) Consequences of Capitalism: Manufacturing discontent and resistance*. Chicago, IL: Haymarket Books.

Chronholm, A. (2009) 'Sweden: Individualisation or free choice in parental leave?' In S. Kamerman and P. Moss (eds), *The Politics of Parental Leave Policies: Children, parenting, gender and the labour market*. Bristol: Policy Press, 227–42.

Citizens Information (2023) 'Your childcare options'. Online. https://www.citizensinformation.ie/en/education/pre_school_education_and_childcare/your_childcare_options.html (accessed 2 November 2023).

Clarkin-Phillips, J. (2016) Fighting the odds to make it even: Mapping an affordance ecosystem in a kindergarten community'. PhD thesis, University of Waikato. Online. https://researchcommons.waikato.ac.nz/bitstream/handle/10289/9991/thesis.pdf?sequence=3&isAllowed=y (accessed 27 October 2023).

Cleveland, G. (2022) 'Give them an inch and they'll take a mile: The story of for-profit child care in Ontario'. Childcarepolicy.net, 25 October. Online. https://childcarepolicy.net/give-them-an-inch-and-theyll-take-a-mile-the-story-of-for-profit-child-care-in-ontario%EF%BF%BC/ (accessed 27 October 2023).

Cleveland, G., Forer, B., Hyatt, D., Japel, C. and Krashinsky, M. (2008) 'New evidence about child care in Canada: Use patterns, affordability and quality'. *IRPP Choices*, 14 (12). Online. https://irpp.org/wp-content/uploads/assets/research/family-policy/new-evidence-about-child-care-in-canada/vol14no12.pdf (accessed 27 October 2023).

Cohen, B., Moss, P., Petrie, P. and Wallace, J. (2004) *A New Deal for Children? Re-forming education and care in England, Scotland and Sweden*. Bristol: Policy Press.

Cohen, B., Moss, P., Petrie, P. and Wallace, J. (2018) '"A New Deal for Children?" – what happened next: A cross-national study of transferring early childhood services into education'. *Early Years*, 41 (2–3), 110–27. https://doi.org/10.1080/09575146.2018.1504753.

Consultative Committee on Pre-school Educational Services (1947) *Report of the Consultative Committee on Pre-school Educational Services.* Wellington: Department of Education.

Coote, A. and Percy, A. (2020) *The Case for Universal Basic Services.* Cambridge: Polity.

Council of Australian Governments ([2020]) *Belonging, Being & Becoming: The Early Years Learning Framework for Australia.* Online. https://www.acecqa.gov.au/sites/default/files/2020-05/belonging_being_and_becoming_the_early_years_learning_framework_for_australia.pdf (accessed 27 October 2023).

Cowan, K. and Flewitt, R. (2020) 'Towards valuing children's signs of learning'. In C. Cameron and P. Moss (eds), *Transforming Early Childhood in England: Towards a democratic education.* London: UCL Press, 119–33.

d'Agnese, V. (2018) *Reclaiming Education in the Age of PISA: Challenging OECD's educational order.* Abingdon: Routledge.

Dahlberg, G. (2000a) 'Early childhood pedagogy in a changing world: A practice-oriented research project troubling dominant discourses'. In New Zealand Educational Institute (ed.), *Policy, Practice and Politics: Te Riu Roa Early Childhood Millennium Conference proceedings.* Wellington: New Zealand Educational Institute, 7–26.

Dahlberg, G. (2000b) 'From the "people's" home – Folkhemmet – to the enterprise: Reflections and reconstitution of the field of early childhood pedagogy in Sweden'. In T.S. Popkewitz (ed.), *Educational Knowledge: Changing relationships between the state, civil society and the educational community.* Albany, NY: State University of New York Press, 201–20.

Dahlberg, G., Moss, P. and Pence, A. (2013) *Beyond Quality in Early Childhood Education and Care: Languages of evaluation,* 3rd edn. Abingdon: Routledge.

Davison, C. (1998) 'Kindergartens and their removal from the State Sector Act'. *New Zealand Annual Review of Education,* 7, 151–67.

Davison, C. and Mitchell, L. (2009) 'The role of the state in early childhood education: Kindergartens as a case study of changing relationships'. *New Zealand Annual Review of Education/Te arotake a tau ao te matauranga i Aotearoa,* 18, 123–41. https://doi.org/10.26686/nzaroe.v0i18.1550.

Deeming, C. (2017) 'The lost and the new "liberal world" of welfare capitalism: A critical assessment of Gøsta Esping-Andersen's *The Three Worlds of Welfare Capitalism* a quarter century later'. *Social Policy & Society,* 16 (3), 405–22. https://doi.org/10.1017/S1474746415000676.

Department for Education (England) (2019) 'Number of children's centres, 2003 to 2019: Annual figures for the number of children's centres from 2003 to 2019'. Online. https://assets.publishing.service.gov.uk/government/uploads/system/uploads/attachment_data/file/844752/Number_of_Children_s_Centres_2003_to_2019_Nov2019.pdf (accessed 27 October 2023).

Department for Education (England) (2021) 'Survey of childcare and early year providers: Main summary, England, 2021'. Online. https://assets.publishing.service.gov.uk/government/uploads/system/uploads/attachment_data/file/1039675/Main_summary_survey_of_childcare_and_early_years_providers_2021.pdf (accessed 27 October 2023).

Department for Education (England) (2023a) 'Early Years Foundation Stage Profile: 2024 handbook'. Online. https://assets.publishing.service.gov.uk/government/uploads/system/uploads/attachment_data/file/1109972/Early_Years_Foundation_Stage_profile_2023_handbook.pdf (accessed 15 January 2024).

Department for Education (England) (2023b) 'Statutory framework for the early years foundation stage: Setting the standards for learning, development and care for children from birth to five'. Online. https://assets.publishing.service.gov.uk/media/65aa5e42ed27ca001327b2c7/EYFS_statutory_framework_for_group_and_school_based_providers.pdf (accessed 27 October 2023).

Department for Education (England) (2024) 'Early years foundation stage (EYFS) statutory framework'. Online. https://www.gov.uk/government/publications/early-years-foundation-stage-framework--2 (accessed 15 January 2024).

Department for Education and Employment (England) (1998) *Meeting the Childcare Challenge: A framework and consultation document.* London: The Stationery Office.

Department for Education and Skills (England) (2005) *Extended Schools: Access to opportunities and services for all: A prospectus.* Online. https://dera.ioe.ac.uk/id/eprint/6326/7/Extended-schools%20prospectus_Redacted.pdf (accessed 10 December 2023).

Department for Education and Skills (England), Department for Work and Pensions, HM Treasury and Women & Equality Unit (2002) 'Inter-Departmental Childcare Review – November 2002: Delivering for children and families'. Online. http://dera.ioe.ac.uk/8814/2/su%20children. pdf (accessed 27 October 2023).

Department of Children, Equality, Disability, Integration and Youth (Ireland) (2022) 'Minister O'Gorman launches "Together for Better" new funding model for Early Learning and Care and School Age Childcare as Core Funding contracts begin for 4,000 services'. 15 September (updated 18 October). Online. https://www.gov.ie/en/press-release/2c040-minister-ogorman-launches-together-for-better-new-funding-model-for-early-learning-and-care-and-school-age-childcare-as-core-funding-contracts-begin-for-4000-services/# (accessed 9 January 2024).

Department of Children, Equality, Disability, Integration and Youth (Ireland) (2023) 'What is a City/County Childcare Committee?' Online. https://myccc.ie/#:~:text=City%20and%20County%20Childcare%20Committees&text=A%20key%20role%20of%20the,child%2Dcentered%20and%20partnership%20approach (accessed 27 October 2023).

Department of Education (Australia) (2023) 'Child Care Subsidy'. Online. https://www.education.gov.au/early-childhood/child-care-subsidy (accessed 15 January 2024).

Department of Health (England) (1997) *Children's Day Care Facilities at 31 March 1997*. London: Department of Health.

Devercelli, A.E. and Beaton-Day, F. (2020) *Better Jobs and Brighter Futures: Investing in childcare to build human capital*. Washington, DC: World Bank. Online. https://openknowledge.worldbank.org/bitstream/handle/10986/35062/Better-Jobs-and-Brighter-Futures-Investing-in-Childcare-to-Build-Human-Capital.pdf?sequence=5&isAllowed=y (accessed 27 October 2023).

Dewey, J. (1939) 'Creative democracy – the task before us'. Address given at a dinner in honour of John Dewey, New York, 20 October. Online. https://www.philosophie.uni-muenchen.de/studium/das_fach/warum_phil_ueberhaupt/dewey_creative_democracy.pdf (accessed 13 January 2024).

Dewey, J. (1980) *The Middle Works, 1899–1924*, 15 vols, ed. J. A. Boydston. Carbondale: Southern Illinois University Press.

Domurath, I. (2022) 'The explicable non-death of neoliberalism in Chile'. *Social Europe*, 14 September. Online. https://socialeurope.eu/the-explicable-non-death-of-neoliberalism-in-chile (accessed 27 October 2023).

Doucet, A. (2023) 'Care is not a tally sheet: Rethinking the field of gender divisions of domestic labour with care-centric conceptual narratives'. *Families, Relationships and Societies*, 12 (1), 10–30. https://doi.org/10.1332/204674322X16711124907533.

Doucet, A., McKay, L. and Mathieu, S. (2019) 'Re-imagining parental leave: A conceptual "thought experiment"'. In P. Moss, A.-Z. Duvander and A. Koslowski (eds), *Parental Leave and Beyond: Recent international developments, current issues and future directions*. Bristol: Policy Press, 333–52.

Doucet, A., McKay, L. and Tremblay, D.-G. (2009) 'Canada and Québec: Two policies, one country'. In S. Kamerman and P. Moss (eds), *The Politics of Parental Leave Policies: Children, parenting, gender and the labour market*. Bristol: Policy Press, 33–50.

Durie, M. (2001) 'A framework for considering Maori educational advancement: Opening address'. Paper presented at the Hui Taumata Matauranga, 24 February, Turangi/Taupo.

Duvander, A.-Z. and Löfgren, N. (2023) 'Sweden country note'. In S. Blum, I. Dobrotić, G. Kaufman, A. Koslowski and P. Moss (eds), *International Review of Leave Policies and Research 2023*. Online. https://www.leavenetwork.org/fileadmin/user_upload/k_leavenetwork/country_notes/2022/Sweden2022.pdf (accessed 13 January 2024).

Early Childhood Care and Education Working Group (1988) *Education to be More*. Wellington: Department of Education.

Early Childhood Education Project (1996) *Future Directions: Early childhood education in New Zealand*. Wellington: New Zealand Educational Institute Te Riu Roa.

Early Years Research Centre (2019) *Early Years Research Centre Submission on Strategic Plan for Early Learning 2019–2029*. Waikato: Wilf Malcolm Institute for Educational Research.

Education Scotland. 2020. *Realising the Ambition: Being me. National practice guidance for early years in Scotland*. Livingston: Education Scotland. Online. https://education.gov.scot/media/3bjpr3wa/realisingtheambition.pdf (accessed 15 January 2024).

EIGE (European Institute for Gender Equality) (2020) *Eligibility for Parental Leave in EU Member States*. Luxembourg: Publications Office of the European Union. Online. https://eige.europa.eu/sites/default/files/documents/mh0219002enn_002.pdf. (accessed 28 October 2023).

Eisenstadt, N. (2011) *Providing a Sure Start: How government discovered early childhood*. Bristol: Policy Press.

Eisenstadt, N. (2012) 'Beyond Sure Start'. Presentation to a Children in Scotland Conference: 'A new era for Scotland's youngest citizens: Getting the legislation right', East Kilbride, 18 June.

Employment New Zealand (2023) 'Good faith in collective bargaining'. Online. https://www.employment.govt.nz/starting-employment/unions-and-bargaining/collective-agreements/collective-bargaining/good-faith/#:~:text=The%20good%20faith%20provisions%20likewise,good%20faith%20under%20the%20law (accessed 28 October 2023).

Esping-Andersen, G. (1999) *Social Foundations of Postindustrial Economies*. Oxford: Oxford University Press.

Eurydice (2019) *Key Data on Early Childhood Education and Care in Europe: 2019 edition*. Online. Luxembourg: Publications Office of the European Union. https://data.europa.eu/doi/10.2797/894279 (accessed 28 October 2023).

Featherstone, T. (2021) '2 ASX listed childcare stocks'. *Switzer Report*, 24 June. Online. https://switzerreport.com.au/2-asx-listed-childcare-stocks/ (accessed 13 January 2024).

Fisher, B. and Tronto, J. (1990) 'Toward a feminist theory of caring'. In E. Abel and M. Nelson (eds), *Circles of Care: Work and identity in women's lives*. Albany, NY: State University of New York Press, 35–62.

Fortunato, P. (2022) 'The long shadow of market fundamentalism'. *Social Europe*, 5 May. Online. https://socialeurope.eu/the-long-shadow-of-market-fundamentalism (accessed 28 October 2023).

Foucault, M. (1988) *Politics, Philosophy, Culture: Interviews and other writings, 1977–1984*, ed. L.D. Kritzman, trans. Alan Sheridan and others. London: Routledge.

Freire, P. (2004) *Pedagogy of Hope: Reliving 'Pedagogy of the Oppressed'*, new edn, trans. R.R. Barr. London: Continuum.

Friedman, M. (1982) *Capitalism and Freedom*, 2nd edn. Chicago, IL: University of Chicago Press.

Frost, N. (2023) 'New Zealand elects its most conservative government in decades'. *New York Times*, 14 October. Online. https://www.nytimes.com/2023/10/14/world/asia/new-zealand-election-national-wins.html (accessed 6 December 2023).

Gallagher, A. (2022) *Childcare Provision in Neoliberal Times: The marketization of care*. Bristol: Policy Press.

Garnier, P. (2016) *Sociologie de l'école maternelle*. Paris: PUF.

Gaunt, C. (2022) 'Government names 75 local areas to operate family hubs'. *Nursery World*, 2 April. Online. https://www.nurseryworld.co.uk/news/article/government-names-75-local-areas-to-operate-family-hubs (accessed 28 October 2023).

Gaunt, C. (2023) 'Will the Chancellor's childcare reforms work in practice?' *Nursery World*, 28 March. Online. https://www.nurseryworld.co.uk/news/article/will-the-chancellor-s-childcare-reforms-work-in-practice-1 (accessed 28 October 2023).

Gee, J.P. (2007). 'Reflections on assessment from a sociocultural-situated perspective'. *Yearbook of the National Society for the Study of Education*, 106 (1), 362–75.

George, S. (1999) 'A short history of neoliberalism'. *TNI*, 24 March. Online. https://www.tni.org/en/article/short-history-neoliberalism (accessed 3 January 2023).

Gillies, D. (2011) 'State education as high-yield investment: Human capital theory in European policy discourse'. *Journal of Pedagogy*, 2 (2), 224–45. https://doi.org/10.2478/v10159-011-0011-3.

Government of Canada (2021) 'Budget 2021: A Canada-wide early learning and child care plan'. Online. https://www.canada.ca/en/department-finance/news/2021/04/budget-2021-a-canada-wide-early-learning-and-child-care-plan.html (accessed 28 October 2023).

Government of Canada (2022) 'Federal Secretariat on Early Learning and Child Care'. Online. https://www.canada.ca/en/employment-social-development/programs/early-learning-child-care.html (accessed 28 October 2023).

Government of Ireland (2021) 'Nurturing Skills: The workforce plan for early learning and care and school-age childcare 2022–2028'. Government of Ireland.

Gramsci, A. (1971) *Selections from the Prison Notebooks of Antonio Gramsci*, ed. and trans. Q. Hoare and G. Nowell-Smith. London: Lawrence & Wishart.

Guardian, The (2022) 'The Guardian view on fixing inflation: A reckoning with free markets is needed'. *The Guardian*, 18 May. Online. https://www.theguardian.com/commentisfree/2022/may/18/the-guardian-view-on-fixing-inflation-a-reckoning-with-free-markets-is-needed (accessed 28 October 2023).

Halkyard, H. (1983) 'Te Kohanga Reo: A transformation'. *Broadsheet*, 13, 16–18.

Hammarström-Lewenhagen, B. (2013) 'Den unika möjligheten: En studie av den svenska förskolemodellen 1968–1998' (The unique opportunity: A study of the Swedish preschool model 1968–1998). PhD thesis, Stockholm University. Online. http://su.diva-portal.org/smash/get/diva2:662145/FULLTEXT01.pdf (accessed 28 October 2023).

Heckman, J. (2022a) 'Invest in early childhood development: Reduce deficits, strengthen the economy'. Online. https://heckmanequation.org/resource/invest-in-early-childhood-development-reduce-deficits-strengthen-the-economy/ (accessed 28 October 2023).

Heckman, J. (2022b) 'The Heckman Curve'. Online. https://heckmanequation.org/resource/the-heckman-curve/ (accessed 28 October 2023).

Helenchilde, I. (2022) '$10-a-day childcare plan threatened by worker shortage across Canada'. *Capital Current*. Online. https://capitalcurrent.ca/10-a-day-childcare-plan-threatened-by-worker-shortage/ (accessed 28 October 2023).

Hill, E. and Wade, M. (2018) 'The "radical marketisation" of early childhood education and care in Australia'. In D. Cahill and P. Toner (eds), *Wrong Way: How privatisation and economic reform backfired*. Carlton, Vic: La Trobe University Press.

Hipkins, C. (2017) 'Terms of reference: Development of a 10 year strategic plan for early learning'. Online. https://www.education.govt.nz/assets/Documents/Ministry/consultations/Strategic-Plan-ToR.pdf (accessed 28 October 2023).

HM Government (England) (2005) *Children's Workforce Strategy: A strategy to build a world-class workforce for children and young people*. Online. https://webarchive.nationalarchives.gov.uk/ukgwa/20130123124929/http://www.education.gov.uk/consultations/downloadableDocs/5958-DfES-ECM.pdf (accessed 29 October 2023).

HM Treasury (England) (2003) *Every Child Matters*. Online. https://assets.publishing.service.gov.uk/government/uploads/system/uploads/attachment_data/file/272064/5860.pdf (accessed 29 October 2023).

HM Treasury (England) (2004) *Choice for Parents, the Best Start for Children: A ten year strategy for childcare*. London: Her Majesty's Stationery Office. Online. https://dera.ioe.ac.uk/id/eprint/5274/2/02_12_04__pbr04childcare_480-1.pdf (accessed 29 October 2023).

Hofkins, D. and Northen, S. (eds) (2009) *Introducing the Cambridge Primary Review: Children, their world, their education*. Cambridge: University of Cambridge. Online. https://cprtrust.org.uk/wp-content/uploads/2013/10/CPR_revised_booklet.pdf (accessed 11 November 2023).

Hopkin, J. (2020) *Anti-System Politics: The crisis of market liberalism in rich democracies*. New York: Oxford University Press.

Hoyuelos, A. (2004) 'A pedagogy of transgression'. *Children in Europe*, 6, 6–7.

Human Rights Commission (2023) *Human Rights and Te Tiriti o Waitangi*. Online. https://tikatangata.org.nz/human-rights-in-aotearoa/human-rights-and-te-tiriti-o-waitangi (accessed 13 January 2024).

Joshi, H. and Davies, H. (1993) 'Mothers' human capital and childcare in Britain'. *National Institute Economic Review*, 146 (1), 50–63. https://doi.org/10.1177/002795019314600104.

Kaga, Y., Bennett, J. and Moss, P. (2010) *Caring and Learning Together: Cross-national research on the integration of ECCE within education*. Paris: UNESCO. Online. https://www.unesdoc.unesco.org/images/0018/001878/187818E.pdf (accessed 29 October 2023).

Kelsey, J. (1997) *The New Zealand Experiment: A world model for structural adjustment?* Auckland: Bridget Williams Books.

Kelsey, J. (1999) 'New Zealand's "experiment" a colossal failure'. 9 July. Online. http://www.converge.org.nz/pma/apfail.htm (accessed 13 January 2024).

Koslowski, A., Blum, S., Dobrotić, I., Kaufman, G. and Moss, P. (eds) (2022) *18th International Review of Leave Policies and Related Research 2022*. International Network on Leave Policies and Research. Online. https://www.leavenetwork.org/fileadmin/user_upload/k_leavenetwork/annual_reviews/2022/Koslowski_et_al_Leave_Policies_2022.pdf (accessed 13 January 2024).

Labaree, D. (2017) 'Futures of the field of education'. In G. Whitty and J. Furlong (eds), *Knowledge and the Study of Education: An international exploration*. Didcot: Symposium Books, 277–83.

Lange, D. (1989) *Before Five: Early childhood care and education in New Zealand*. Wellington: Department of Education.

Lee, W., Carr, M., Soutar, B. and Mitchell, L. (2013) *Understanding the Te Whāriki approach: Early years education in practice*. Abingdon: Routledge.

Lenz Taguchi, H. and Munkhammar, I. (2003) 'Consolidating governmental early childhood education and care services under the Ministry of Education and Science: A Swedish case study'. UNESCO Early Childhood and Family Policy Series no. 6. Online. https://unesdoc. unesco.org/ark:/48223/pf0000130135 (accessed 29 October 2023).

Leonhardt, M. (2022) 'Staff shortages are crippling childcare centers across the U.S., and that's only the beginning of the problem'. *Yahoo! finance*, 15 November. Online. https://finance.yahoo. com/news/staff-shortages-crippling-childcare-centers-201534309.html (accessed 29 October 2023).

Lepper, J. (2022) 'More than 1,000 Children's Centres closed over last decade'. *Children & Young People Now*, 30 June. Online. https://www.cypnow.co.uk/news/article/more-than-1-000-children-s-centres-closed-over-last-decade (accessed 29 October 2023).

Lewis, J. (2011) 'From Sure Start to Children's Centres: An analysis of policy change in English early years programmes'. *Journal of Social Policy*, 40 (1), 71–88. https://doi.org/10.1017/S0047279410000280.

Lloyd, E. and Penn, H. (2014) 'Childcare markets in an age of austerity'. *European Early Childhood Education Research Journal*, 22 (3): 386–96. https://doi.org/10.1080/1350293X.2014.912901.

Local News Plus (2023) 'Cheaper child care a win for thousands of local families: PM'. 21 April. Online. https://www.localnewsplus.com.au/pm-visits-to-talk-education-child-care/ (accessed 9 January 2024).

Luc, J.-N. (2010) '"Je suis petit mais important": La scolarisation des jeunes enfants en France du début du XIXe siècle à nos jours'. *Carrefours de l'éducation*, 2010/2 (30), 9–22. https://doi.org/10.3917/cdle.030.0009.

MacDonald, C. and Kelly, R. (2022) *Better Childcare: Putting families first*. Policy Exchange. Online. https://policyexchange.org.uk/wp-content/uploads/2022/08/Better-Childcare.pdf (accessed 29 October 2023).

Malaguzzi, L. (1994) 'Your image of the child: Where teaching begins', trans. B. Rankin, L. Morrow and L. Gandini. Online. https://www.reggioalliance.org/downloads/malaguzzi:ccie:1994.pdf (accessed 13 January 2024).

Marquand, D. (2004) *Decline of the Public: The hollowing-out of citizenship*. Cambridge: Polity.

Martin, D. (2016) *Whatever Happened to Extended Schools? The story of an ambitious education project*. London: UCL IOE Press.

Martin Korpi, B. (2016) *The Politics of Preschool: Intentions and decisions underlying the emergence and growth of the Swedish preschool*, 4th edn, trans. B. R. Turner and Ministry of Foreign Affairs. Online. https://www.government.se/contentassets/4b768a5cd6c24e0cb70b4393eadf4f6a/the-politics-of-pre-school---intentions-and-decisions-underlying-the-emergence-and-growth-of-the-swedish-pre-school.pdf (accessed 11 November 2023).

Mathers, S., Sylva, K. and Joshi, H. (2007) *Quality of Childcare Settings in the Millennium Cohort Study (Research Report SSU/2007/FR/025)*. London: Department for Education and Skills. Online. https://dera.ioe.ac.uk/id/eprint/8088/7/SSU2007FR025_Redacted.pdf (accessed 11 December 2023).

Mathieu, S., Doucet, A. and McKay, L. (2020) 'Parental leave benefits and inter-provincial differences: The case of four Canadian provinces'. *Canadian Journal of Sociology/Cahiers canadiens de sociologie*, 45 (2), 169–94.

May, H. (1996) 'Training at the crossroads – again'. *Kuaka Kōrero*, 4, 5.

May, H. (2013) *The Discovery of Early Childhood*, 2nd edn. Wellington: NZCER Press.

May, H. (2019) *Politics in the Playground: The world of early childhood education in New Zealand*, 3rd edn. Dunedin, New Zealand: Otago University Press.

May, H. and Bethell, K. (2017) *Growing a Kindergarten Movement in Aotearoa New Zealand: Its people, purposes and politics*. Wellington: NZCER Press.

May, H. and Mitchell, L. (2018) '"Turning the tide": Suggestions for discussion'. Unpublished paper presented to the Early Learning Strategic Plan Working Group.

Mayall, B. (1996) *Children, Health and the Social Order*. Buckingham: Open University Press.

McDonald, C. (2022) 'What is childcare for?' *Analysis*, BBC Radio 4, 11 July. Online. https://www.bbc.co.uk/programmes/m00193v9 (accessed 30 October 2023).

McDonald, G. (1981) 'The story of a recommendation about care and education'. In M. Clark (ed.), *The Politics of Education in New Zealand*. Wellington: New Zealand Council for Educational Research, 160–73.

McGinn, D. (2022) 'How much parents benefit from the national child-care plans depends on where they live'. *The Globe and Mail*, 9 July. Online. https://www.theglobeandmail.com/canada/article-10-a-day-child-care-fees-canada/ (accessed 30 October 2023).

Meade, A. (1990) 'Women and children gain a foot in the door'. *New Zealand Women's Studies Journal*, 6 (1/2), 96–111.

Meade, A. (ed.) (2005) *Catching the Waves: Innovation in early childhood education*. Wellington: NZCER Press.

Meade, A. (ed.) (2007) *Cresting the Waves: Innovation in early childhood education*. Wellington: NZCER Press.

Meade, A. (ed.) (2009) *Generating Waves: Innovation in early childhood education*. Wellington: NZCER Press.

Meade, A. (2011) 'Centres of innovation: Gaining a new understanding of reality'. *Early Education*, 50 (Spring/Summer), 7–10.

Meade, A., Robinson, L., Smorti, S., Stuart, M. and Williamson, J. with Carroll-Lind, J., Meagher-Lundberg, P. and Te Whau, S. (2012) *Early Childhood Teachers' Work in Education and Care Centres: Profiles, patterns and purposes*. Wellington: Te Tari Puna Ora o Aotearoa.

Ministry of Education (New Zealand) (1988) 'Tomorrow's schools: The reform of education administration in New Zealand'. New Zealand Department of Education, Wellington.

Ministry of Education (New Zealand) (1995) *Report on the direct (bulk funding) of kindergartens to the Education and Science Select Committee, 10 October 1995*.

Ministry of Education (New Zealand) (1996) *Te Whāriki: He whāriki mātauranga mō ngā mokopuna o Aotearoa/Early childhood curriculum*. Wellington: Learning Media.

Ministry of Education (New Zealand) (2002) *Pathways to the Future: Ngā Huarahi Arataki*. Wellington: Ministry of Education.

Ministry of Education (New Zealand) (2005) *Foundations for Discovery: Supporting learning in early childhood education through information and communication technologies: A framework for development*. Wellington: Ministry of Education.

Ministry of Education (New Zealand) (2006) *Ngā Arohaehae Whai Hua/Self-review Guidelines for Early Childhood Education*. Wellington: Learning Media.

Ministry of Education (New Zealand) (2009) *Te Whatu Pōkeka*. Wellington: Learning Media.

Ministry of Education (New Zealand) (2017a) *Te Whāriki a Te Kōhanga Reo*. Te Whāriki Online. Online. https://tewhariki.tki.org.nz/ (accessed 10 December 2023).

Ministry of Education (New Zealand) (2017b) *Te Whāriki: He whāriki mātauranga mō ngā mokopuna o Aotearoa/Early childhood curriculum*. Online. https://www.education.govt.nz/assets/Documents/Early-Childhood/ELS-Te-Whariki-Early-Childhood-Curriculum-ENG-Web.pdf (accessed 31 October 2023).

Ministry of Education (New Zealand) (2019*) He Taonga te Tamaiti/Every Child a Taonga: Early learning action plan 2019–2029*. Wellington: Ministry of Education. Online. https://conversation-space.s3-ap-southeast-2.amazonaws.com/SES_0342_ELS_10YP_Final+Report_Web.pdf (accessed 31 October 2023).

Ministry of Education (New Zealand) (2021a) 'Annual ECE census 2020: Fact sheets'. Online. https://www.educationcounts.govt.nz/publications/ECE/annual-early-childhood-education-census/annual-ece-census-2020-fact-sheets (accessed 31 October 2023).

Ministry of Education (New Zealand) (2021b) 'ECE staffing: Early childhood education remuneration summary'. Online. https://www.educationcounts.govt.nz/statistics/staffing (accessed 11 November 2023).

Ministry of Education (New Zealand) (2021c) 'ECE services. Number of services. Pivot table: Number of ECE services'. Online. https://www.educationcounts.govt.nz/statistics/services (accessed 31 October 2023).

Ministry of Education (New Zealand) (2023a) 'Cabinet paper: Pay parity for certificated teachers in education and care services: Deferring full pass-on of recent kindergarten salary increases'. Online. https://assets.education.govt.nz/public/Documents/our-work/information-releases/Advice-Seen-by-our-Ministers/September-2023/541.-Pay-Parity-Pass_on-Kindergarten-Salary-Increases_Redacted.pdf (accessed 13 January 2024).

Ministry of Education (New Zealand) (2023b) 'ECE services. Number of licensed ECE places. Pivot table: Number of licensed ECE places'. Online. https://www.educationcounts.govt.nz/statistics/services (accessed 4 December 2023).

Ministry of Education (New Zealand) (2023c) *Kōwhiti Whakapae: Strengthening progress through practice*. Online. https://kowhiti-whakapae.education.govt.nz/ (accessed 7 December 2023).

Ministry of Health (UK) (1945) 'Nursery provision for children under five'. Ministry of Health Circular 221/45, 14 December.

Mirowski, P. (2014) 'The political movement that dared not speak its own name: The neoliberal thought collective under erasure'. Institute for New Economic Thinking Working Paper No. 23. Online. https://www.ineteconomics.org/uploads/papers/WP23-Mirowski.pdf (accessed 31 October 2023).

Mitchell, J. (2022) 'Child care costs set to come down to $10-per-day by 2025 for parents of young children: Here's what you need to know'. *The Peterborough Examiner*, 10 June. Online. https://www.thepeterboroughexaminer.com/local-kawartha-lakes/news/2022/06/10/child-care-costs-set-to-come-down-to-10-per-day-by-2025-for-parents-of-young-children-here-s-what-you-need-to-know.html (accessed 31 October 2023).

Mitchell, L. (1996) 'Crossroads: Early childhood education in the mid-1990s'. *New Zealand Annual Review of Education*, 5, 75–92. https://doi.org/10.26686/nzaroe.v0i5.1113.

Mitchell, L. (2002) 'Currents of change: Early childhood education in 2001'. *New Zealand Annual Review of Education*, 11, 123–43. https://doi.org/10.26686/nzaroe.v0i11.1418.

Mitchell, L. (2005) 'Policy shifts in early childhood education: Past lessons, new directions'. In J. Codd and K. Sullivan (eds), *Education Policy Directions in Aotearoa New Zealand*. Southbank, Vic: Thomson Learning, 175–98.

Mitchell, L. (2011) 'Enquiring teachers and democratic politics: Transformations in New Zealand's early childhood education landscape'. *Early Years: An International Research Journal*, 31 (3), 217–28. https://doi.org/10.1080/09575146.2011.588787.

Mitchell, L. (2012) 'Markets and childcare provision in New Zealand: Towards a fairer alternative'. In E. Lloyd and H. Penn (eds), *Childcare Markets: Can they deliver an equitable service?* Bristol: Policy Press, 97–114.

Mitchell, L. (2015) 'Shifting directions in ECEC policy in New Zealand: From a child rights to an interventionist approach'. *International Journal of Early Years Education*, 23 (3), 288–302. https://doi.org/10.1080/09669760.2015.1074557.

Mitchell, L. (2019). *Democratic Policies and Practices in Early Childhood Education and Care: An Aotearoa New Zealand case study*. Singapore: Springer.

Mitchell, L. and Carr, M. (2014) 'Democratic and learning-oriented assessment practices in early childhood care and education in New Zealand'. Early Childhood Care and Education Working Papers Series 2. UNESCO. Online. https://unesdoc.unesco.org/ark:/48223/pf0000226550 (accessed 18 October 2023).

Mitchell, L., Cowie, B., Derby, M., Kahuroa, R., McMillan, H., Carr, M. and Soutar, B. (2022) 'A critical review of draft Practice and Progress Tools (Kōwhiti Whakapae) Social Emotional Learning (SEL)'. Unpublished report submitted to Ministry of Education (New Zealand).

Mitchell, L., Meagher-Lundberg, P., Davison, C., Kara, H. and Kalavite, T. (2016) *ECE Participation Programme Evaluation: Stage 3*. Wellington: Ministry of Education. Online. https://www.educationcounts.govt.nz/publications/ECE/ece-participation-programme-evaluation-delivery-of-ece-participation-initiatives-stage-3 (accessed 31 October 2023).

Mitchell, L., Meagher-Lundberg, P., Mara, D., Cubey, P. and Whitford, M. (2011) *Locality-Based Evaluation of 'Pathways to the Future – Ngā Huarahi Arataki': Integrated report 2004, 2006 and 2009*. Wellington: Ministry of Education. Online. https://www.educationcounts.govt.nz/__data/assets/pdf_file/0017/100916/973_ECE-Strategic-Plan-web.pdf (accessed 9 November 2023).

Mitchell, L., Royal Tangaere, A., Mara, D. and Wylie, C. (2006) *Quality in Parent/Whanau-Led Services*. Wellington: New Zealand Council for Educational Research. Online. https://ww.educationcounts.govt.nz/__data/assets/pdf_file/0004/117184/Quality-in-Parent-Whanau-led-Services-Summary-Report.pdf (accessed 3 January 2023).

Mitchell, L. and Wells, C. (1997) 'Negotiating pay parity in the early childhood sector'. In New Zealand Council of Trade Unions (eds), *Closing the Gap: Forum on equal pay*. Wellington: New Zealand Council of Trade Unions, 163–72.

Monbiot, G. (2016) *How Did We Get into this Mess? Politics, equality, nature*. London: Verso.

Monbiot, G. (2017) *Out of the Wreckage: A new politics for an age of crisis*. London: Verso.

Morton, K. (2021a) 'Busy Bees Childcare buys Irish nursery group'. *Nursery World*, 23 September. Online. https://www.nurseryworld.co.uk/news/article/busy-bees-childcare-buys-irish-nursery-group (accessed 31 October 2023).

Morton, K. (2021b) 'Busy Bees Childcare moves into New Zealand'. *Nursery World*, 22 October. Online. https://www.nurseryworld.co.uk/news/article/busy-bees-childcare-moves-into-new-zealand (accessed 31 October 2023).

Moss, P. (2009) 'There are alternatives! Markets and democratic experimentalism in early childhood education and care'. Working papers in Early Childhood Development 53. Bernard van Leer Foundation and Bertelsmann Stiftung. Online. https://discovery.ucl.ac.uk/id/eprint/10005608/ (accessed 31 October 2023).

Moss, P. (ed.) (2013) *Early Childhood and Compulsory Education: Reconceptualising the relationship*. Abingdon: Routledge.

Moss, P. (2014) *Transformative Change and Real Utopias in Early Childhood Education: A story of democracy, experimentation and potentiality*. Abingdon: Routledge.

Moss, P. (2018) '"To aspire toward ECEC systems that support broad learning, participation and democracy": Reflections on John Bennett's final words on *Starting Strong*'. In N. Hayes and M. Urban (eds), *In Search of Social Justice: John Bennett's lifetime contribution to early childhood policy and practice*. Abingdon: Routledge, 26–37.

Moss, P. (2021) 'Democracy as first practice in early childhood education and care'. In *Encyclopedia on Early Childhood Development*. Online. https://www.child-encyclopedia.com/pdf/expert/child-care-early-childhood-education-and-care/according-experts/democracy-first-practice-early (accessed 3 January 2023).

Moss, P. and O'Brien, M. (2019) 'United Kingdom: Leave policy and an attempt to take a new path'. In P. Moss, A.-Z. Duvander and A. Koslowski (eds), *Parental Leave and Beyond: Recent international developments, current issues and future directions*. Bristol: Policy Press, 57–74.

Moss, P. and Petrie, P. (1997) *Children's Services: Time for a new approach, a discussion paper*. London: University of London Institute of Education.

Munkhammar, I. and Wikgren, G. (2010) 'Caring and learning together: A case study of Sweden'. Early Childhood and Family Policy Series no. 20. Online. https://unesdoc.unesco.org/ark:/48223/pf0000187923 (accessed 31 October 2023).

National Council for Curriculum and Assessment (Ireland) (2009) *Aistear: The early childhood curriculum framework*. Dublin: National Council for Curriculum and Assessment. Online. https://ncca.ie/en/resources/aistear-the-early-childhood-curriculum-framework/ (accessed 15 January 2024).

National Evaluation of Sure Start Team (2012) *The Impact of Sure Start Local Programmes on Seven Year Olds and Their Families*. Department for Education Research Brief, DFE-RB220. Online. https://www.ness.bbk.ac.uk/impact/documents/DFE-RB220.pdf (accessed 31 October 2023).

New Zealand Government (1991) *Employment Contracts Act 1991 (1991 No. 22)*. Online. https://www.nzlii.org/nz/legis/hist_act/eca19911991n22280/ (accessed 31 October 2023).

New Zealand Government (2000) 'Kindergarten teachers to return to State Sector'. Press release, 13 March. https://www.beehive.govt.nz/release/kindergarten-teachers-return-state-sector (accessed 29 October 2023).

New Zealand Government (2022) 'Māori population estimates: At 30 June 2022'. Online. https://www.stats.govt.nz/information-releases/maori-population-estimates-at-30-june-2022/ (accessed 1 November 2023).

New Zealand National Party (2023) 'National's back pocket boost: Tax relief for the squeezed middle. Online. https://www.national.org.nz/delivering_tax_relief (accessed 15 January 2024).

New Zealand National Party & New Zealand First (2023) *Coalition Agreement: New Zealand National Party & New Zealand First*. Online. https://assets.nationbuilder.com/nationalparty/pages/18466/attachments/original/1700778597/NZFirst_Agreement_2.pdf?1700778597 (accessed 13 January 2024).

Noonan, R. (2001) 'Early childhood education: A child's right?' In B. Webber and L. Mitchell (eds), *Early Childhood Education for a Democratic Society: Conference proceedings, October 2001*. Wellington: New Zealand Council for Educational Research, 61–8.

Nuffield Foundation (2021) *The Role of Early Childhood Education and Care in Shaping Life Chances*. Online. https://www.nuffieldfoundation.org/wp-content/uploads/2021/10/Role-early-childhood-education-care-life-chances-Nuffield-Foundation.pdf (accessed 20 November 2023).

Nursery World (2015) 'Busy Bees expands into South-East Asia with acquisition of 60 nurseries'. *Nursery World*, 2 February. Online. https://www.nurseryworld.co.uk/news/article/busy-bees-expands-into-south-east-asia-with-acquisition-of-60-nurseries (accessed 31 October 2023).

Nursery World (2017) 'Busy Bees gains major shareholder'. *Nursery World*, 21 December. Online. https://www.nurseryworld.co.uk/news/article/busy-bees-gains-major-shareholder (accessed 31 October 2023).

Nursery World (2018) 'Busy Bees expanding in China'. *Nursery World*, 6 February. Online. https://www.nurseryworld.co.uk/news/article/busy-bees-expanding-in-china (accessed 31 October 2023).

Nuttall, J. (ed.) (2003) *Weaving te Whāriki: Aotearoa New Zealand's early childhood curriculum document in theory and practice*. Wellington: New Zealand Council for Educational Research.

O'Brien, M. and Moss, P. (2020) 'Towards an ECEC system in synergy with parenting leave'. In C. Cameron and P. Moss (eds), *Transforming Early Childhood in England: Towards a democratic education*. London: UCL Press, 203–19.

OECD (2000) 'Early childhood education and care policy in the United Kingdom'. OECD Country Note. Online. https://www.oecd.org/unitedkingdom/2535034.pdf (accessed 31 October 2023).

OECD (2001) *Starting Strong: Early childhood education and care*. Paris: OECD. Online. https://read.oecd-ilibrary.org/education/starting-strong_9789264192829-en#page3 (accessed 11 November 2023).

OECD (2006) *Starting Strong II: Early childhood education and care*. Paris: OECD. Online. https://www.oecd.org/education/school/startingstrongiiearlychildhoodeducationandcare.htm (accessed 11 November 2023).

OECD (2011) 'Investing in high-quality early childhood education and care (ECEC)'. Online. https://www.oecd.org/education/preschoolandschool/48980282.pdf (accessed 31 October 2023).

Office of National Statistics (2022a) 'Population estimates for the UK, England, Wales, Scotland and Northern Ireland: Mid-2021'. Online. https://www.ons.gov.uk/peoplepopulationandcommunity/populationandmigration/populationestimates/bulletins/annualmidyearpopulationestimates/mid2021#:~:text=We%20estimate%20the%20UK%20population,2021%20censuses%20for%20these%20countries (accessed 31 October 2023).

Office of National Statistics (2022b) 'Births by parents' country of birth, England and Wales: 2021'. Online. https://www.ons.gov.uk/peoplepopulationandcommunity/birthsdeathsandmarriages/livebirths/bulletins/parentscountryofbirthenglandandwales/2021#:~:text=5.-,Live%20births%20to%20non%2DUK%2Dborn%20women%20by%20geography,2020%20to%2029.6%25%20in%202021 (accessed 31 October 2023).

Ofsted (2022a) *The Annual Report of His Majesty's Chief Inspector of Education, Children's Services and Skills 2021/22*. Online. https://www.gov.uk/government/publications/ofsted-annual-report-202122-education-childrens-services-and-skills/the-annual-report-of-his-majestys-chief-inspector-of-education-childrens-services-and-skills-202122 (accessed 31 October 2023).

Ofsted (2022b) *Main Findings: Childcare providers and inspections as at 31 March 2022*. Online. https://www.gov.uk/government/statistics/childcare-providers-and-inspections-as-at-31-march-2022/main-findings-childcare-providers-and-inspections-as-at-31-march-2022#figure-8 (accessed 3 January 2023).

Partnership for the Public Good (2021) *A New Funding Model for Early Learning and Care and School-Age Childcare: Report of the Expert Group to Develop a New Funding Model for Early Learning and Care and School-Age Childcare*. Online. https://first5fundingmodel.gov.ie/wp-content/uploads/2021/12/Funding-Model-FINAL-REPORT-2.pdf (accessed 31 October 2023).

Paull, G. (2012) 'Childcare markets and government intervention'. In E. Lloyd and H. Penn (eds), *Childcare Markets: Can they deliver an equitable service?* Bristol: Policy Press, 227–56.

Paull, G. and Popov, D. (2019) *The Role and Contribution of Maintained Nursery Schools in the Early Years Sector in England*. London: Department for Education. Online. https://assets.publishing.service.gov.uk/government/uploads/system/uploads/attachment_data/file/912995/Frontier_Economics_MNS_report_REVISED_v2.pdf (accessed 31 October 2023).

Pelling, L. (2019) 'The Swedish face of inequality'. *Social Europe*, 17 January. Online. https://socialeurope.eu/the-swedish-face-of-inequality (accessed 31 October 2023).

Pelling, L. (2022) 'Sweden's schools: Milton Friedman's wet dream'. *Social Europe*, 16 May. Online. https://socialeurope.eu/swedens-schools-milton-friedmans-wet-dream (accessed 31 October 2023).

Penn, H. (2019a) 'Putting childcare at the heart of the social market economy'. Wilfried Martens Centre for European Studies Policy Brief. Online. https://www.martenscentre.eu/wp-content/uploads/2020/06/childcare-social-market-economy-europe-1.pdf (accessed 31 October 2023).

Penn, H. (2019b) 'Understanding the contexts of leadership debates'. *Contemporary Issues in Early Childhood*, 20 (1), 104–9. https://doi.org/10.1177/1463949118800768.

Penn, H., Burton, V., Lloyd, E., Mugford, M., Potter, S. and Sayeed, Z. (2006) 'Early years: What is known about the long-term economic impact of centre-based early childhood interventions?'. Technical report. EPPI-Centre, Social Science Research Unit and Institute of Education, University of London. Online. http://eppi.ioe.ac.uk/cms/LinkClick.aspx?fileticket=l5do4A7UCSo%3D&tabid=676&mid=1572 (accessed 31 October 2023).

People for Education (2022) 'Ontario joins the rest of Canada with new child care agreement'. Online. https://peopleforeducation.ca/our-work/ontario-joins-the-rest-of-canada-with-new-child-care-agreement/ (accessed 31 October 2023).

Péralès, D., Chandon-Coq, M.-H. and Rayna, S. (eds) (2021) Les Passerelles, tout un art! *Crèches, centres de loisirs, écoles maternelles*. Toulouse: érès.

Prka, R. (2021) 'Childcare assets increasingly desired by larger funds'. *The Market Herald*, 21 September. Online. https://themarketherald.com.au/childcare-assets-increasingly-desired-by-larger-funds-2021-09-21/ (accessed 31 October 2023).

Property Council of Australia (2022) 'Government investment drives interest in childcare assets'. *Property Australia*, 15 November. Online. info.propertycouncil.com.au/property-australia-blog/government-investment-drives-interest-in-childcare-assets (accessed 3 January 2023).

Radio New Zealand (2022) 'Early educator operator to sell 105 centres, citing impact of pandemic restrictions'. 30 August. Online. https://www.rnz.co.nz/news/business/473768/early-education-operator-to-sell-105-centres-citing-impact-of-pandemic-restrictions (accessed 31 October 2023).

Raper, A. (2022a) 'NSW and Victorian governments plan new free year of preschool schooling within a decade'. ABC News, 15 June (updated 16 June). Online. https://www.abc.net.au/news/2022-06-16/nsw-victoria-plan-for-new-preschool-year-education/101155350 (accessed 31 October 2023).

Raper, A. (2022b) 'NSW government reveals $5 billion childcare plan in state budget'. ABC News, 13 June (updated 14 June). Online. https://www.abc.net.au/news/2022-06-14/nsw-government-childcare-state-budget-5-billion/101149014 (accessed 31 October 2023).

Raworth, K. (2017) *Doughnut Economics: Seven ways to think like a 21st century economist*. London: Random House Business Books.

Redwoods Dowling Kerr (2022) 'Childcare & education market report: January 2022'. Online. https://redwoodsdk.com/wp-content/uploads/2022/01/RDK_ChildcareBrochure_Jan2022.pdf (accessed 31 October 2023).

Reedy, T. (2003) 'Toku rangatiratanga na te mana-matauranga: "Knowledge and power set me free …"'. In J. Nuttall (ed.), *Weaving te Whariki: Aotearoa New Zealand's early childhood curriculum document in theory and practice*. Wellington: New Zealand Council for Educational Research, 51–77.

Rinaldi, C. (2021) *In Dialogue with Reggio Emilia: Listening, researching and learning*, 2nd edn. Abingdon: Routledge.

Rizvi, F. and Lingard, B. (2009) *Globalizing Education Policy*. Abingdon: Routledge.

Roberts-Holmes, G. (2021) 'School readiness, governance and early years ability grouping'. *Contemporary Issues in Early Childhood*, 22 (3), 244–53. https://doi.org/10.1177/1463949119863128.

Roberts-Holmes, G. and Moss, P. (2021) *Neoliberalism and Early Childhood Education: Markets, imaginaries and governance*. Abingdon: Routledge.

Robinson, C.-L. (2002) 'Playgroup paper'. Report for Early Childhood Development. Wellington: Early Childhood Development.

Rose, N. (1999) *Powers of Freedom: Reframing political thought*. Cambridge: Cambridge University Press.

Rowson, J. (2019) 'Bildung in the 21st century: Why sustainable prosperity depends upon reimagining education'. Online. https://cusp.ac.uk/wp-content/uploads/09-Jonathan-Rowson-online.pdf (accessed 31 October 2023).

Royal Commission on Social Policy (1988) *The April Report. Volume III, part two: Future Directions: Associated papers.* Wellington: Royal Commission on Social Policy.

Royal Tangaere, A. (1997) 'Te kōhanga reo: More than a language nest'. *Early Childhood Folio*, 3, 41–7. https://doi.org/10.18296/ecf.0268.

Sahlberg, P. (2012) 'Global educational reform movement is here!'. Blog. Online. https://pasisahlberg.com/global-educational-reform-movement-is-here/ (accessed 31 October 2023).

Seth, A. (2021) *Being You: A new science of consciousness*. London: Faber & Faber.

Simon, A., Penn, H., Shah, A., Owen, C., Lloyd, E., Hollingworth, K. and Quy, K. (2021) *Acquisitions, Mergers and Debt: The new language of childcare: Main report.* Online. https://discovery.ucl.ac.uk/id/eprint/10142357/7/Childcare%20Main%20Report%2020010222.pdf (accessed 31 October 2023).

Sims, M. (2017) 'Neoliberalism and early childhood', *Cogent Education*, 4 (1). Online. https://www.tandfonline.com/doi/pdf/10.1080/2331186X.2017.1365411 (accessed 31 October 2023). https://doi.org/10.1080/2331186X.2017.1365411.

Skolverket (2000) *Child Care in Sweden*. Stockholm: Skolverket. Online. https://www.skolverket.se/download/18.6bfaca41169863e6a653a14/1553956850507/pdf633.pdf (accessed 12 November 2023).

Skolverket (2008) 'Ten years after the pre-school reform: A national evaluation of the Swedish pre-school'. Stockholm: Skolverket. English translation. Online. https://web-archive.oecd.org/2012-06-14/90684-48990164.pdf (accessed 12 November 2023).

Skolverket (2018) *Curriculum for the Preschool*. Lpfö 18. English translation. Online. https://www.skolverket.se/download/18.6bfaca41169863e6a65d897/1553968298535/pdf4049.pdf2019 (accessed 31 October 2023).

Slaughter, M. (2023) 'Newsable: Is this the most right wing government since the 90s?'. *Stuff*, 24 November. Online. https://www.stuff.co.nz/national/politics/301014821/newsable-is-this-the-most-right-wing-government-since-the-90s (accessed 13 January 2024).

Smith, A.B. (2016) *Children's Rights: Towards social justice*. New York, NY: Momentum Press.

Smith, A.B. and May, H. (2006) 'Early childhood care and education in Aotearoa–New Zealand'. In E. Melhuish and K. Petrogiannis (eds), *Early Childhood Care and Education: International perspectives*. Abingdon: Routledge, 95–114.

Smith, G., Sylva, K., Smith, T., Sammons, P. and Omonigho, A. (2018) 'Stop start: Survival, decline or closure? Children's centres in England, 2018'. Online. https://www.suttontrust.com/wp-content/uploads/2018/04/StopStart-FINAL.pdf (accessed 31 October 2023).

Social Prosperity Network (2017) 'Social prosperity for the future: A proposal for Universal Basic Services'. UCL Institute for Global Prosperity. Online. https://www.ucl.ac.uk/bartlett/igp/sites/bartlett/files/universal_basic_services_-_the_institute_for_global_prosperity_.pdf (accessed 31 October 2023).

Sosinsky, L. (2012) 'Childcare markets in the US: Supply and demand, quality and cost, and public policy'. In E. Lloyd and H. Penn (eds), *Childcare Markets: Can they deliver an equitable service?* Bristol: Policy Press, 131–52.

Sousa, D. (2020) 'Towards a democratic ECEC system'. In C. Cameron and P. Moss (eds), *Transforming Early Childhood in England: Towards a democratic education*. London: UCL Press, 151–69.

Sousa, D. and Moss, P. (2023) 'Towards democratic culture and political practice in early childhood education for transformative change at a time of converging crisis: The case for transformative change at a time of converging crisis', *ETD – Educação Temática Digital*, 25:e023067, 1–23. http://dx.doi.org/10.20396/etd.v25i00.8672067"10.20396/etd.v25i00.8672067.

Spinoza, B. (1996) *Ethics*, trans. Edwin Curley. London: Penguin Books.

Standards and Testing Agency (England) (2023) 'Reception baseline assessment'. Online. https://www.gov.uk/government/collections/reception-baseline (accessed 31 October 2023).

State Services Commission (1980) *Early Childhood Care and Education: A report of the State Services Commission Working Group*. Wellington: State Services Commission.

Statham, R., Parkes, H. and Nanda, S. (2022) 'Towards a childcare guarantee'. Institute for Public Policy Research. Online. https://www.ippr.org/files/2022-09/towards-a-childcare-guarantee-sept-22.pdf (accessed 31 October 2023).

Statistics Canada (2021) 'Survey on early learning and child care arrangements, 2020'. Online. https://www150.statcan.gc.ca/n1/daily-quotidien/210407/dq210407b-eng.htm (accessed 31 October 2023).

Stedman Jones, D. (2012) *Masters of the Universe: Hayek, Friedman, and the birth of neoliberal politics*. Princeton, NJ: Princeton University Press.

Stiglitz, J. (2019a) 'After neoliberalism'. Online. *Project Syndicate*, 30 May. https://www.project-syndicate.org/commentary/after-neoliberalism-progressive-capitalism-by-joseph-e-stiglitz-2019-05 (accessed 31 October 2023).

Stiglitz, J. (2019b) 'The end of neoliberalism and the rebirth of history'. *Social Europe*, 26 November. Online. https://www.socialeurope.eu/the-end-of-neoliberalism-and-the-rebirth-of-history (accessed 31 October 2023).

Stover, S. and New Zealand Playcentre Federation (2003) *Good Clean Fun: New Zealand's playcentre movement* (repr.). Auckland: Playcentre Publications.

Stuart, M. (2011) 'Cradle and all; rocking the cradle of wealth: Human capital theory and early childhood education in New Zealand,1999–2008'. PhD thesis, Auckland University of Technology. Online. https://openrepository.aut.ac.nz/bitstream/handle/10292/4452/StuartMJ.pdf?sequence=3&isAllowed=y (accessed 31 October 2023).

Sutton Trust (2018) '1,000 children's centres "lost" since 2009'. Press release, 4 April. Online. https://www.suttontrust.com/news-opinion/all-news-opinion/1000-childrens-centres-closed-since-2009/ (accessed 31 October 2023).

Sylva, K., Melhuish, E., Sammons, P., Siraj-Blatchford, I. and Taggart, B. (2004) 'The effective provision of pre-school education (EPPE) project: Findings from pre-school to end of Key Stage 1. Online. https://dera.ioe.ac.uk/18189/2/SSU-SF-2004-01.pdf (accessed 31 October 2023).

Tizard, B. (2003) *The Thomas Coram Research Unit, 1973–1990: A memoir*. London: Thomas Coram Research Unit, Institute of Education.

Tizard, J., Moss, P. and Perry, J. (1976) *All Our Children: Pre-school services in a changing society*. London: Temple Smith/New Society.

Tobin, J. (2022) 'Learning from comparative ethnographic studies of early childhood education and care'. *Comparative Education*, 58 (3), 297–394. https://doi.org/10.1080/03050068.2021.2004357.

Tobin, L. (2022) 'The £1bn debt pile behind children's nursery giants Busy Bees and Bright Horizons'. *The Times*, 4 December. Online. https://www.thetimes.co.uk/article/the-1bn-debt-pile-behind-childrens-nursery-giants-busy-bees-and-bright-horizons-bg2g6qchw (accessed 31 October 2023).

Tooze, A. (2021) 'Has Covid ended the neoliberal era?' *The Guardian*, 2 September. Online. www.theguardian.com/news/2021/sep/02/covid-and-the-crisis-of-neoliberalism (accessed 31 October 2023).

Tronto, J. (1993) *Moral Boundaries: A political argument for an ethic of care*. London: Routledge.

Tronto, J. (2017) 'There is an alternative: *Homines curans* and the limits of neoliberalism'. *International Journal of Care and Caring*, 1 (1), 27–43. https://doi.org/10.1332/239788217X14866281687583.

UK Parliament (2010) 'The development of Children's Centres'. Online. https://publications.parliament.uk/pa/cm200910/cmselect/cmchilsch/130/13006.htm (accessed 14 January 2024).

UN Committee on the Rights of the Child (2006) 'General comment No. 7 (2005): Implementing child rights in early childhood', 20 September, CRCC/GC/7Rev.1. Online. https://www.refworld.org/docid/460bc5a62.html (accessed 31 October 2023).

Unger, R.M. (2004) *False Necessity: Anti-necessitarian social theory in the service of radical democracy*, 2nd edn. London: Verso.

Unger, R.M. (2005) 'The future of the Left: James Crabtree interviews Roberto Unger'. *Renewal*, 13 (2/3), 173–84.

United Workers Union (2021) '"Spitting off cash": Where does all the money go in Australia's early learning sector?'. Online. https://bigsteps.org.au/wp-content/uploads/2022/08/spitting-off-cash-uwu-report.pdf (accessed 31 October 2023).

Vandenbroeck, M. (2020) 'Discussion: Early childhood education as a locus of hope'. In M. Vandenbroeck (ed.), *Revisiting Paolo Freire's Pedagogy of the Oppressed: Issues and challenges in early childhood education*. Abingdon: Routledge, 186–202.

Vandenbroeck, M., Lehrer, J. and Mitchell, L. (2022) *The Decommodification of Early Childhood Education and Care: Resisting neoliberalism*. Abingdon: Routledge.

Vecchi, V. (2010) *Art and Creativity in Reggio Emilia: Exploring the role and potential of ateliers in early childhood education*. Abingdon: Routledge.

Verba, D. (2014) *Le Métier d'éducateur de jeunes enfants*. Paris: La Découverte.

Waitangi Tribunal (2023) *The Treaty of Waitangi/Te Tiriti o Waitangi*. Online. https://www.waitangitribunal.govt.nz/treaty-of-waitangi/meaning-of-the-treaty/ (accessed 13 January 2024).

Watson, P. (2010) *The German Genius: Europe's third renaissance, the second scientific revolution, and the twentieth century*. London: Simon & Schuster.

Wells, C. (1999) 'Future directions: Shaping early childhood education policy for the 21st century – a personal perspective'. *New Zealand Annual Review of Education*, 8, 45–60. https://doi.org/10.26686/nzaroe.v0i8.1368.

Westberg, J. and Larsson, E. (2022) 'Winning the war by losing the battle? The marketization of the expanding preschool sector in Sweden'. *Journal of Education Policy*, 37 (5), 705–22. https://doi.org/10.1080/02680939.2020.1861338.

White House (2021) *The Build Back Better Framework: President Biden's plan to rebuild the middle class*. Online. https://www.whitehouse.gov/build-back-better/ (accessed 3 January 2023).

Wintour, P. (2012) 'Labour conference 2012: A cerebral address on moral limits of markets'. *The Guardian*, 30 September. Online. https://www.theguardian.com/politics/2012/sep/30/labour-conference-2012-markets (accessed 31 October 2023).

Wolfe, K. (2023) 'Open letter to the Prime Minister: Five-point call to action from Te Rito Maioha Early Childhood New Zealand'. Online. https://www.ecnz.ac.nz/Public/News/Articles/Open-letter-to-the-Prime-Minister.aspx (accessed 31 October 2023).

World Bank (2023) 'World Population 2022'. Online. https://databankfiles.worldbank.org/indicator/SP.POP.TOTL (accessed 13 January 2024).

Wright, E.O. (2012) 'Envisioning real utopias: Alternatives within and beyond capitalism'. David Glass Memorial lecture. Online. https://www2.lse.ac.uk/assets/richmedia/channels/publicLecturesAndEvents/slides/20120522_1830_EnvisioningRealUtopias_sl.pdf (accessed 31 October 2023).

Wylie, C. (1992) *First Impressions: The initial impact of salary bulk funding on New Zealand kindergartens*. Wellington: New Zealand Council for Educational Research.

Wylie, C. (1993) *The Impact of Salary Bulk Funding on New Zealand Kindergartens: Results of the second national survey*. Wellington: New Zealand Council for Educational Research.

Wylie, C. (1998) *Can Vouchers Deliver Better Education? A review of the literature, with special reference to New Zealand*. Wellington: New Zealand Council for Educational Research.

Zigler, E. (2003) 'Forty years of believing in magic is enough'. *Social Policy Report*, 17 (1), 10.

Index

United States, 32–3, 34, 58–9
public funding, Aotearoa New Zealand, 18–19,
  189–90
  1986–1990, 166–8
  1990–1999, 169, 170, 175
  1999–2008, 179–80
  2008–2017, 181, 183
  historical context, 156
  State Services Commission Report (1980),
    161
'Public Futures', 223
public provision, essential in transforming early
  childhood in Anglosphere, 206–7, 213–17
public services, 12, 206

Quadrant Private Equity, 51
quality of services, 68, 69
Quality Rating and Improvement Systems
  (QRIS), 71–2, 75
Québec, parenting leave, 23–4, 55, 76

Raworth, Kate, 81, 203–4
real estate investment trusts (REITs), 53, 76
Realising the Ambition: Being me, 31
recruitment and retention of 'childcare' staff,
  64–7
Redwoods Dowling Kerr, 46–8
Reggio Emilia, 44, 76, 204, 206–7, 209, 210,
  220–1, 226
Republic of Ireland, 13, 14
  Busy Bees in, 49
  'childcare discourse', 41
  extent of integration of ECEC services, 39
  proposals for change, 58, 59–60
  summary of early childhood systems,
    28–30
review, need for, 202–3
Rizvi, Fazal, 85
Rose, N., 206
Rowson, J., 209, 210
Royal Tangaere, A., 159, 163–4

salles d'asiles, 99
Sandel, Michael, 214
school choice, 224–5
school-dominant split system, France, 96–9
  emergence of stable system, 99–102
  extent of integration of ECEC services, 39
Scotland, 13
  'childcare discourse', 41
  extent of integration of ECEC services, 39
  school choice, 224–5
  summary of early childhood systems, 30–2
  universal entitlement, 57
Seth, Anil, 82
Simon, Antonia, 46
Sims, Margaret, 3–4
Smith, A.B., 154, 176, 181
Smith, G., 144–5
social construction, 82
social democracy and Social Democratic party,
  Sweden, 105–6, 111, 120
social democratic welfare regime, 118
social skills, 85–6
Somers, M., 203, 214

split systems. *See* childcare-dominant split
  system; school-dominant split system,
  France
staff. *See* pay, teachers and staff; teachers and
  staff; teachers and staff, Aotearoa New
  Zealand; teachers and staff, England
standardised assessments of childcare services,
  71–5, 76–7
Starting Strong project (OECD), 137–40, 177
'start' programmes, 92
State Services Commission Report on Early
  Childhood Care and Education (Aotearoa
  New Zealand), 161–3
Statham, R., 69
Stiglitz, Joseph, 201
Stover, S., 157
Strategic Plan for ECE (2022) (Aotearoa New
  Zealand), 193
Stuart, Margaret, 85–6
Sure Start programme (England), 131–2, 137,
  149–50, 152
  National Evaluation of Sure Start (NESS),
    142
Sweden. *See* fully integrated system, Sweden
Sylva, K., 140–2

Targeted Assistance for Participation (TAP)
  grants (Aotearoa New Zealand), 183
teachers and staff, 64, 212
  Australia, 21, 65, 66
  Canada, 24–5, 66
  and confusion about purpose of early
    childhood services, 62–3
  consequences of childcare-dominant split
    system, 64–7
  employment conditions, 64–5, 67
  France, 98–9, 101, 102
  images of, 205–6
  and neoliberalism, 83
  OECD reviews on, 138, 139
  Republic of Ireland, 29–30, 58, 60
  Scotland, 32
  Sweden, 104, 109–10, 111, 116
  United States, 34, 66–7
  See also teachers and staff, England
teachers and staff, Aotearoa New Zealand,
  18–19, 166, 168–9, 170, 178–9, 188–9
  in kindergartens, 155, 156, 167–8, 170–1,
    189
  Pathways to the Future plan, 178–9
  pay, 18–19, 58, 173–6, 179, 185–6, 189,
    194, 195
  proposed changes, 58
  qualifications, 166, 169, 174, 181–2, 183,
    185, 188–9
  staff education, 166, 169
  undermining of collective bargaining, 170
teachers and staff, England, 27, 64–5, 125, 144,
  146–8, 152
  Children's Centres, 133
  Effective Provision of Pre-School Education
    (EPPE) study, 141
  improving qualifications, 130
  lack of radical reform by New Labour, 151
  recruitment and retention, 65–6
Te Kōhanga Reo movement, 158–9, 163

Milton Keynes UK
Ingram Content Group UK Ltd.
UKHW020647290524
443256UK00006B/90